SLIDING ON THE SNOW STONE

by

ANDY SZPUK

ISBN-10 1499740441
ISBN-13 978-1499740448

All rights reserved. No part of this book may be reproduced or transmitted in any form or by any means, electronic or mechanical, including photocopying, recording, or by any information storage and retrieval system, without permission in writing from the copyright owner.

'Sliding on the Snow Stone' is the copyright of the author, Andy Szpuk, 2011. All rights are reserved.

The cover design by Isabel Szpuk and Simon Klymyszyn, incorporating a photograph by Paulo Brandão: (http://www.paulobrandao.com).

Refer to sections in the back for pronunciations and translations.

Stefan, a lifetime later ...

You should see how many tablets I have to take: about a dozen every morning. But before I dose myself up, I have to get out of bed. So, once I'm awake and feel the shooting pains in my arms and legs, I push myself up and swing my legs around on to the floor. It takes some effort. Then I sit on the edge of the bed for a minute or two, getting my breath.

I get up, walk out of the bedroom and make my way downstairs carefully, making sure I use the handrail. Then I make myself a cup of tea and some breakfast. Or sometimes my wife Maria makes it for me. Then I take my tablets.

I've been in this world for more than 80 years now and it feels like it. It's no fun getting old, I can say that much, but the fact I'm actually still here is a miracle in itself. I give thanks to God every day for each precious moment of life. I wash the tablets down with my tea. During the course of the day I have to take another dozen. If I could jump up and down I reckon I'd rattle.

Then I get myself dressed and walk to the bus stop. I can only walk slowly with a stick. When the bus comes I sit near the front. I enjoy the ride into town, after all it doesn't cost me anything with my pensioner's bus card. I usually go for coffee with my friend Bronec. He's Polish. I'm Ukrainian. He's all right. I've known him a few years now. We talk about all sorts of things, have a laugh and a joke, but today Bronec's not around. So, I've got my son with me, Andriy. He's a man now, he's got a family of his own, but he's come to see me today. He asks me what language is spoken when I meet up with Bronec. I shrug my shoulders and explain that I speak in Ukrainian to Bronec, while he speaks Polish, and we fill any gaps in English.

Andriy's been asking me lots of questions just lately, about what happened all those years ago. The trouble is, my memory's not so good these days, and it was a long time ago. I don't know if I really even want to remember some of the things that happened.

We all have memories, they're a big part of us. There's no escape from them. We can try and block them, or shut them out, but it's futile. We always remember the good times: The Christmases, the birthdays, the weddings, the laughter and the smiles. They make us feel good, but some memories have to be pushed down. They have to be buried so deep it becomes a form of torture. When the Second

World War ended, many people celebrated, all over the world. Don't get me wrong. I was relieved just like everyone else, but what happened to me leading up to the end of the War affected me for the rest of my life. There are many things I'd like to forget, but can't.

Chapter 1

Ukrainian proverb: There are many lies but barely one truth

My first memory is of Soviet soldiers carrying corpses away. Looking from a window of our house, this is what I saw. I was five years old, not old enough to fully understand what was happening. A horse drawn wagon clattered along the road, and there was a small group of uniformed soldiers picking the bodies up and throwing them onto the bed of the wagon.

I ran to my father. He was sitting on an old wooden chair in our kitchen with his elbows on his knees and his head in his hands. His face was pale, and his cheeks were sunken in, all hollow. His eyes glistened in the gloom.

'Father! What's happening? What's wrong with all those people out there? Are they sick?' He didn't reply, but he looked up at me.

'What is it, Father? What's going on?'

'Stefan, I can't answer your questions now.' He spoke softly, his voice shaking.

'Why are the soldiers taking all those people?'

'Be quiet Stefan!' When Father raised his voice we knew that was the end of it. That's how it was then. We children did as we were told when an adult's voice was raised. So, I ran round to our neighbour's house where my friend Bohdan lived. I knocked on the door. There was no answer. The door was slightly ajar so I pushed it open a little further. I peered through the crack and I saw his mother and father sitting together on their old sofa. They were hugging each other and sobbing. The door creaked and opened still further. They looked up at me.

'Come in Stefan, come in.' Bohdan's father beckoned to me.

I stepped through the doorway and walked towards them. Bohdan's mother pulled me to her and hugged me tight.

'Where's Bohdan?' I asked.

'He's gone! He's gone!' She began to wail.

'When will he be back?'

'He won't be coming back,' replied his father, unable to control the tremor in his voice.

In Ukraine, it was the time of the Holodomor*; the year was 1932.

It was a famine created by the Soviets. They began by taking away all our grain, and once they'd done that, they stripped rural Ukraine of all its food produce. There was nothing left to eat. Of course, back then I didn't know all that. I was just a boy.

As I walked back home from Bohdan's house I looked back down towards the road, and in the beautiful summer sunshine, lingering upon a background of a deep blue sky, there was something strange in the air. It was a smell like nothing I had ever known. It made me feel sick. I watched the soldiers dragging away the dead bodies and throwing them onto their wagons. They were chatting to each other as if it were just another day's work, as if what they were doing was perfectly normal. I didn't understand. It didn't seem real. Was it some sort of game? It couldn't be. These were neighbours and friends, turned into skeletons, just skin and bone. Some of the bodies were collected from the neighbouring houses, some from front gardens, and others from near the communal well that gave us its precious gift of water. Some of the bodies were strewn along the side of the road. Many of them were our neighbours, people whose homes I'd visited to play with their children, like Bohdan. I watched more and more bodies being thrown onto the wagon, there were men, women and even some children. I realised then where Bohdan had gone.

It was close to dinner time, and one of the soldiers walked away from the wagon, leaving the other four to cover up the bodies with canvas sheets. He came back a few minutes later with a pail of water from the well. He clunked it down onto the end of the wagon and the soldiers got hold of a tin mug each from a storage box. They took a good, long drink and splashed water on their faces and hands. Then, each of them pulled out a hunk of bread and a piece of meat, again from that storage box, and they slumped down on the grass verge with their hats pushed back. Their eyes lit up as they bit chunks from the thick slices of bread and meat. I couldn't believe what I saw. These men had food, while all around them was starvation and death. They sat in the middle of all this and ate their meal, without a care, without even a tear of remorse. Along the side of our approach was a row of stones that separated the grass from the track, and I had an urge to get hold of one and throw it at the soldiers, so I bent down and picked one up. It was the size of a large potato, and how I wished it was one, so I could forget about those soldiers, and take it inside for Mother to cook and fill myself up with it. It was just a stone though, hard, smooth and solid. In my mind, I had this idea I could run down our approach with the stone raised above my head, yelling at the top of my voice until I was close enough to hurl it right at one of those grinning Soviets, and split his head right open, causing blood to spurt out and for him to feel some pain. Let him wail like some of the mothers of the dead children in our village. He wouldn't be sat around shoving bread into his face and joking with his friends then. Before I could do anything else, Father appeared next to me and he saw the stone raised above my head. He looked down the approach and saw the soldiers having their dinner, 'Stefan, come on. Come inside now. Keep away from those soldiers. They've got guns. If you bother them, they'll use them. I've heard about soldiers killing children around here. You mustn't go near them.'

I lowered my arm and the stone rolled onto the ground. Father and I went inside where we joined Mother and my brother, Volodimir, for our midday meal. All we got on this occasion was half a cup of cold milk. Some days we got nothing at all. After this meagre lunch, I went outside once again and the soldiers weren't around. I ran down the road to look for my friends, the ones I played with most days, the few that were still around.

At the end of our road lived an old couple, Viktor and Katrina. They worked in the Kolhosp, the Soviet state controlled collective farm. I remember hearing Father talking about them and cursing them for collaborating with the Soviets. Viktor and Katrina kept themselves to themselves, but sometimes when my friends and I ran down the road playing our games, Viktor would shout at us from the front of his house, 'Hey, you boys! Keep the noise down will you? Can't a fellow get some peace around here?' We stopped to look at him, just long enough to see he was a bit mad with us. Then we turned and ran off, kicking up a cloud of dust behind us which spiralled away in the breeze. Many people, such as Viktor and Katrina, accepted the Soviet yoke and got on with living that life. They were peasants, used to leading a simple life. They were those of the village who hadn't prospered on their own, so didn't have much to lose. They adopted Soviet rule almost without thinking. And of course there was also the fear. It was in the air all around us. The Soviets showed no sense of justice. If anyone dared to speak out against them, it was one of two things. The salt mines in Siberia, or a bullet in the back of the head. In some ways the second option was more attractive. Siberia was a desolate, barren, freezing place, and to work there in such atrocious conditions was a worse fate.

Even with threats such as those hanging over us, there were those who didn't agree with Soviet rule and all that went with it.

There were many who despised the Soviets, but were careful who they spoke to. Sometimes, Father could be heard having whispered conversations in the kitchen with one or two of his oldest, most trusted friends. We couldn't always make out very much of what was being said, but these were people who were proud to be Ukrainian. They longed for Ukraine to be free.

It was just the four of us in our house, Mother, Father, my brother Volodimir and me. Mother and Father worked hard to bring us up, to put food on the table. After all, is that not what family life is all about? Sitting down to eat together is something all families do, but it got so bad that our parents couldn't provide for us. There was simply no food. Father told us of the old days when there was plenty; he tried to make us understand that things could be better. It was hard for us to comprehend, because for us children, this was our world. Maybe this was how life was? It didn't show signs of getting any better.

That's why, whenever I could, I ran around the village and the surrounding area with my friends, although there were many times, without much in the way of food inside us, we were so weak we just sat inside our homes.

That summer was a glorious one, with blue skies and licks of warm sunshine wrapping around us just about every day. We boys had chores, and a usually fruitless daily quest for food, but whenever we could, we'd call round for each other. Bohdan would knock on our door, in the days when he was still around, and Mother would shout to me. My boots would be on in a matter of seconds and Volodimir usually joined us. Another boy, Miron, also accompanied us, and we charged out of the village into the nearby woods. We were skin and bone, there was nothing on us, but we could still run. In our minds we were like the wind, flying through the village. This was our escape, our way of getting away from the sickness and suffering around us, and of course we did what all children do, we played games.

'Come on, Stefan!' yelled Bohdan as he snapped a suitably thick stick and swished it around him like an expert swordsman, 'the Poles are coming!'

Determined to outdo him, I got hold of a thicker, longer stick and tried to snap it away from its tree trunk, 'I'm right here!' I yelled back, as the stick put up a struggle, until a final tug made it mine, 'Chaarrrge! There are too many for you, my Hetman. I'm on my way!'

Bohdan always insisted on being Hetman* Bohdan Khmelnytsky, the greatest of all Kozak commanders, and how could any of us argue with him? He had the right name. So he led us. Miron and

Volodimir also got themselves sticks and the three of us followed our Hetman.

'This way, men! We take the higher ground and then we ride down into them. Slash them to pieces, boys!'

As supreme horsemen and the bravest of warriors, we battled deep into the evening, repelling wave after wave of invaders. We didn't care about the cool, evening breeze creeping through the holes in our ragged clothes.

'Cut them down, boys! Destroy them!' cried Bohdan, and we slashed and charged until our arms and legs wobbled like jelly.

'Back to the camp!' he shouted, but not so loud that time. Like the rest of us, his bones were weary and his breath was short, and so we trudged to our usual spot, a fallen tree trunk; the biggest one in those woods. The Poles were a fierce enemy. Our battles with them through the history of our Ukrainian nation were legendary, with our borders switching back and forth countless times; every inch of our land has been paid for in Kozak blood.

And so, after sitting down to rest for a few minutes, further commands were issued from Bohdan, 'Right! This camp will be our kingdom. We must build a castle here!'

'Yes, sir!' cried back we three, and all of us went in search of fallen logs and sticks. We hauled as many as we could back to that tree trunk and leant them either side, covering them with smaller sticks and long grass. It wasn't the biggest castle in the world, and a wobbly construction, but it was our fortress. We'd defend it to the death. No one would ever take it from us, we'd drive them away.

The sunsets in those woods were beautiful, the red and orange of the sun formed a delicious glowing crescent on the horizon that I wanted to grab hold of and eat. Those flickering stabs of light cut through the trees, they sliced through the twisted branches, giving us our own magic garden of light to play in. The real world was forgotten.

Eventually, darkness began to fall on us, and we were forced to return to our homes. We breathed hard on the way back, and passed many bodies lying in the road, of people who had simply dropped and died of starvation. The road we walked along to get home was the one that led to the town. In desperation, these people had tried to escape, tried to get to the town, in the vain hope they might find food there.

As we walked along we could feel the hunger in our bellies, and I wondered when I would next eat. There were times, even as a boy of five, when I thought about what the future might hold for me, my family and friends.

Would we be next? Would it be our mothers and fathers, or our brothers and sisters? Who could tell? We'd just been in the woods slashing away with our wooden swords, believing we could defend our land, but could we really? It was like the whole of Ukraine was waiting to die.

The Soviet soldiers came back the next day and it was always the same routine. First of all, they searched all the houses and dwellings for food. They turned everything upside down. Any possible hiding place was invaded by prying Soviet fingers. With Father already at his place of work, the local nail factory, it was left to my mother to deal with the soldiers. One of them came into our kitchen with a pair of large metal, lidded pails and slammed them onto the floor,

'Fill them.' The soldier fixed a sneer on Mother and ran his eyes up and down her.

'Yes, y-yes, sir.' Mother turned towards a pair of buckets that were positioned in the coolest part of the kitchen. With shaking hands she poured milk from the buckets into the two pails, trying not to spill any. The milk was from our cow. Even though the Soviets stripped every scrap of food away from our village, they allowed us to keep livestock, on the principle that animals would produce food such as milk and eggs for their ever increasing food demands. Of course, without grain and food, most of the animals perished, or were slaughtered, cooked and eaten. Somehow, we kept our cow alive.

Without another word, the soldier picked up the pails and marched out of our house. Once the others soldiers had finished turning our house upside down and searching our barns and outhouses, they left to search the next house.

Our cow was such a good-natured beast and we made sure she had a plentiful supply of either grass or hay. There was no meat on our bones due to lack of sustenance, but we used every last ounce of energy to make sure the cow was fed, and she gave us shooting streams of warm, frothy milk twice a day. The Soviets collected two bucketfuls every morning, and later that day Mother milked the cow again, collecting another two bucketfuls. Mother took the milk and chopped in beetroot leaves, and put in whatever seasoning she could find and made up a soup. That's what we ate, day after day. That cow was a miracle sent from the Lord above, I have no doubt about that.

Our village, Novi Khutyry*, near the town of Vinnitsya*, was such a wonderful place to grow up. The land around us stretched out towards the horizon, with golden fields of wheat and corn all around. The light summer breeze blew on the heads of corn and the ears of wheat, forming ripples that spread across the fields in flowing curves. It was a sin that such a landscape should be tarnished by the murderous acts of the Soviets. There were soldiers dotted all around, patrolling the fields, to make sure nobody took away any of the crops. The starving population was being driven, either into the arms of the Lord, or into acts of destruction.

I remember on one occasion I was passing by a small group of houses, on my way to a friend's house, when I stumbled across a Soviet wagon outside a small, beaten up house. It needed a lick of paint, and the thatched roof was ragged. As I got closer I could hear what was being said,

'You've taken everything! I've got nothing left! Nothing! My husband's dead. My children are all dead. What else do you want? Tell me what you want!'

'Listen, lady, we're just here doing our job.' They were piling corpses onto a wagon. The bed of the wagon creaked as the pile got higher.

'Please! Let me fetch a priest! To get a blessing for him. You can't just take him like this. Can't he have a decent burial?'

'Lady, we're just following orders.'

Warily, I stole a glance at her. She was pacing up and down, wringing her hands and every so often she stopped and held her head in her hands. Then, without any warning she rushed into the house and returned holding a burning rag.

'Well, you won't take anything else from this house! I'll make sure of that.'

She threw the burning rag onto the roof. The house was soon ablaze. The Soviet soldiers retreated. One of them took off his cap and scratched his head, and the two of them smiled at each other. Then, they simply carried on about their business. Some neighbours tried to console the woman. I walked on. This sort of thing was a common sight. The spirit to resist was there, but there was no way to fight the battle. Not really. All we had left was to destroy our own homes before the Soviets got their hands on them.

That's how things were. Too many of us had shown signs of resistance, and so, the Soviets came down on us like a hammer. They wanted to take everything we'd worked so hard for, but why should we give it to them? Many in the village were resentful of the grain quota demanded by the Soviet state. It was like slavery. No one dared to speak out against them. They tried to crush us, but our spirit was too strong with that Kozak blood inside us. They may have forced us to walk with our heads bowed, just thinking about the next piece of bread, but they couldn't stop us being who we were.

Autumn arrived and all the children over the age of seven returned to school. I was thankful for that in some ways, because Volodimir came home with a bagful of books and I'd sit and look at them, and try to read some of the words. Books were something I developed a passion for from a very young age. They gave me something to focus on rather than food.

While Volodimir was at school, I was sent out to look for firewood. It was one of my chores. I'd scour around the lanes and meadows, putting all I could find into a small sack. Before his departure into the arms of the Almighty, Bohdan would usually join me, and of course, we'd end up running along together. Bohdan was a fast runner, he usually won our races. Then we'd watch as our breath turned to steam. We'd be breathing hard. Thinking back now, we didn't run far. We didn't have the energy. The meadows and scrub areas were eerie and quiet. Whatever animal life that was left out there had gone deep into the ground. Otherwise, whatever it was, it would've been eaten.

'Shhh! Stefan, look!' Bohdan was crouching down and keeping very still. He lifted a finger up to his lips. I looked across into a small wooded area, and there perched on a boulder was a sparrow. Not a fat bird, but big enough to our hungry eyes. Trying not to make any sudden moves, Bohdan reached down and picked up a rock that was lying next to his foot. Carefully, he raised his arm above his head, and with a swift motion he threw the rock at the sparrow. 'Blast it!' His throw was off target and the sparrow flew away. Thing is though, I'd seen him hit one before, and we'd roasted the sparrow and eaten it. This time it wasn't meant to be, so we hurried along and gathered more wood before going home.

Our kitchen had a big, wooden table where our family sat for our evening meal, a bowl of that thin, milky broth. Father always led us in prayer before each meal. All around our house were framed icons of Bible scenes. We had at least one in every room. They were big, imposing frames, constructed of wood and coated in gold paint. The frames were carved and shaped into curves with some very fine decorative detail. I loved looking at those icons, they seemed to soothe me somehow. The colours were so bright and vivid. It was as if I could jump right into the picture and sit there inside it. The golden frames glinted in the candlelight. One of those icons was mounted above the kitchen table. It was a painting of the Last Supper. I remember, on more than one occasion, looking up at it and giving thanks to God we were still alive. On another occasion I recall a conversation between Bohdan's father, Petro, and my own, when he'd called in one evening.

'These icons are beautiful, Mikola. I know I've been round here many times before, but I've never really appreciated how good they really are. They're wonderful. They must be worth a lot.'

'Well, I bought them at the bazaar just after Volodimir was born. You see, I wanted to bring God into this house. To bring our children up as Christians. I got them for a good price, but you're right, they weren't cheap.'

'Don't take this the wrong way, but maybe you could take them to the town and sell them to get bread.'

'No. The icons stay right here. With God here we'll get through this.'

'But surely it's worth it? To try and feed your wife and children.'

'The icons stay.'

Those paintings were there to remind us that maybe there could be some good in the world, because Lord knows, we were surrounded by dark forces, by those who wished to wipe us from the map. They sat in their den of power, plotting to destroy us. The leader of these devils was Stalin. He was evil. His Soviet followers and henchmen were mindless murdering scum. Many times I've had a vision, where a dark cloud gathers above them. All of them. And then lightning strikes them down. Havoc rains down on them, and they are annihilated. In my heart I want vengeance for what they did to us. I hope they rot in Hell.

It doesn't sound very Christian I know, to say such things, but the scale of what was done is hard to believe. To take food away from millions of people so that they starve to death is a crime of such a proportion that it cannot be seen as anything other than evil.

It's hard to describe. When you're so hungry, it tightens up inside you. It's like there are spiders crawling in your belly. So many times I felt like I could just sit down and eat, and never stop. I remember my brother Volodimir and me bursting into the house and saying to our Mother, 'Mama! We're hungry! Can we have something to eat?'

'My beloved children,' she said looking down at us, and what she said next breaks my heart. It hurts me to even think about it. She said, 'Take *me* and eat *me*.'

The famine raged on as the Soviet drive to take all our food continued right up to the winter. There were fewer people around. We were being wiped out. I remember that winter as being a very bitter one. We stamped our feet in our battered *choboti** and pulled our woollen hats down over our ears, those of us that had them, and then it was open warfare as we ventured out into that snow-covered terrain that was our village. Volodimir would start things off by pulling off my hat and running away with it.

'Hey! Give me my hat back!' I'd shout at him. Then I'd turn around and four or five of the other boys would be lined up with snowballs in their hands. They threw them at me, spattering me. The melting ice would stream through my hair, creep under my collar and slide down my back. But I fought back. I might have been little but I was damned quick. I'd plunge my hands into the snow, make snowballs and launch into them. I'd fire the snowballs at them, and Volodimir would then take my side. He was a good thrower, everyone got ice down their backs when he got going. We loved it. Running down the road to school, it was all we needed. Sometimes we'd get hold of a big *doshka**, maybe an old door or something like that. We'd all jump on and carve through the ice as we slid down the hills, kicking up a snow spray. We'd get to the bottom of the hill and one of us would shove a toe end into the snow causing the *doshka* to spin around. We'd all go skidding off in different directions. We loved it. A huge white playground of powdery snow. Who needs toys when you've got that stuff? There was a small lake near our village and, when it got really cold in the evenings, so cold you could hardly feel your fingers and toes, we'd run down there to skid around on the ice that formed on and around it. On a clear evening, the moonlight reflecting off the frozen water gave us plenty of light, and it was like being in some kind of magical kingdom. On the far side of the lake was a steep slope which led down to a wooded area, and where there was a beaten up old shack. An old man called Matviyko lived there who was well known in the village, even though he was hardly ever seen. How he survived down there all on his own I don't know. It was rumoured that he was a bit crazy, so we boys kept away from that shack. On one occasion we were sliding down that hill which was frozen as hard as glass. Some of us slid down on our boots, waving our arms wildly to keep our balance, others managed to find a piece of wood to sit on. Well, the ground was so frozen that, once we'd reached the bottom, we all struggled to find our feet again and slipped around, grabbing each other for support and then falling over again. As we lay on the floor, we heard a rasping chuckle. We looked across at the shack and there he was! He was a stout old man with wild eyes staring out from baggy cheeks and wild grey, thinning hair sprouting in every direction. He was wrapped in a thick, grey coat with a red scarf tucked right up to his chin.

'Boys, boys,' he said in a voice like a rumble from Heaven, 'this is what happens when you come down here and slide around on the snow stone, you end up spending time with Matviyko.' He lifted his face up to the moonlight and laughed, his breath a cloud of steam. We didn't hang around, we scrambled up that slope almost as quickly as we'd come down, and then we walked home. Matviyko's words puzzled me as we made our way back in the light from the moon. Then I realised that, to him, snow stone was ice. He was an odd sort of fellow and I guessed that living alone might cause someone to act strangely and use peculiar language.

When we got home, Mother sat us next to the stove to warm us up. We gazed into the fire. The flames jumped around in the stove and I let my mind wander. I thought about the Kozaks on the steppes. Now that was freedom. What a life they must have led, underneath the stars, with no one to tell them what to do. Riding into battle ready to die if need be, but with the strength and the swordsmanship to slay any army, no matter how powerful. Mother would usually interrupt my dreaming. She'd pass me a cupful of warm milk and then scold us a little for getting so drenched and dirty, but that was it, there was very little else.

Visitors to our village could've sensed that something wasn't quite right. The cry of eagles overhead was no more. Village life had changed. There were never any dogs around, or cats. Anything that could be eaten had disappeared. A silence hung over us. A black gloom. Life was being drained away, day by day.

Father would come home from his work at the local nail factory. They gave him one slice of bread to feed the four of us. So we split it into four pieces. That's all we got. A piece of bread two inches square! It was barely enough to feed a mouse. It was enough to send you mad, and people did lose their reason. These were ordinary families, ordinary people, but they were driven to do the unthinkable.

One day, a villager arrived at the local bazaar with a quantity of meat for sale. Many people rushed towards him waving money, desperate to buy some of the meat. Others stood back. Where had the meat come from? There were hardly any animals left in the area. Perhaps just those such as our own cow, which were kept purely for producing milk. He laid out the slices of red meat on several dishes. There was enough to almost fill a table. The meat looked fresh and many people, as they queued, debated about how they would cook it. Some talked about making a stew which would maybe last a few days. Others talked of mincing the meat to make sausages, which would last even longer, but those who had stood back were ones who had worked on the local councils before the Soviets took over. The elders of the village. They were compelled to speak out, 'Wait! Wait! You must tell us where this meat has come from. Is it beef or pork? Or what is it? You must tell us before anyone can have any of this meat.'

Of course, the man broke down and it soon became clear. It was human meat. People were killing their children and eating them. Later that evening, I lay in bed and heard Father's voice from down below,

'Those damned Soviet sons of bitches! Look what they've done to us! They've turned us into beasts. I know that man who killed his own children, he works at the factory with me, but look what he's done!'

I heard another voice, it sounded like Petro, Bohdan's father,

'How could anyone do that to their own children though, eh? When we lost Bohdan, it would never have entered our heads to do anything like that! It's the work of the devil!'

'Yes and that particular devil's name is Stalin!' thundered Father.

I didn't sleep so well that night. I drifted in and out of dreams, where images of the man who'd killed and eaten his own children kept appearing. There he was, only a few feet away, waving a carving knife in front of a twisted stare, and with his face sliced into a gap-toothed grin. I woke up screaming and ran to Mother in the bed she shared with Father. She hugged me and calmed me down. Those nightmares continued for many nights.

Somehow our family survived. While all around us people were dying. We were lucky, I guess. We made sure our cow got fed and, in return, she gave us milk. Mother made up the soup. Maybe it wasn't the tastiest soup I've ever had, but when you're hungry you savour it well enough.

Sometimes, Mother would send me along to the factory to take some of the milky broth to Father for his lunch. It was hardly a meal fit for a working man, but it was more than most of the others got. I could sense some unease from him as I gave him the jar of broth. There were other men around who could smell the aroma of warm food and all eyes shifted across to where we were, like cats eyes squinting through the gloom. I could feel them peering out of every corner of that place when that jar of soup arrived. Father drank it down quickly, gave me the jar back and I hurried away. It felt shameful somehow, to be bringing food for my father when others went without.

So, this was how my life began. I was born into a catastrophe, but I didn't know it at the time, I just thought this was our life.

Chapter 2

Ukrainian proverb: Those sitting above can easily spit on those below

At first, all we could see was a speck in the distance. We watched, and we had an idea what was happening; it wasn't the first time.

'They're coming! They're coming!'

Miron stood in front of us breathing hard. We'd just watched him run all the way down the full length of the road that ran from the village into Vinnitsya. It was a straight stretch of road, it must have run for about a half a mile. It always seemed like a long way to me. Like it stretched on and on to the rest of the world.

Volodimir and I, and some other boys were playing a game of football with an old ball that was past its best. At the age of seven I was the youngest, so the older boys always chose me to be goalkeeper. I didn't mind anyway. I liked throwing myself around.

It was two years after the famine. We had a little bit more to eat, not a great deal, but people weren't starving to death anymore. We were getting stronger and when we saw Miron standing in front of us, and heard his words, it was a call to arms. The older boys took control. They sent us little ones back into the village to get as many boys as we could and bring them to join us. The Moscali were on their way!

The Moscali were the Soviet boys that lived in the town. Every now and then they would walk out of the town up to where we lived in the village. They thought they could lay into us. They had some stupid idea in their heads they could beat us. We were having none of that and collected as many boys together as possible and waited. As the seconds ticked by we became more and more determined.

'Come on you Moscali! Come and get some!' we hollered down the road, ready for anything. They'd need to kill us, each one of us, before we gave up, or before we'd let them get past us.

It wasn't too long before they came into view. There were about 20 of them, and we had about the same number. It would be an even fight. Well, it would have been if they weren't such a bunch of soft city boys. As they got closer we saw their slicked back hair, and their fancy shirts and trousers. They thought they were really something, so we did what we always did. We shouted at them, 'Katsap! Katsap!' and made bleating noises, mocking them.

They hated that, because katsap* means billy goat. Now, that may not seem like such a big insult these days, but the Moscali boys hated it. It got right under their skin. They really saw themselves as refined and modern, so to be mocked as farm animals was like spitting in their faces. We could see the wounded look in their eyes as we yelled and mocked them. So they called back, 'Hohli! Hohli!*'

This was another word for billy goat, but also referred to the Kozak haircut. Somehow they thought this would belittle us, but it made us laugh even more. Was that the best they could come up with? These boys with their city education and sophisticated ways. We laughed louder and flapped our hands at them to show our scorn.

Then they started. Big stones flew through the air at us, and we had to be quick to dodge them. But then *we* started. A supply of big stones was all ready. My job was to pass them up to the bigger boys. I darted back and forth to keep the supply line well fed much of the time but every now and then one of the boys would turn to me, 'Come on Stefan! We need more stones!' It was at times like this when I thought of Bohdan. He would have helped if he was still around. He was so quick on his feet he would have lifted twice as many stones as me and passed them up to the bigger boys. Mind you, I expect he'd have wanted to be stood at the front throwing the stones at the Moscali.

Our boys launched the stones as if they were firing rockets, straight and true. Volodimir was right at the front and was our best thrower. He had big broad shoulders and was built solid like a barn. He hit a couple of the Moscali boys, one square on the chest and the other on his arm. They both scrambled away.

The Moscali boys scattered and tried to regroup. Some carried on throwing at us, but stones were flying through the air at them non-stop. They couldn't cope.

The battle raged and, amid the hail of stones, two of the older boys in our group reached inside their jackets and pulled out sawn-off shotguns. The boys throwing stones at the front stepped aside. Those holding the shotguns stepped through the gap and took aim in the general direction of the Moscali. They fired. We covered our ears as the twin blast of the sawn-off shotguns echoed all around us. Two arcs of fire flashed over the heads of the Moscali. They all threw themselves onto the ground, and then ran like rabbits as wisps of gun smoke hung in the air. They fled. Back where they came from.

We all jumped and cheered as they retreated back down the road, until they just looked like a swarm of flies in the distance. We wiped the sweat off our brows with our sleeves or with our shirts as we walked back into the village. Our heads were high and we smiled and joked with each other. The evening sun beat down on us. The older boys lit cigarettes and each bragged about how many Moscali he had hit. I enjoyed listening to their talk. It was a victory for all of us. It lifted us for a day or two. It made us feel like we were a force to be reckoned with. Volodimir and I went home, and after a big mugful of hot milk, we went to bed with the glow of victory still warming us inside.

Following one such occasion I remember waking up the next morning feeling elated, just like I always did. The stone fights with the Moscali didn't occur that often, maybe every few months, but it was enough to stir the Kozak blood inside us. Even with the Soviet boot trampling all over us we found a way to fight back. Driving the Moscali boys away showed that we could defend ourselves. In reality of course, the overwhelming might of the Soviets was too much for our nation. The stone fight victories were just a shred of hope, a flicker of something.

I got dressed and went downstairs and sat down at the kitchen table. The smell of warm bread filled the room. It made my mouth water, it always did. Mother was standing by the stove heating up some milk. She looked across at me and we said 'good morning' to each other with a smile.

I sat and watched her as she busied herself around the stove and the cupboards. Her hair was tied back and flowed like a waterfall down her back. It was black as a raven, the same as my own untidy mop. I loved to watch her. She opened up one of the cupboards and lifted some plates out and placed them on a table. She moved so gracefully. Then she turned to me, 'Stefan, fetch me some more logs from the yard, please.'

Without hesitation, I stood up. For her, I would have done anything, my beloved Mother. I would have walked through fire, through storms, across deserts or through deep waters, anything at all for her. I rubbed the sleep out of my eyes with the backs of my hands, yawned and stepped out of the door to our yard. There was a chill in the air that summer morning so I didn't hang around and collected a bucket of logs from our shed and carried them back in. I knelt down by the stove, opened the grate, and fed a few logs in watching the flames lick around them, enjoying their warm glow.

Mother came and stood next to me to check the milk. She removed it from the stove and poured it into cups. She put the pan down and brushed a strand of hair out of her face. I jumped up and wrapped myself around her. I can still remember her warm aroma even now. She ruffled my hair and picked me up. She looked into my eyes and we smiled at each other.

'Stefan, you have such beautiful blue eyes. Just like your father. You're my lovely, beautiful, blue eyed boy.'

I loved the softness of her voice. I could have listened to her talk all day. She sat me back down on a chair and brought me over a cup of steaming hot milk. I blew on it to cool it down. Mother sliced some bread, buttered it and set down a couple of slices on a plate in front of me. It may not sound like much of a breakfast but, believe me, this was a feast compared to what we had during the years of the Holodomor.

A few mouthfuls later it was all gone, and I washed it down with the hot creamy milk. Of course I asked for more, but Mother just looked at me and said, 'Later Stefan, later. Now go and get ready for school. And tell your brother to get out of bed. You'll both be late if you don't get moving!'

I got up and went to the bedroom I shared with Volodimir, put on my jacket and picked up my schoolbag. Volodimir was already sitting up in bed with his elbows on his knees.

'You're going to be late for school again and Father won't like it if he finds out.' I said.

'Don't worry Stefan, I'll get there on time today.' He looked at me and grinned. I knew what he was thinking and I grinned right back. We didn't need to say anything, but we were both still feeling good about the stone fight with the Moscalis.

He said, 'You get going Stefan, and I'll catch you up.'

'Okay.'

He leapt up out of the bed and stood stretching his arms around his head. I left him to get dressed and walked back out into the hallway, and put my shoes on. Then I grabbed a kiss off Mother and left for school. I walked down our path and stepped out onto the street.

There was a golden sun in the sky, it was still rising, but the morning was still a little chilly, so I didn't hang around. I put my head down and marched on. I knew I would probably meet up with some of my friends along the way, but I didn't expect Volodimir to catch me up. It always took him a long time to get himself up and about in the mornings. Not like me. As soon as I woke up and opened my eyes I was ready for the day. I wanted to get dressed, get as much breakfast down me as I could and then I just wanted to be out there.

No one else was around this particular morning. The street was completely deserted. That suited me. Sometimes, I liked to feel as though I was the only person in the world, walking along with the birds singing in the trees, with the road stretching out in front of me and a horizon waiting for me. What would the day bring?

The school was right on the other side of the village, it took about half an hour to get there. So I walked along. A gentle breeze shook the leaves in the trees around me.

I didn't mind going to school, not that I would have admitted it to my brother or my friends, but, in actual fact, they were the reason I liked it. Break times were the best times. We'd play football or running games in the schoolyard. We'd tease each other and there would be the occasional fight when things went too far. But despite any differences we may have had, and putting aside any disagreements or hostilities that may have taken place, we knew we were all brothers and sisters. Descended from Kozaks. Our time would come one day, that's what we believed. We had to. Whatever the Soviets did to us we had to keep our faith, and our identity as Ukrainians.

Aside from the games we played, there were other things at school that were beginning to have a real effect on me. In my schoolbag I had a battered copy of the poems of Taras Shevchenko. Many of them I knew off by heart. They'd planted themselves right inside me. As long as I live his words will echo inside me. The images he conjured up of our beautiful land were so true. The majestic honesty of his poetry stirred up a storm inside me. I'd never felt such passions. The way he used words was like a Kozak would use them. It was as if he had dug them up from the soil. There was a rawness, a wonderful earthiness. He touched the whole Ukrainian nation with his words. Shevchenko was a visionary, he gave us ideas like no one else, and he made us think about our place in the world:

The days pass, the nights pass,
As does summer. Yellowed leaves
Rustle, eyes grow dim,
Thoughts fall asleep, the heart sleeps,
All has gone to rest, and I don't know
Whether I'm alive or will live,

Or whether I'm rushing like this through the world,
For I'm no longer weeping or laughing…
My fate, fate, where are you now?
I have none;
If you begrudge me a good one, Lord,
Then give me a bad one!
Let a walking man not sleep,
To die in spirit
And knock about the entire world
Like a rotten stump.
But let me live, with my heart live
And love people.
And if not… then curse
And burn the world!
It's horrible to end up in chains
To die in captivity,
But it's worse to be free
And to sleep, and sleep, and sleep—
And to fall asleep forever,
And to leave no trace
At all, as if it were all the same
Whether you had lived or died!
Fate, where are you, fate where are you?
I have none!
If you begrudge me a good one, Lord,
Then give me a bad one! A bad one!

While I was walking along, with my eyes following those words across the page, from the corner of one eye I saw a figure emerge from one of the side streets. I looked across and saw it was one of the older boys of the village, one of Volodimir's friends. He was walking slowly with his head bowed. At the junction, I stopped and waited for him. He stopped a few yards away. It was Sasha, one of the boys who blasted a shotgun at the Moscali only the day before. Tears were streaming down his cheeks. It wasn't like Sasha to cry. He was a hero to me. Sasha was fearless, he'd take anyone on. If there were ten Moscali in front of him he'd fly into them like a hurricane. Never before had I seen him like this, I didn't know what to say or do, but eventually, after an awkward moment which hung in the air like an over-ripe apple on a tree, I took a step towards him and said, 'Sasha, what's the matter?'

He took a few breaths and raised his head. Clearly, he was struggling to speak, but he eventually blurted out, 'They've taken him. They've taken my father.'

There was a stunned silence for a few seconds, but as soon as he said those words I had an idea what may have happened. He carried on, 'Last night they came for him. Soviet soldiers. There must have been about ten of them. I was in bed, almost asleep when I heard noises. So I went downstairs, and I heard them say it, Stefan, I heard them.'

He was talking about a phrase every Ukrainian dreaded:

Without right of correspondence.

The scholars, the educated, the successful, or anyone who spoke out against Soviet rule was taken away, and their families were denied contact. None came back. It was never made clear what happened to them, and no information was given by the Soviets. But we knew only too well where they were taken. There was a park in the town where the Soviets had built a compound with a 12-foot high wooden fence. The compound was guarded by armed soldiers. We boys went down there many times to observe. Nearby was a tree that we climbed up. We couldn't see into the compound from the tree, but we got a better view of the comings and goings. It also concealed us from the soldiers. On many occasions we saw people escorted in there under armed guard. A period of time later the Soviets would start up several vehicles within the compound. The engines made a terrific amount of noise - enough to drown out the sound of rifle fire. We never saw any of the people escorted in there come back out.

Sasha's father was a hard worker; he'd managed his land well, so much so that he acquired a few more acres over the years. He employed several of the local peasants on his land and was a well-liked, successful farmer. Until the time came when the Soviets decided on collectivisation, and then most of his land was taken from him. It must have been a shock to him. At first, he reacted in the same way as everyone else, by keeping quiet. To speak out against the Soviets, to make a fuss in any way was a death sentence, so people held back. Tongues didn't wag and people's mouths stayed zipped up tight. Sasha's father must have finally lost his patience and said or done something, but we didn't know what it was he might have done. We just knew he'd been taken away.

'I'll kill them! I swear I'll kill them all. I'll go down to their compound and burn it down!' Sasha stopped crying and was shaking.

I looked around and saw that, for once, Volodimir had dragged himself out of bed and was approaching and I was glad about that. Straight away Volodimir realised that Sasha was in some distress. I quickly told him what had happened, as much as I knew anyway. Volodimir put an arm round Sasha's shoulders. Tears started to flow again.

'Sasha. I know you want to fight them, but if you go down to that compound you'll just get shot and that'll be that.' Volodimir tried to reason with Sasha.

'I've lost my father. He's gone. They've killed him.' Sasha collapsed in a heap by the roadside and lay there sobbing. Volodimir and I looked at each other. We'd lost many friends and relatives over the years, but to lose your own father was something you just didn't even want to think about.

Sometimes I think we grew up too fast. I was seven, Volodimir was nine, and Sasha was 11. The things we'd seen and the world we lived in were too terrible for children. Sasha was the oldest child in his family and he would now be the head of the house. It was all wrong. His father hadn't done anything to anybody. He hadn't stolen anything or mistreated anyone. The Soviets were merciless. If you disagreed with them, they got rid of you. Not only that, they wiped away all trace of you, as if you never existed.

We gathered ourselves together and carried on walking. None of us said very much. Well, what could you say? The day passed by in something of a haze. We were all in shock I guess. Sasha didn't say much all day, and at the end of school, as we all walked home; he stormed off with his head down. We let him go, but we hoped he'd be all right.

Later that night I was lying in bed just dozing. I was nearly asleep, when I heard a noise. It was coming from the window. It sounded like a spray of small stones clattering onto the glass. Volodimir was already asleep, so I jumped out of bed. I threw the window open and poked my head out. I looked down into the darkness, but I couldn't see anything and screwed up my eyes to try and focus. I saw a blurred pair of arms waving at me and looked harder until I made out a face in the darkness, 'Sasha! What are you doing here at this time?'

'Stefan, I've come to let you know I'm leaving.'

'What?'

'I've got to get out of here, before they come for me. I know I won't be able to keep my mouth shut. One day, and it could be any day, might even be tomorrow, I'll say something against them and they'll find out. They'll take me away, just like they took my father. I can't live like this. I'm going west, to the mountains. I'm going to join the Resistance. We have to fight back. I just know this is what I have to do. Wish me luck.' He turned away before I could say anything and ran off into the black curtain of the night, but I wished him luck all the same.

We'd heard many stories about the Resistance. They were a band of men living in the Carpathian Mountains, fighting for a free Ukraine, taking on our old enemies, the Poles and the Soviets.

I didn't know what to think. I closed the window and got back into bed. I lay there for a while thinking about Sasha. Part of me envied him. He was off on a big adventure, but he was leaving everything behind. He was going into the unknown, and that was something I was uneasy about. Even though the Soviets mistreated us and were trying to destroy us, or so it seemed, I loved the place where I lived. Okay, our house wasn't the biggest around but it was enough for us. I had my family. My grandmother on my mother's side lived in the next village. We saw a lot of her. We had many friends in our neighbourhood, it was a real community. There were good and bad things about it, but it was where I belonged.

Father came from Stanislaviv, further west. Sometimes we'd go and visit his sisters over there, but I was always glad when we came back. I didn't know what to make of what was happening to us all. Sasha had run away, that's how bad it had become. It seemed like my whole world was always in some sort of turmoil. Eventually, I managed to drift off to sleep again.

The next day I was on my way to school again. It was another bright sunny day. I was just strolling along when I got to the junction where I'd met up with Sasha the day before. My thoughts turned to him and I hoped he was okay. He'd done the right thing in my eyes. Sasha was a true Kozak, ready to fight at any time and tough as they come. And he liked to say what was in his head and in his heart. That was a problem, and that's why it was better that he'd gone.

The Soviets were a cunning lot. They infiltrated our community. There were boys in the school who were new to the village, and they didn't really mix. We didn't trust them, so we kept our distance. Something wasn't quite right about them. Often we'd see them hanging around on the fringes of our group trying to listen in to what was being said. We kept away from them and certainly didn't say anything to them, but their eyes followed us everywhere.

And there were also plenty of uniformed Soviet Secret Police officers around, but it was the plain clothes ones you really had to watch out for. They stood in doorways swallowed up in dark shadows, and they watched every move we made. Every word we spoke could have been used against us. We learned to keep our mouths shut, and we changed our language in the way we spoke. We used a mix of lots of different dialects to confuse them. I don't know if it worked but, anyway, most of the time, we were out in the woods or in the fields playing football or running races. We had to escape. That's what they did to us. They carved us up. Divided us. They made it so that no one spoke to their neighbour for fear of Soviet reprisal. Anyone could be listening and whoever we mixed with could be a Soviet informer. We couldn't trust a soul and quickly learnt to keep quiet. It was as if there was a deafening shroud of silence hanging over us. Engulfing us and suffocating us.

One day, not long after Sasha left, Father took Volodimir and me for a walk down to the river in Vinnitsya. He wanted to show us some of the sights in the town, and get us away from the daily drudgery in the village. The three of us walked along together talking about everything and anything. As we were just arriving in the town a man approached. It was one of the Soviet officials who sometimes came to our village; one of the lower ranks. 'Good morning Mr Szpuk, how are you and your family today?'

Father looked at him with maybe a hint of suspicion in his eyes, but without giving much away, and then he said, 'Good morning. I'm well. We're all well. But can you tell me the whereabouts of one of my neighbours? He was taken away just over a week ago?'

'Mr Szpuk, you know I can't tell you anything at all about any particular individual. That information is classified.'

'But he didn't do anything wrong.'

The official narrowed his eyes, 'Mr Szpuk, I would advise you not to say any more. You are in a better position than you may imagine.'

'What do you mean?'

'Well, we have it on record that you've been to America. But you rejected their bourgeois lifestyle and returned to our glorious Soviet heartland. That is highly commendable and it stands you in good stead. But you still need to be careful.'

With that he stepped aside and walked on, leaving us standing there open mouthed. What he said was true. Father did go to America when he was a young man in search of work, but there was none. It was no better over there, so he came back.

To the Soviets this was a victory. It proved to them they were right with their Bolshevik ideas and plans. So, perhaps for this reason, Father survived the Soviet purges. Not many did. We had our walk around the town. Father pointed out some of the landmarks, some of the old churches and buildings, and as he spoke to us I couldn't help thinking to myself how lucky we were he hadn't been taken away. I didn't want to lose him.

In those years following the Holodomor, our situation was better in that we had a little more food. No-one was starving anymore and that was a blessing, but even so, our rations were sparse. Each person was allowed a slice of bread, and we were permitted to grow vegetables in the small plot that was still our own. Mother struggled to stretch our rations to feed us. Sometimes, in the summer, she would collect up a selection of the vegetables, if we had enough to spare, and walk into the town. It was a long way. There she would sell the vegetables and buy some cuts of meat for us, if any were available at the right price, but those occasions were few. Most days I woke up hungry and went to bed hungry. Everybody did what they could to get more food, from wherever they could.

Not far from where we lived was a carp farm. It was constructed in a small lake where we boys went to swim in the summer. The lake was patrolled by guards, and there were numerous signs everywhere forbidding fishing, but that didn't stop us boys. What we did was get hold of a small length of sturdy stick, about one inch in diameter and about six inches long. We also got some very fine twine and some hooks. With these we each constructed a fishing line and concealed the stick in one of the tufts of grass on the bank of the lake, digging it in to make it secure, and keeping it concealed. Sometimes when we were doing this a guard would appear in the distance. At such times Volodimir would dive into the water with Miron and they'd clown around to distract the guard, even just for a few moments while we finished digging the sticks in and cast our lines, using worms for bait.

Volodimir was a strong swimmer. He'd turn somersaults and do handstands in the water. That always got a laugh from the guard. Then he'd carry on walking towards us. 'Hello there, boys.'

We all replied loudly, 'Hello Mister!' We grinned up at him. Brashness and bravado was usually enough to take his attention away from ever finding our secret fishing lines. He smiled at us, 'Enjoy your swim boys. You've picked a beautiful day for it.'

So then we'd take turns to swim or to keep an eye on the sticks. We couldn't use floats because the guard would be able to work out what was happening so it was simply a case of pulling each line in every so often to see whether we'd got a bite. On several occasions I came home with a lovely big carp tucked inside my shirt. Mother would prepare it and we'd all eat well those evenings. Those carp were tasty.

Otherwise, we survived on very little. Not only was food in short supply, there was also a shortage of fuel. We bought a supply of coal in for the winter but again, this was rationed. Many times, after dark, I went with Father to a nearby railway depot where freight trains sometimes stopped overnight. One of these carried logs and, whenever we could, we helped ourselves to as many as we could carry. They were heavy. Of course, we were stealing, and it was best not to think what the Soviets might do if they caught us, but we had no choice. It was either steal the logs in the pitch black of night or freeze.

It was as if they were slowly trying to erase us. Our village looked like it might crumble away. The local church had been shut down and boarded up and the churchyard was completely overgrown. It was like a jungle. When going to and from school we'd pass by houses with their windows smashed in or boards nailed across them. Their front gardens would be covered in weeds and rubbish, and their rusty gates swung back and forth, creaking in the breeze. We saw duck ponds that had become overgrown and infested, cowsheds that were falling apart, and abandoned vegetable plots which had rotted down and turned to foul smelling mush. Worst of all, every now and then we'd walk past the charred remains of what had once been dwellings. Their smoky fumes lingered in the air and the stench locked itself into the air. To look across and see what remained was truly heartbreaking. It was a black landscape. Charcoal dust still hung in the air and, if we weren't careful, drifted into our throats, making us cough and splutter, so we hurried away from them. Anyhow, they were spooky. There was something quite eerie about the smallholdings that had been set on fire, as if they were still occupied in some way.

One day, someone from our group of boys suggested going into one of these deserted houses. I can't recall who it was. I reckon it may have been Sasha before he ran off to join the Resistance, but I'm not sure.

There was Volodimir, Miron, Sasha and me. We cautiously walked up the cobbled approach. The wind was howling around our ears and I swallowed. It was a bright, sunny day, but goose bumps formed on my arms and shoulders as we approached that house. We walked up a set of steps to a side entrance door. There were cobwebs everywhere, and we dragged them out of our hair with our fingers. Miron tried the handle. The door creaked open. We walked in, feeling our way and bumping into each other, it was pitch black in there. The air smelt sickly sweet like treacle. We stumbled in and disturbed the thick layer of dust that lay inside. Coughing and spluttering, we walked around banging into furniture and tripping over until Volodimir said, 'Let's get out of here!'

We scrambled to get out. It was a relief to get out into the daylight. We walked back down the approach. It felt as if we'd just been walking around in a tomb. As if we'd just been inside the death of our nation.

Would we just watch as we were systematically destroyed one by one? Or would we fight back? I was glad that Sasha had run away to join the Resistance. He was a born warrior, a true Kozak. With more like him maybe we stood a chance.

This was how we lived, always looking over our shoulders and taking care what we said. The Soviets were everywhere, waiting and listening. It was as if we were hiding, or sleeping. One day we'd wake up and the nightmare would be over. That's what we hoped. We just wanted to be free.

The Soviets kept us in our place, we were in their grip, and of course they fed lies, to us and the outside world. They were forever proclaiming how glorious and wonderful their Soviet Republic was. It was as if the outside world couldn't see or hear, and we had no way of telling them anything. We were cut off. So, when one day Father came home with a radio, we were fascinated. He flicked a switch and it crackled into life. He played with the controls and there was a good deal of high-pitched whining, and then a voice. It spoke in German. Now, Father was a keen scholar of languages, and we all learned German in school, so we all had some understanding. Volodimir and I were quick to recognise the odd word or phrase and call them out but Father raised a finger to his lips and told us both to shush. He had a much greater command of the language. He listened closely for a good few minutes, then he spoke to us, 'It's a news broadcast from Berlin. The German army has invaded Czechoslovakia. They're moving east. God help us, let them come and free us from the Bolsheviks.'

The signal then faded, and Father carried on tuning until he got another strong signal. This time the voice spoke in Russian, '*All citizens of the Soviet Union have a duty to fight for our glorious Motherland, Russia. The German menace is getting closer. They are barbarians. They will come and slaughter us. They will murder our children. They will rape our women, and they will steal or destroy everything we have. We must drive them away. We must stand together shoulder to shoulder like good Bolsheviks. We will never give in to the vicious Hun. Remember, it is your duty.'*

Those words sent a chill through us. We knew that the Soviets would gladly send us all to our deaths to save themselves, and if we refused then we'd most likely be shot.

We wondered what would happen should the Germans invade. Surely it couldn't be any worse than life under the Soviets? The three of us, Father, Volodimir and I all leant over the radio listening closely, but then we heard a noise behind us which made all three of us turn around. Mother was sitting on a chair with her face in her hands, sobbing. She looked up at us, tears streaming down her cheeks, 'No! Please no. No more war. I can't stand it. We can't take any more death. Surely we've had enough? Please God, don't let it happen.' She clasped her hands together and looked up towards the ceiling.

The three of us stood there feeling some shame. She was right. She had every reason to cry. Her first husband had died during the First World War. He'd joined the Imperial Russian Army and died in combat, probably killed by a fellow Ukrainian fighting for the Austro-Hungarians. We never knew, but it was senseless. As always, we Ukrainians got caught up in the crossfire of a bloody conflict between our neighbours. Volodimir and I put our arms around her, and Father fiddled with the radio once again until he found some music. It was a cheery, folksy sort of tune, with a young girl singing in a shrill voice, accompanied by mandolins and accordions. It didn't quite fit the moment, none of us were in the mood to sing along or dance, but we listened all the same. It certainly filled an awkward moment.

That radio became a part of our everyday lives. Father had to limit our listening to an hour every evening, so we listened to stories and songs as often as we could. It freed us from our daily slog even if only for a short time. It helped us to forget how hungry we were, and how we were crushed beneath the Soviet boot of Bolshevism. It put a smile on our faces. Later, when we'd gone to bed I often heard the radio's high-pitched whine, and I knew Father was tuning in to news broadcasts.

All through the village a sense of anticipation started to grow. More and more people were getting hold of these radio sets, which the Soviets encouraged. We knew they wanted to feed us propaganda, and so we tried to listen in to broadcasts from other parts of the world.

The air was alive with expectation, but not only that, there was a real sense of foreboding. None of us knew what was coming. Whatever it was, and whatever might happen, there was a shred of hope, that we might be freed from Soviet rule.

The summer of 1939 was one which I would never forget. We boys spent our time swimming at the lake and trying to catch fish. We ran races and played football in the beautiful sunshine. I was 11 years old and I was due to return to school within the coming week.

Volodimir and I returned home one evening right at the end of the summer to find Mother and Father in a state of some excitement. Mother was pacing up and down wringing her hands and occasionally stopping to say to herself, 'Oh dear God help us! Please help us!'

Father, on the other hand, was standing upright, head high like a Kozak. He looked at us, his cheeks flushed. 'It's started boys. It really is happening. The Germans have invaded Poland. They're on our doorstep.' The radio was blaring away in the background. Volodimir and I looked at each other. We didn't know what to say. None of knew what was around the corner, but we hoped and prayed it might lead to better times.

Chapter 3

Ukrainian proverb: The devil always takes back his gifts

If I could go back in time and change one thing, I know what that would be. For Mother to live her life in peace. She'd been through so much. Never once did I hear her complain, through the toughest of times, and with the mountain of hard work she faced every day in bringing up a family on a smallholding. She cooked, cleaned and worked our land. The cow got milked and fed before sunrise, and after that she never stopped all day. She seemed to survive on very little sleep. If I was up early at five or six, I'd find her in the kitchen baking or cooking with what little was available to her. She did the very best she could for us from virtually nothing. We were a close family and I think she feared for us. It was 1939 and the Nazis had just invaded Poland. I was 12 and Volodimir was 14. Although we were still boys it was common for those of our age to be conscripted into the Red Army and sent out into battle. The Nazis were becoming more of a threat and they were getting too close for comfort, certainly we thought the Soviets would be alarmed at the prospect of Nazi jackboots crossing their borders. All we could do was wait and see what the Soviets would do next.

I was very young when I first became aware of how Mother liked to sing. That was how I knew she was nearby. A melody would drift through the air, just ever so gently, it always made me lift my head up. Then she'd appear, usually carrying a load of washing or a basket of vegetables, but with a look of rapture on her face, as if she was lost in some world inside herself. Where everything was how it should be, with angels looking over us and with plenty of everything.

Many times Mother and Father sat down together after our evening meal and sang. Between them, they knew many traditional Ukrainian folk songs with real strong melodies. Some of them were humorous, others were sad. Volodimir and I loved the funny ones. Now and again the radio would play some of these old tunes, and we all sang along. It lifted our spirits and it made sure we never forgot who we were and where we'd come from. This was our land. We just wanted to be left alone to live our lives in peace, but our neighbours wouldn't let us. Both the Poles and the Soviets had invaded us throughout our history. We were stuck in between them and we'd been ravaged from both sides many times down the ages. Was it all about to come down on us once again?

Father spent more and more time listening to the radio. Sometimes he'd sit next to it for hours tuning into different stations trying to find out what was going on. All we knew was that the Nazis had advanced into Poland and were driving towards us. All we could do was sit and listen. The radio gave us some information, but there was no way of knowing what was true and what was a lie. That was what the Soviet regime did to us, they turned us inside out with their propaganda.

So, we got our information from other sources. Whispers drifted across to us from all corners of the land, not from announcements on the radio. It filtered through by word of mouth. From village to village and town to town. It got muttered in so many Ukrainian ears. They were on the march. None of us said very much to each other about the rumours. We knew what the Soviets were capable of. Would they come for us in the middle of the night? At gunpoint. To force us to join them and march to the front. Once we got there they'd most likely send us out with one rifle between five to try and do battle with the Nazis.

We didn't want to wear the Red Army uniform and be part of what that stood for. What we really wanted was a free Ukraine, but that seemed more out of reach than ever, so we held our breath and waited. It was like we were frozen. As if we'd seized up. Every day we went about our business as normal. To school or work, and the endless struggle to get fed and keep warm kept us occupied. It was as if we were waiting for something to happen. All the time, our eyes were on the horizon.

Then one night, it must have been close to midnight, a big commotion came our way. The handle on our bedroom door rattled, and the glass in the window trembled. There was a low rumble in the distance. Volodimir and I woke up wondering what was happening.

'Volodimir! What's going on?'

'I don't know! What in Heaven's name can it be?'

The rumbling increased. It seemed to be underneath us, on top of us and all around us, all at once. Was the ground about to swallow us up? At that point Father burst into our room, 'Boys, stay quiet and keep your heads down!'

We both buried our heads in our pillows and pulled our blankets right up. The vibrations got stronger and gradually the noise grew even more, it pounded in my ears as if our village were being bombarded by large rocks and boulders from a landslide. I sat up, and in the moonlight creeping through our curtains, saw that Volodimir had done the same. The noise got louder and louder. The three of us edged across to the window and looked through the curtains. There was a flickering line of white light hovering in the sky. It was growing and getting closer. The roar of engines filled the air. I don't know about Father or Volodimir but I remember very well my heart beating so hard in my chest I thought I might explode. Then we saw them. Soviet trucks, one after the other, driving right past our house. They were all different sizes. Some were covered, others carried machinery or armoured vehicles. The procession seemed to go on forever. This was it. The Red Army was right in amongst us. They were heading west, towards the border we shared with Poland. I really hoped they wouldn't hang around. Occasionally they seemed to slow down as if they might stop and my heart pounded again, but thankfully, they picked up in speed once again and after about 20 minutes the procession tailed off. The noise and the glow faded into the distance. We breathed again. This time we'd been spared, but for how long? There was no way of knowing whether the trucks would stop somewhere nearby and then visit all the local villages to conscript men and boys, or whether they would head straight to the border. The silence and the darkness were back with us.

'They've gone. I hope they don't come back this way again. Don't worry boys. Just get back to bed and I'll see you in the morning.' Father closed our bedroom door. But could we sleep? Not a chance.

'What do you think'll happen Volodimir?'

'I don't know. But we need to find out. I know. Let's get up early. Then we can have a walk down the road. See if they're still nearby or whether they've travelled further.'

'Okay.'

That was our plan. I was nervous. I'll admit that, but we were accustomed to seeing Soviet soldiers around anyway and we'd learned how to keep out of their way. We knew the lanes and the meadows around our village and beyond, so we'd just make sure we weren't seen. That was one of Volodimir's great talents. He loved the countryside, and he seemed to also have an instinct when it came to travelling across the land. He'd navigate us through without being seen. I had no doubts about that.

Sleep was slow to come that night, which was not surprising with the Red Army so near. I hoped they'd keep going, right on into oblivion for all I cared. We lay in bed, talked a little, and then just waited, hardly daring to breathe. A minute would pass. Then another. And another. I felt like screaming. In my head I could still see the line of trucks going by, I was sure I could still hear them. I broke into a sweat. I half expected to hear a banging on the door and loud Russian voices demanding to come in. I tried to sleep. We needed to find out what was happening, but to do so we needed daylight and it was slow coming.

Eventually, slivers of sunlight appeared through the gaps in the curtains. I sank down into the bed and breathed a little easier, but I could hardly keep my eyes open. I closed them and started to doze.

'Stefan. Come on, wake up.'

I eased my eyelids back up. Volodimir was standing over me. 'Come on Stefan. We said we'd make an early start.' I rubbed my eyes and pulled the covers off. I staggered up out of bed and quickly pulled on my trousers, shirt and socks. Volodimir was already dressed. I followed him out of the bedroom and into the kitchen. I looked at the clock. It was five thirty.

Mother was standing at the sink washing some vegetables. She turned around,

'Boys! You're up early. Is there an occasion of some sort? You two usually stay in bed later on a Saturday.' Volodimir and I looked at each other. Straight away we knew that Mother didn't know what had happened. Somehow, she hadn't heard the commotion from the Red Army trucks. Well, she survived on so little sleep, I guess she must have been in some deep, deep slumber not to have heard that almighty row.

'One of the boys at school says there are a lot of blackberry bushes in the woods between here and the next village. They're in a secluded spot, so not many know about them, but I reckon I can find them. We thought we'd try and get there early before they get picked by all the other children,' said Volodimir.

'Blackberries eh? Don't forget to bring some back. I can bake us a nice pie. Well, you'd both better sit down and have some breakfast before you go.'

Volodimir and I shuffled our feet. We didn't want to hang around too long in case Father got up. Just lately he'd got into the habit of staying up late on a Friday night and listening to the radio into the early hours. It usually meant he got up a little later on a Saturday. He could have appeared any time and would have been suspicious. Certainly, he would not have allowed us to go out that morning under the circumstances. Not with the Red Army in the area. Volodimir persuaded Mother to pack us up some bread and butter and some bottles of milk instead of having breakfast at the table. After all we didn't want to miss out on those lovely, juicy blackberries did we? We pulled on our boots and threw on our jackets while Mother packed up our bag of provisions.

'Be careful boys. Get back for some dinner won't you?'

'Of course, Mama.'

She gave us both a peck on the cheek, handed us our bag of supplies, and we hurried out of the door. We ran down the road away from the house until we were almost out of sight. The early morning gloom swallowed us up, we could just about see where we were going. There was a chill in the air.

'You shouldn't lie to Mother.' I scolded Volodimir.

'I wasn't. There are blackberries out in the woods. We'll find some, trust me.'

I wasn't convinced, but soon forgot about it as we crunched through the autumn leaves to the edge of the village. Although the darkness still hung heavy over us, a golden shimmer lingered on the horizon. The sun was coming up. We weren't all that far out of the village when we saw some deep tyre tracks in the mud. We looked at them closely in the half-light. They were from big trucks. It showed the Soviets meant business. We looked at each other. Neither of us said anything but perhaps our thoughts were the same. The Soviets had put together an army big enough to fight a full scale battle, but would they come looking for more soldiers once they'd lost some?

We clambered up a bank and walked across some fields using whatever cover we could to shield ourselves from the road. In some places the grass was long, in others there were shrubs and bushes for us to weave in and out of. We ducked in and out of the trees and tried to make ourselves invisible as best we could. On and on we walked. There were a few signs of life stirring around us. The birds sang to us, and the autumn sun finally came up and threw piercing orange rays through the trees. Otherwise, there was little sign of life. There was no sign of any Soviet trucks either.

A mile or two further on, we still hadn't seen anything and we were about ready for some food. My stomach was making noises.

'Can we stop and have the bread and milk now?' I asked Volodimir.

'Yes, let's just get across to those trees over there and we can sit down.'

Fifty or so metres further on we reached those trees and walked through them with the sunlight flickering through from further beyond. It was slightly damp around us but we managed to find a small clearing with some good sized rocks to sit on. It was a sunny spot and quite dry. We threw ourselves down onto them and Volodimir started to unpack our breakfast. Just then I spotted something nearby. It was a movement in the trees next to us. I froze. Was it a small animal? Maybe a rabbit? Or a fox?

'Volodimir,' I hissed, 'what was that?' He turned his head to listen closer.

There was a rustling sound and it was getting stronger. We stood up and watched as two figures emerged from the trees right in front of us.

'Don't move! Stay right where you are and put your hands up!' Volodimir dropped the bag and we slowly raised our hands above our heads.

It couldn't have been any worse for us. The pair inching closer to us were Soviet soldiers, one of them holding up a rifle and pointing it at each of us in turn. We kept very still. They walked towards us not saying anything and I couldn't believe what was in front of me. They were just boys! They weren't much older than us. Their uniforms were too big for them and their helmets looked like giant mushrooms. Their belts hung limp around their waists. They looked more like clowns than soldiers. I stopped myself from smiling.

'What's in the bag?' yelped the smaller one, the one without the rifle. He spoke in Russian which we understood.

'J – Just some bread and milk,' replied Volodimir. The bag was snatched up and the smaller one pulled out one of the pieces of bread and tore into it, shoving it down like he hadn't eaten for days. Then he took some swigs of the milk. They swapped over. The smaller one kept the rifle on us, while the larger one took some bread and milk. The smaller one paced from side to side, never taking his eyes off us. The larger one didn't speak at all.

'Right! We need some information from you. You'd better tell us the truth or we'll blast you to Hell!'

'W-what is it you want to know?' replied Volodimir.

'We want to know how to get to the mountains. To join the Resistance. You tell us how to get there from here, and tell us good!'

'What about the Red Army? Shouldn't you be with them?'

Still holding the rifle, the smaller one stepped closer until we could see right down the barrel of the rifle. I caught a whiff of gunpowder.

'You want to know about the Red Army? Okay, we'll tell you about the Red Army. They make us march on empty stomachs. They give us weapons, but don't show us how to use them. And anyway, not all of us get weapons. They treat us like dogs, but expect us to fight for the glory of Stalin and his Bolshevik ideals. We've had enough. Now tell us how to get to the mountains!'

Well, in their situation, the two young Soviet soldiers couldn't have struck it luckier. Volodimir's love of the countryside, together with the fact that, as a family, we'd travelled west many times to visit relatives, meant that he was able to tell the two young soldiers the best way to get to the Carpathians in Galicia where it was common knowledge that the Resistance was based. The two of them listened to Volodimir closely and what he said to them must have rung true. To head south west, stay near to the waterways and the southern border. It all made perfect sense. While they listened to him they finished off what was left of the bread and milk. The smaller one threw down the bag, took a step closer and shoved the rifle in our faces. 'Right you two! Lie down on the ground! Face down!' We dropped to our knees and lay down.

'Put your hands out flat in front of you, and don't move!'

Then everything went quiet. Everything stopped. I don't know for how long. Even the blades of grass brushing my face seemed to stand still. The birds weren't singing. I searched inside my head for a prayer.

The silence was broken by two pairs of feet swishing through the grass. We didn't move a muscle until the sound was very faint, until we couldn't hear it. Then we pushed ourselves up onto our knees and turned around. We took a few deep breaths. In the distance we saw the two boys. They'd raced off so quickly they were already more than a hundred metres away on the other side of the road. Volodimir and I stood up and brushed off the soggy leaves and the dirt. My hands were shaking. Even though we were used to seeing armed soldiers around, it was the first time I'd ever had a rifle pointed at me at such close range. Volodimir put his arm around my shoulders, 'Come on Stefan, let's go home.' I just nodded. I couldn't speak. We stood up. My legs were heavy, as if they were rooted into the ground. I took a few steps and we walked back the way we came. It was a slow walk, but I was never happier to be going home and lifted my face up to soak up the sun which was now shining down on us. Once we'd gone about a mile we stepped back onto the road where it was easier to walk. We thought it unlikely that any Soviets were in the immediate area.

As we got closer to the village Volodimir jumped up off the road onto the verge and climbed up onto the top of a wooden fence.

'Where are you going?' I asked.

'Come on Stefan, let's have a look around here.'

We were some distance away from the place where we'd run into the Soviet soldier boys and I was feeling a little better. So I jumped up and we climbed over the fence. We were in an overgrown meadow area with trees, shrubs and long grass all around us. Wild flowers of all shapes and sizes flicked around our knees as we made our way through this lovely glade. Volodimir led us through some trees until right in front of us were three or four bushes with luscious ripe blackberries covering them. We got to work. I felt a lot better after we'd filled ourselves up with the blackberries. We just about stripped those bushes. It was typical of Volodimir to find them.

'Have you been here before Volodimir?'

'No.'

'How did you know these blackberries were here?'

'I didn't. I just got a feeling, from the way it looked when we were walking by.'

As brothers Volodimir and I were close. I could usually tell when he was lying. On this occasion it was clear to me he was telling the truth. This was typical of him. He was a real country boy, it was almost as if he'd sprouted up from the earth himself, his bond with nature was just like the early morning dew on a blade of grass - he was part of the natural world around him. From an early age he helped Mother in our smallholding with planting out and tending crops. Well, we both did, but the difference was, Volodimir was a natural. Everything he touched in our garden bloomed and flourished. He seemed to know what the weather would do, he had an instinct for it. He could tell us when it was going to rain, or when to expect snow. Most of the time he was right. He had a way with the animals too, as soon as he walked into our barn they all turned to look at him and walked towards him. He'd pat and stroke them and make cooing noises in their ears. They loved him. He always knew if one of them was sick or not so well.

Volodimir and I filled our bag with blackberries to take home for Mother and made our way back down to the road. We carried on walking, and before long we reached the outskirts of the village. There were a few villagers around, going about their daily business. It was a warm morning. Volodimir and I were tired from our exertions.

Thirsty too. The blackberries had filled us up but their sweet juices left our mouths sticky. I wanted a drink of milk or water to freshen up my mouth, but inside I was shaking. I ran my fingers through my hair and, as we got closer to our house I slowed right down.

'Stefan, what is it? Come on, we're nearly home.'

'But Volodimir, Father'll ask us questions, you know he will.'

'Don't worry. He might shout at us, but Mother'll be pleased to see us. She'll look after us.'

We walked up to the front door and opened it. All seemed quiet and we stepped inside, hoping to sneak into our room without being seen, but there was no chance of that. Mother and Father were sitting at the kitchen table looking right at us. As soon as Mother saw us she rushed over and hugged us tight. 'Boys! I'm so glad you're all right! I've been so worried. Where have you been?'

It was still early. We hadn't been out that long, but Father obviously suspected that we'd been up to no good and must have shared his concerns with Mother.

'We've brought some blackberries back for you.' Volodimir handed the bag to Mother.

'Oh that's lovely! Look at this lot! There's enough to make us a big juicy pie here.'

'Yes, we found a whole lot of bushes right inside the deepest part of the wood.'

'You've done well, my boys,' Mother beamed at us, 'what a lovely lot of blackberries.'

Father, however, was looking at us with furrowed brows, 'So boys, did you see any Soviet trucks out there?'

'Well, we walked a while, and then we saw some deep tracks in the mud and decided not to go any further.'

Volodimir was a sly one. He could talk his way out of most things. I'm not entirely convinced Father believed us, but like Mother, he was glad to have us back safely. He forbade us to leave the village from that time onwards. He was right to do so. It was too dangerous. Anyhow, we weren't exactly eager to relive the experience. Mother poured us each a long cool glass of milk and we drank it down. I felt safe again, inside the cosy walls of our little house. It was familiar. God looked over us in our home.

Village life carried on, just like always. In fact, because of the situation in Poland we were able to go about our daily routine with less interference from the Soviets. They were occupied in taking back Western Ukraine from the Poles and securing that border. We lived our lives one day at a time.

Father listened to the radio more and more. The Nazis broadcast their propaganda, the Soviets theirs, as ever it was impossible to tell what was true and what was not.

I immersed myself in school, and in particular Ukrainian literature. The words of writers such as Taras Shevchenko and Ivan Franko seared into my heart and soul. They truly defined what it is to be Ukrainian, and Lord knows all our enemies had tried so hard to take that away. I enjoyed my studies. I wanted to know about the world around me, and all about the rest of the world across the seas, oceans, deserts and plains. We had some good teachers and I was always interested in how people lived in other parts of the world.

I had an aptitude for the practical side of things too. When I was 12 our class was instructed in woodwork. As we walked into the workshop for the first time the industrial smell of it filled my nostrils and I gazed in wonder at the rack upon rack of tools that were neatly stored in large cupboards. We learned about each one of them, and before very long, I was sawing, planing and chiseling joints. We practised the basics until we were deemed to be proficient enough to begin a project. Within a few weeks the woodwork teacher, Mr Markovych, took me to one side, 'Stefan, you are doing very well in this class. It's time for you to start a project.'

'Thank you Mr Markovych.' I was truly excited about making something rather than just cutting joints for practice. He passed me a sheet of paper. I examined it and my eyes lit up. It was a plan of a model aeroplane. It was perfect. I hoped I'd be allowed to keep it.

'So Stefan, make a good job of this and you can take it home. It has to be perfect though, otherwise we'll keep it here and reuse the wood.' It was as if he'd read my mind. Mr Markovych gave me a bundle of rough timbers of various sizes. He helped me sort through them and work out which to use for each section of the aeroplane and then I was away. I planed each piece of wood, taking care to keep them perfectly square. Then I cut out the right lengths. Before long I was planing again and shaping each section, cutting joints and sanding down. Within a few weeks I was ready to assemble the aeroplane. I was nervous. Mr Markovych saw how hesitant I was and stepped in to help me at the gluing up stage. With his help I successfully put the aeroplane together. It looked fantastic! The propeller and the wheels all rotated perfectly and it looked just right. I lifted it above my head and made a whirring engine noise to give it its maiden flight.

'Stefan! Put that down. You haven't finished it just yet.' Mr Markovych explained that I would need to apply a final rub down to the aeroplane with fine sand paper, wipe it down and begin the process of varnishing. It took another two weeks to apply enough coats of varnish, and just before the final coat I painted a Ukrainian flag on the fuselage. A strip of blue and a strip of yellow, our national colours. Mr Markovych smiled at me when he saw this and ruffled my hair. 'Well done Stefan.' While I was waiting for the coats of varnish to dry I was left without much to do in the workshop so Mr Markovych came to me, 'Stefan, another student started an aeroplane project some time ago but he never finished it. His family moved out of the area, so we haven't seen him. Would you like to finish it off?' Of course I was only too happy to take his offer up and, a couple of weeks later was walking home with a pair of beautifully polished, gleaming wooden aeroplanes.

When I got home I gave one of them to Volodimir. They became part of our daily games. The only other toys we had was a box of old tin soldiers that our Grandmother had given us, a relic from one of the abandoned houses. We played war games. We launched our Ukrainian fighter planes and they dived down over enemy lines and destroyed the invaders. It didn't matter who the enemy were, they might have been Soviets or Poles. We drove them back, away from our land. That was all we wanted, nothing more.

The days passed by. The radio played and we listened as much as we could, or were allowed. When we heard about the Nazis invading France, and North Africa, we took notice. According to news reports the Nazi army was strong, organised and heading our way. Maybe we'd be free of our Soviet oppressors once and for all. Some people thought the Nazis would help us Ukrainians get our freedom. We waited. None of us really knew what lay ahead. All around us were the warmongers. The Red Army guarded our border, the Nazis on the other side, but there was no invasion. It was a stalemate and none of us could understand why. The Nazis were invading and conquering most of Europe. Why had they stopped at our border?

Two years of tension passed by, and we arrived at the year of 1941. Every day our eyes looked to the west. We wondered what was to come. Winds of turmoil blew across the mountains and the plains right into our homes. We knew there were many battles and conflicts taking place. It was as if the wind howled with the wails of those who had perished. The Nazis were sweeping through everything in their path. The British, and only the British it seemed, were out to stop them. France was already in Nazi hands. That much we knew.

Despite all the unrest and uncertainty we carried on living our lives. We liked to laugh and have fun just like boys and girls all over the world. We'd gather together in the village square. Once the icy winter had passed, we were there most evenings. Volodimir, Miron and I were always together. In the early spring it was often still chilly so we'd be wrapped up in hats and jackets. Other boys gathered there and, sometimes, one of them would dish out cigarettes. We were growing up you see, and we wanted to be just like the adults. Girls would walk past and we'd shout to them,

'Hey! My lovely, you look beautiful! Come and talk to us.'

Most of them would keep walking, their cheeks flushed, but one or two came over and we chatted to them. All the boys would try to impress the girls. We all tried to make them smile, by goofing around and with lots of clowning. All the jumping around kept us warm. The girls just watched and giggled. One of them I became quite fond of. Her name was Natasha. She had long black curls, lovely blue eyes and skin so soft and smooth it was like the dough that Mother made for baking bread. She would come up to me and stand very close. We'd hold hands and she'd whisper,

'Stefan, you're my little Kozak.' I loved that. Her breath on my neck made me tingle all over. She was an angel. At this time I was 13 years old. I'd only ever kissed my beloved Mother and Grandmother. To be honest I'd always been a little shy with girls. Volodimir and the other boys teased me about Natasha, but one evening, in the spring, I was there in the village square with her. None of the others were around. As usual we were holding hands. Our breath turned to mist in front of us. Then we turned towards each other and kissed. It was a sweet moment if a little awkward. We held onto each other tightly. Her lips were so soft. We kissed several times and then she rested her head on my shoulder. We stood there together. I wanted to be with her like that for ever. The moment was shattered by the arrival of Volodimir, Miron and several other boys, 'Ooh, look at the two lovebirds! Aahhh! Don't they look lovely together?' Natasha and I stepped away from each other but we shared a secret smile. It was a moment I would never forget. In the weeks leading up to Easter I met with Natasha almost every night. We'd meet in the square. Then we'd walk to the nearby woods to find a secluded spot. I'd bring along my copy of *Kobzar** by Taras Shevchenko and I'd read aloud to her. Her favourite was always *Why*

Should I Have Black Eyebrows? She'd laugh out loud and say, 'Stefan, that's just like you. Your eyebrows are black as coal.' I loved being next to her. She was a year older than me and a little bit taller, so I always preferred it when we were sitting down together rather than standing up. I suppose you could say she was my first girlfriend. Well, Volodimir, Miron and all the other boys never tired of reminding me of that. They'd often disturb us, just when we'd found somewhere quiet to be together and talk. They'd sneak up on us just when we'd got close and were about to kiss, 'Stefan!! The boys are here! It's good to see you two lovebirds. You always find the best places. Can we join you?' Volodimir grinned mischievously. There was no point in trying to get away from them. Anyhow, we were a band of brothers, I could never turn these Kozaks away. We had a code, to stand together on our land and carry the fight as best we could. We would never surrender who we were to anyone.

Easter came and the whole village celebrated, as usual. I didn't see Natasha for over a week because she lived on the other side of the village. At home, Mother and Father arranged for our traditional offering of painted eggs, ham, soft cheese, bread and *paska** to be blessed by the local priest. Then, after prayers we'd all sit down and Mother would slice up some bread and the *paska*, we'd butter them well and partake of our Holy meal.

All around nature bloomed, the grass, the greenery and the spring flowers returned with all their fragile, delicate beauty. Our winter coats were put away and we left our boots indoors, we wore our summer shoes in the spring. It sounds silly I know, but in the really hot days of summer we'd go barefoot to save on shoe leather. Father forever scolded us for scuffing up our footwear and, every few weeks, we'd see him at his workbench in a corner of the barn repairing someone's boots or shoes.

I hadn't seen Natasha for two or three weeks. I wouldn't have admitted it to anyone but I was missing her. Even though I liked to hang around with the boys, at times I walked around the village on my own, hoping to see her. I even went to her house one day and knocked on the door. Her mother answered and said that Natasha wasn't home.

Anyway, I hung around with Volodimir, Miron and the other boys and I can't say I didn't have fun. Summer was approaching and the glorious sunshine bathed us in its glow, but some days the weather was bad and the rain was often heavy. On those occasions I'd play indoors with Volodimir. We had the wooden aeroplanes and the soldiers. In our bedroom we'd mark out a battleground. Ukraine always emerged victorious with piles of tin soldiers flattened along its borders.

There was still no sign of Natasha. Until one day in June when we boys were walking through the village. There was a big gang of us, maybe about eight or nine. We turned a corner and there she was. There was no mistaking her. She was with another boy and they were kissing with some passion. My heart twisted around and turned somersaults inside me. I wanted to reach out to her but I couldn't move my arms. I wanted to run up to her, get hold of her and hold her tight, and tell the other boy she was mine, but my legs wouldn't move. I thought about calling out to her but my throat was too dry and when I opened my mouth nothing came out. The next thing I knew Volodimir was beside me, with his arm around my shoulders.

'Come on Stefan, let's go home.'

Thinking back now, she wasn't right for me anyhow. She was too old, and too tall. It was just a teenage infatuation, but at the time it was as if my whole world had collapsed around me. It was getting late, close to supper time, so we made our way home. I sat through supper quietly and went to bed early. I was tired. I thought about Natasha while I lay in bed. It took me some time to get to sleep, but eventually I nodded off.

Of course I dreamt of her. We were walking hand in hand, barefoot, through a meadow caressed in golden rays from the sun. Laughing and smiling we chased each other. Then we stopped and I picked flowers and gave them to her. All around us was a peace, a kind of calm, as if there was no one else in the world, just the two of us. Then we looked up and a dark cloud sat in the sky above us. We shivered, and then there was a crack of thunder.

I woke up, but the crashing sounds continued and, once again, our house was shaking. On a shelf in the corner of the bedroom were the two wooden aeroplanes I'd made. The vibrations caused them to slip to the edge of the shelf, and then a thunderous boom thudded through the air causing the planes to topple off the shelf down into the army of tin soldiers below. The soldiers scattered all over the floor. Volodimir sat up with a start. I jumped out of bed and ran to the window. I looked through the curtains. There was fire in the sky.

Chapter 4

Ukrainian proverb: A hungry wolf is stronger than a satisfied dog

At daybreak, we cautiously wandered out of our houses. Many of our neighbours were already outside. Father walked down our approach with Volodimir and me following while Mother stayed indoors. There was a silence amongst us, our neighbours and ourselves were gripped by a collective dread. We walked down the road with our heads bowed. What would we find? A man, one of our neighbours, came running up to us. It was Miron's father, Ivan.

'I've seen it, I've seen it! Come with me! It's not far, come on! It's this way!'

We followed him back down where he'd come from, and about 400 metres away we found ourselves standing at the edge of a crater. The earth was scorched a deep red, and was still smouldering slightly. It was liquid black in places, like melted sugar. The smell was strange, with a sourness that made us screw up our faces.

'Nazi bombs,' said Ivan. Nobody responded, and I don't think he was expecting anyone to. He was just saying it out loud. We walked further and saw more craters, and then some dwellings that had taken an impact. God save us, somehow the damage had all been to outhouses or barns. None of the actual houses had been hit.

Villagers stood in a line from the well passing down bucket after bucket of water to finally put out the flames which had been raging all night. People had lost some of their livestock, but there had been no human loss. We'd been lucky for once, but would our luck last?

'Come on, boys.' Father, Volodimir and I turned away from the scenes of devastation and trudged home. We walked up our approach, and through our gate. To our left was a wooden enclosure built by Father, with a little help from me, to house our geese. There were a dozen of them and they all rushed towards us as we passed, honking away madly. We looked across at them, and I don't know what Father or Volodimir were thinking, but I was glad of the geese. They filled an unbearable silence, and perhaps they showed us that to make ourselves heard we needed a voice – a loud one, a voice which wouldn't stop. Mother came out of the house with a bucket of cornmeal to feed them and they soon calmed down. She turned towards Father,

'Did you find out what the noise was?'

'Yes, Olha. It's what we've feared for a while. We've been bombed, but people have only suffered damage to livestock and outbuildings, so far anyway. But it looks like the Nazis are coming our way. There's no doubt about that.'

Mother walked up to the three of us and pulled us together in an embrace,

'Oh, Mikola. Oh, boys. What will become of us?' Her eyes were red around the edges and there were tears in them. Eventually, she released the three of us, and then Father spoke, 'All we can do is wait and see. In the meantime we have work to do around here. Let's keep ourselves busy.' He put his arm around Mother and walked into the house with her. Volodimir and I followed. Once inside, he instructed us to put on our work shirts and trousers, the ones we used around our smallholding when helping out with the daily tasks. Then, Volodimir took our cow out to the pasture while I followed Father into the barn, 'Stefan, it's going to be a long, hard winter. We need to prepare ourselves.' He rolled up his sleeves and took up a position next to a large pile of logs. He picked one of them up, placed it on a chopping block and raised the axe above his head. With a muscular swing of the axe he split the log in two, and then put the axe through each of the smaller pieces again. I gathered them up and put them in a small barrow. Once it was full, I wheeled it across the barn where we had a large crate to store our firewood, and stacked them neatly inside. We worked liked this for quite some time, without stopping or speaking to each other. The sweat poured off Father as, over and over again, he swung the axe down. The sound of the splintering wood shuddered through me again and again. The crate was beginning to overflow, but Father continued to chop the logs, paying no heed to this. I started a small, neat, pile of firewood in front of the crate.

Then, it must have been almost two hours later, Volodimir came back with our cow, and it was only then that Father stopped. He watched as Volodimir led the cow back into its place in the barn. Then he hung the axe up and said, 'Come on, boys, let's get a drink.' Wearily, he led us boys into the house. Mother was standing at her stove, busy as ever with a steaming pot. There was a melody floating through the air. I smiled to myself. How I cherished that sound, it sent shivers up and down me every time I heard it. Mother's singing was truly beautiful, like that of a nightingale. She turned around and smiled at us. She poured us all a glass of milk and we drank it down.

'Well,' said Father. 'This is it. We're in the middle of a war now. Things are going to get difficult for us. We have to try to hold on to what we've got and stick together.' As we sat in the kitchen and drank our milk, I never for one minute thought that we'd ever be apart. I prayed to God we'd all stay together.

The radio fizzed, whined and crackled more than ever as Father tried to find out what was happening. The Soviet broadcasts had stopped, there was nothing from Moscow, no propaganda broadcasts, no public information, nothing.

Meanwhile the Nazis' voice was all too clear. *'We are here as liberators. You have been ruled by the dictatorial power of the Bolsheviks. Germany will conquer them! Join us in our quest for freedom. The Soviet Union has treated you like slaves. The military might of the German Army will drive them back.'*

It was 1941 and I'd just turned 14. I'd grown up in some very tough times. None of us expected things would improve much, but we wouldn't be sorry to see the back of the Soviets.

Like a spider spinning its web, the Nazis infiltrated and occupied every corner of our beloved Ukraine. The disorganised and bedraggled Soviet soldiers were easily driven back. Many times we cowered in the darkness of our homes in the chilly autumn evenings, listening to bombs exploding, some far away, others very close. Too close. It wasn't long before the Nazis were amongst us.

As they drove through the village, some people greeted them with traditional offerings of bread and salt, and a large crowd assembled to cheer them. The procession of Panzer tanks, armoured vehicles, and Nazi soldiers on motorbikes was truly impressive. Everything about them, the vehicles, their uniforms, their weapons, all seemed superior. Would this mean the end of the purges and the terrors? Maybe people wouldn't just disappear anymore. Soviet rule had left its scars on us. Surely things couldn't be any worse under the Nazis?

The Nazi convoys drove to the far side of the village and headed towards Vinnitsya, stopping only to take over the local village hall and install a radio communications team there with a unit of armed soldiers to oversee them, and patrol the village. The main body of the convoy marched on towards the city.

'What do you think?' I asked Volodimir as we watched the Nazis in action.

'I don't know, Stefan. The Soviets have gone and that's good, but I'm not sure about these Nazis. As Father says, we'll have to wait and see, I suppose. But to be honest, Stefan, they look like a whole lot of trouble to me.' I'd learnt to trust Volodimir's instincts. He was such a good judge of people and situations.

The following Monday morning, Volodimir and I walked to school in the bright, cool sunshine of early summer. To me, that sunshine seemed more golden than ever before, because the Soviet menace that had inflicted so much misery on us was no longer around. Further down the road, we came across an armoured car full of German troops. They were dishing out chocolate bars to all the passing children. As soon as Volodimir and I saw this, we broke into a sprint. A few minutes later, we were cramming chocolate into our mouths.

'You see Volodimir, the Germans aren't so bad are they?' I said between mouthfuls of chocolate.

'Hmmm, we'll see.' he replied.

The school day passed slowly. With the summer upon us, we boys and girls just wanted it to end so we could be out in the sunshine. We'd had enough of sitting in a dusty classroom. At the end of the day, we charged through those school gates without looking back, with little regard for those crumpled books stuffed into our overflowing wooden desks. There was still plenty of daylight left and we had games to play, and girls to tease, and plenty more besides. Volodimir and I ran up our approach, ready to dump our schoolbags, grab a slice of bread and butter if one was available, and then be out again as soon as we could, to meet our friends.

We burst through the door to see Mother and Father sitting at our kitchen table drinking from tea mugs. 'Hello Mama', I said, 'is there anything for us to eat?' But I froze when I saw Mother's tear-stained face.

'Boys, boys, come in and sit down,' said Father in a voice that was more of a whisper than his usual authoritative tone, 'we need to talk . . .'

Volodimir and I sat down with some uncertainty inside us. I wondered what could be troubling Mother and Father.

'Let me tell you what happened today,' resumed Father, regaining some composure, 'I went to work at the nail factory as usual to find everything completely wrecked. The machines had been ripped out and most of the tools were gone, it was a hollow shell. My workmates and I just stood there looking at it all when we heard the sound of engines from outside. We looked out of the window and saw a couple of armoured cars. Soldiers jumped out of them and came into the building.'

Father paused to take a swig from his mug of tea.

'The officer in charge came up to me, because I was standing at the front, and asked me all about the factory. I told him all I knew in my best German, and then he and the other soldiers kicked us out. That officer, who went by the name of Wulf, he wanted to use the factory, for the war effort I guess, and it means we've all lost our jobs. Some of the fellows began to complain and wave their arms around, but the soldiers lowered their guns and pointed them at us, so that was that.'

Father stopped again and drank down the rest of his tea.

'Don't worry, Father,' said Volodimir, 'we'll manage somehow. Stefan and I can catch lots of fish through the summer months and we can store plenty to keep us going through the winter.'

Father smiled at Volodimir, but we sensed there was more, Mother was still motionless at the kitchen table with fresh tears flowing from her.

'Thank you, Volodimir, I know you and Stefan'll help out and I really appreciate that, but it's not quite so simple.' Father stood up from his chair and paced up and down, and finally stood next to the stove, facing us.

'We milled around outside for a while. Many of us were angry and some of the fellows made comments about damn soldiers. The next thing we knew, that officer fellow, Wulf, and his men came marching out of the factory and over to us. He ordered us to line up, and with several soldiers pointing guns at us we didn't have much choice. Wulf was looking for recruits, fit men who could do heavy work, starting in the morning. He ordered a soldier to take our names and addresses, and then told us to report there first thing. One of us asked him what the nature of the work would be, and he replied: *digging holes*.'

Father reached into his trouser pocket, took out a pack of cigarettes and lit one. Mother lifted her head up and then dried the tears from her face using her apron. She sighed heavily. Father blew out a large cloud of smoke and continued,

'All the while, Wulf kept a hand on his pistol, so we couldn't refuse. As we left, he said: *I never forget a face, so make sure you're all here tomorrow morning, or I'll make it my business to come and find you.*'

Volodimir and I listened and the full horror of what might lie ahead pushed its way into our heads like weeds sprouting across a field.

Neither of us spoke, so Father carried on, 'I'm hoping the Germans only want us digging for a day or two,' Father appeared to tremble a little as he said those words, 'so boys, what I'm more concerned about is how we'll manage without any money coming in. That's what was in my mind as I walked home, so I decided to keep myself busy. I got back and I collected all our jars of marinated vegetables and fish and took them across to the barn. You see, my boys, we've got hard times ahead of us, so I hid those jars in the darkest corners of the barn. I also took all our sacks of grain and hid those too. Then I heard a song floating through the air and that made me turn my head.'

Father looked across at Mother. Her composure was back and she managed a small smile before she spoke, 'I'd been to visit Grandma in Schitky, to take her some bread and a few jars of pickles, and I came up the approach. Of course, those noisy geese rushed up to me and honked away, so I sang a song to them just like I always do. They soon settled down and I turned towards the house and saw Father standing there. I was surprised to see him, but when he explained why he was back early, I was shocked. Why does this have to happen to us? Why?! We're good people, we've never hurt anyone, just got on with our own lives. Now, your Father is being taken away, and Lord knows what'll happen to him!' Mother threw her head down onto her knees and wept. Father pulled a chair across, placed an arm around her, and whispered to her, to soothe her.

I looked at Volodimir and between us, we couldn't find any words. Well, what could you say? We'd been through a period of terror with the Soviets where people were taken out to dig their own graves and then shot in the back of the head, and I wondered whether the Nazis used similar methods. Inside my head I was praying, desperately hoping this was not to be Father's fate. There was no way of escape. There were soldiers guarding all access routes in and out of the village, they were everywhere. A curfew had been imposed on us. No one was allowed out of their homes after ten. Anyhow, Father wished for us all to stick together. There's no way he would have left us and run away. We sat through our supper in a silence that threatened to suffocate us all. Father couldn't eat. He drummed his fingers on the table as he tried to get through his meal of potato pancakes and soured cream. He shuffled his feet. We sat and watched him, hardly daring to move. It was agony. In the end he stood up and threw his chair back, 'It's no good. I don't like to see food go to waste, but right now I need a drink.'

He walked across the kitchen and opened up the cabinet in the corner. He took out a bottle of *horilka**, got himself a glass, and poured a generous measure. He took a mouthful and then topped up his glass again. His shoulders dropped and he seemed to relax a little. He strolled across the room and walked through the door, into our parlour. He sat down on the sofa and breathed deeply. Volodimir and I left the kitchen table and joined him. We sat either side of him, just as we'd done when we were little.

'Boys, whatever happens to me, you must take care of your mother, you know that don't you?' Yes was the only answer we could give to that question. Father smiled at us in turn, and ruffled our hair, almost spilling his glass of *horilka*. He somehow managed a small throaty laugh. I held onto him tight. So did Volodimir.

Mother finished up her tidying in the kitchen and came through to sit with us. She brought the bottle of *horilka* through, 'Here Mikola, have one more, but then that'll be enough. You need a clear head for the morning.' Father drained the rest of his glass and Mother poured him another large one. The atmosphere became a little warmer. Mother turned on the radio, but instead of tuning into news broadcasts, she found a music station. We listened for a while, even whispering some of the words under our breath at times, but we couldn't fully lose ourselves in the music, our minds were occupied. Inside our heads we were fighting to hold off images of devastation, of tragedy, of what might be to come.

There were many hugs exchanged that evening before we went to bed. Mother's eyes reddened, and so did those of mine and Volodimir, but we fought the tears back. The Kozak blood inside us diluted the fear. One day I hoped we'd assemble an army. A mass of men, on horseback with blades and bullets. With righteousness on our side and with the wind behind us, we'd crush all who'd oppose us. Destroy them, all those who brought misery upon us, tear out their hearts and watch as the soil beneath our feet drank down their blood. Free ourselves from the chains of the invaders. Those were my thoughts as I lay down in my bed.

Sleep wouldn't come. I thought about Father. All about our lives and how we'd grown up. The memories soothed me, despite everything. Even with all the terror and hunger around us, we'd stayed together and survived. He'd always done his best for his family. Eventually, I drifted off to sleep.

When morning came, the piercing autumn sun poured through the cracks in our curtains and filled the bedroom with stabs of radiant warmth. I threw my blankets back and got out of bed. I made my way to the kitchen where Mother was silently occupied at a work table, 'Stefan, hurry up, or you'll be late for school.'

'Where's Father?'

'He's gone.' For a second or two, the finality of that statement, of those two small words, struck me like hammer blows. Then we carried on. As if nothing was wrong. I ate some bread, then got dressed and walked to school with Volodimir.

The day creaked along, like an old barn door flapping in a gale. My head was full of so many thoughts, I couldn't focus on anything. The teachers scolded me for daydreaming. I just wanted to go home.

At the end of the school day, Volodimir and I made our way home together. We didn't know whether to walk or run. A gentle breeze blew dead leaves around our legs. At first we dragged our feet, and then we ran as fast as we could until we reached the next bend in the road. Then we walked a short way until we got some of our breath back. Then we ran again. We continued in this fashion all the way home. Whether we were walking or running, we gasped for breath, sometimes hard, sometimes not so hard. This meant we couldn't talk to each other; we couldn't even think. We didn't want to think.

At last we arrived home. All was quiet. We walked up our approach. The geese waddled up to us honking away and flapping their wings, but for once I didn't want to hear them and hurried indoors with Volodimir. Mother was sitting on a chair in the kitchen. She looked worn out with worry. We both ran over to her and hugged her,

'Oh, boys, boys! My beautiful boys. It's like a breath of fresh air when you come home. You make the sun shine in my heart, you know that don't you?' We both smiled at her, but those smiles soon faded, 'Is Father back yet?' ventured Volodimir.

'Not yet, no. But, he'll be here, I'm sure he'll be here soon.' She wiped her eyes with her apron, stood up and poured us both a glass of milk.

It began to get dark. Volodimir lit our oil lamps while Mother dished up our supper. None of us said very much while we ate. The wind was howling around our house. We heard the rustle of the trees and a nearby fence rattled and groaned. The noises made us lift our heads up. We sat and ate with one eye on the door.

Finally, with God's mercy, we heard footsteps and the door opened. Father walked in. He stood there with filthy black hands and face, covered in what looked like earth, but in spite of this, he smiled at us. We ran over to him, but he held his palms up, 'Well, I have to say I'm glad to be back, but let me get myself cleaned up, and then we can all sit down together.'

Mother poured some hot water into a bucket and passed it to Father who carried it out to our back yard. I jumped up and took an oil lamp out for him. The wind had dropped and the evening was calmer. Father stripped off and washed himself down as best he could in the low light from the lamp. He towelled himself down and came inside where he got changed and combed his hair.

He came through to the kitchen to eat his supper and flopped down onto a chair. We let him eat his supper in peace. He demolished his cabbage stuffed with buckwheat in very little time. Then he stretched his arms up and placed them on the back of his head for a few seconds. He looked like the life had been drained out of him. 'Well, I expect you want to hear all about what happened today, so let's go through to the parlour eh?' He picked up a hot cup of tea that Mother had made him, and led the way. We all trooped through. He dropped himself down on the sofa, and we all sat around him.

'There were four open trucks, and about thirty of us all climbed in and tried to make ourselves comfortable. It was a bumpy ride. The driver had little or no thought at all for us, his human cargo. He flew around all the bends at crazy speeds. Eventually we were in open countryside. It must have been quite a few miles away from here. I didn't recognise where we were. They ordered us out of the trucks and, as we climbed out, we were given a spade. Then we set to work. They wanted us to dig up the soil from the land around us and load it into the trucks. We had barrows and planks of wood to ferry the earth. But as soon as they told us to load the soil into the trucks I knew we were to be spared the bullet. Otherwise they'd have left the soil next to the ditch to cover the evidence. We worked all day, like dogs. They gave us a cup of water twice a day, and some thin vegetable soup for our lunch. They worked us hard. If any one of us stopped, we were cuffed by a soldier and told to carry on. It was harsh, very harsh.'

'But what did they want the soil for?' asked Volodimir.

'Well, that's a very good question, Volodimir. And it was one that puzzled us all. Until word got round. Someone overhead one of the drivers joking about what he was going to do later that evening when he got back home to Germany.'

'Germany?' Volodimir frowned.

'They're stealing our land. Our beloved black soil. You know they call us the Breadbasket of Europe don't you? Well, of course you do boys, and everyone else in Europe knows it too.'

We'd been taught this in school. Ukraine's earth was rich and fertile, perfect for growing just about anything you wanted. Father carried on, 'They're thieves, no better than the Soviets. They may turn out to be even worse, who knows?' The Nazi invaders had got their feet firmly planted on our land in a very short space of time, and their intention was to steal it from beneath us and shift it back to Germany. Father endured this backbreaking work until the end of the week until he was no longer needed. The Nazis had taken all they wanted. There was no payment. It must have been heartbreaking for him to be an instrument in the Nazis' crime. We Ukrainians didn't have much. The soil beneath us was one of our most valuable assets. In high summer the rolling fields of golden wheat were a truly wonderful sight. The vegetables we grew were plump and delicious with rich colours. The grass sprouted in thick juicy clumps and provided a nutritious source of food to make our cows fatter. To take this land away was a violation.

He arrived back home a little earlier than usual on the Friday afternoon. He walked up our approach. Mother was standing at the gate. He walked up to her and he could see she was upset, 'Olha, what's the matter?'

'Listen.' she replied.

Father listened, but he couldn't hear anything. He furrowed his eyebrows and cocked his head to one side to try and hear something, 'I can't hear anything, Olha.'

'Look.' She pointed to the enclosure. The one which housed the geese. It was empty.

'Where are they?' said Father.

'The soldiers came this morning. They said they needed food for their troops, and they just ripped the fence down and took them. I tried to stop them, but the Officer, it was the one called Wulf, he gave me such a look I thought he was going to kill me. I was scared, Mikola, I'm sorry.'

'No, Olha, you did the right thing. These damned Nazis are here to take everything from us. We know that now. God damn them to Hell!'

Mother and Father stood there together in a silence which lasted a few seconds until it was broken by the sound of honking! A lone goose wandered out from the enclosure, looking a little sorry for itself.

'Right,' said Father, 'see this goose? I'm going to make sure the Nazis don't get their thieving hands on it.'

He grabbed hold of the goose around its neck. It honked and flapped frantically, like it knew it was on borrowed time. Father took it to a small outhouse at the side of our barn and butchered it. That evening we had something of a feast. The goose was roasted and Mother prepared potatoes and fried cabbage to go with it. We hadn't eaten such a meal for some time. I remember sitting there with my belly full and with a big smile on my face. Of course it meant we wouldn't have any more goose eggs, but I could see Father's reasoning. Better that we should eat the goose before the Nazis took it.

This was how things unfolded. We'd hoped that the Soviet style of collective farming would be eradicated under the Nazis. We were wrong. The soldiers, upon the command of Wulf, took two thirds or maybe even three quarters of our land. They just charged in, with their rifles and bayonets and took everything. They kept us toiling on our own land, but for their own benefit, to feed their own soldiers. We kept many of our supplies well hidden, but we had to be careful. The soldiers were always around. They visited all the local smallholdings on a daily basis to collect whatever food they could to feed their army. We were left with the scraps.

One day, Wulf marched onto our back yard. Mother and Father went out and greeted him. He stood upright, with his legs apart and his arms folded across his chest. Flanked by armed infantrymen, he fixed Father with his iron gaze, 'So. I'm informed you have a cow here?'

'We do, Sir. She gives us milk. We make butter and cheese with it. That cow is a blessing to us, Sir.'

Wulf strode up to the barn and looked at our cow, 'Well then, you must provide for our soldiers. After all, we are here to offer you and your family protection from the damned Bolsheviks, therefore I must insist that you supply milk, butter and cheese on a regular basis. I'll assign a soldier to collect the rations. You won't let me down, will you?' We all breathed a collective sigh of relief, but tried not let it show. We stood impassive, like nothing could touch us. Our faces betrayed nothing. That was something we'd learned under the Soviets, never give anything away. Father nodded and agreed to provide some supplies, but secretly, inside he was glad the Nazis weren't taking the cow away. We all were. Because our cow was a lifeline. Even if we gave the Nazis half of what she produced we'd still have enough for ourselves, but again, Father took steps to hide extra rations. Just enough for those times when we were running short, or enough to pass on to our grandmother in the next village.

If we thought times were hard under the Soviets then we were fools to think Nazi rule would be any better. They were an army on the march and wherever they went they took what they needed. They didn't care about anyone else.

Our village was on the outskirts of Vinnitsya, and we had suitable sites in the surrounding area with potential for factory buildings, and so we had ended up with quite a number of industrial premises, similar to the nail factory where Father worked. Over a number of years, despite Soviet rule, the factories had provided paid work for the local population. A level of prosperity had flowed from these factories. The Nazis took them all over. This meant there was no work for the majority of the men in the village. We were all thrown back into yet another struggle to feed ourselves.

Winter began to draw closer. The blackness of the night lowered itself onto us like a big trapdoor over our heads. The Nazis had us in their grip. They squeezed every ounce of life out of us. They were all around us. It was like being trapped in a tomb.

As during the time of the famine, we eked out an existence through our cow's produce, and with bread, potatoes and other vegetables. When Christmas came we had a small celebration. We prayed for peace. We just wanted to be left alone to live our lives. When the New Year came I hoped it would bring change and defeat for the Nazis. I dreamt of a free Ukraine. Then we received a proclamation. Work was available! The Nazis delivered a series of announcements. Men of working age were required in Germany. They would provide transport across the border and there would be plentiful work and improved conditions. This is what they said.

Many signed up and made the journey. Others chose to stay at home. It was a difficult decision. Whether to stay at home and survive on starvation rations or to seek out a better life. Those who signed up were transported across the land to various parts of Germany. It didn't take long before word came back to us. The conditions in Germany were atrocious. It was slave labour. There was no pay and the food was terrible. There were some reports that our people were fed with cabbages that were infested with worms. When this was pointed out to the Germans they just laughed and said it was extra meat. That was what we heard anyhow. It didn't take long for the Nazis to step right into Soviet boots, and treat us like dirt.

Meanwhile, in the background, we had the Resistance. We also had Russian Partisans operating in the area. Both of these factions opposed the Germans and fought a guerrilla war. Sabotage was one of their weapons. They'd disable the Nazi trucks by slashing tyres. They'd steal whatever equipment they could, they firebombed sentry outposts, and they'd position big rocks along the roads in the early hours of the morning to create a hazard for the Nazi truck drivers.

This was all very well, but it had its consequences. Every time such an incident occurred we knew about it all right. Wulf and his men would speed into the village in their armoured trucks, usually around midday when the local bazaar was at its busiest in the village square. They'd round up all the men they could find there. Then they'd pull out a few of them. Maybe about ten, or twenty. It was like the Soviet purges all over again. Except this time we were left with no doubt that these men were to be executed for the latest actions of the Partisans or Resistance.

'*Achtung*!* Yet again, our glorious German army has been sabotaged by the insurgents among you! We don't know which of you have done this, but we must take action to stamp this out! Line up for the execution squad!' Wulf slapped a baton into his gloved fist as he spoke. The men lined up. Wulf walked along the line and made his selection. His infantrymen pulled out the poor unfortunates and they were bundled into the back of a covered wagon, never to be seen again.

It was worse than the Soviet regime in some respects, because we were in a war zone. No one knew what would happen from one day to the next. At least under the Soviets we had some relative periods of stability.

One dark evening in the early weeks of the New Year, in the year of 1942, we were all sat down having dinner when we heard the growl of an engine and the squeal of brakes on our yard. We all looked around, and Father stood up. We heard rapid footsteps and then there was a fierce banging at the door. The door flew open. It was Wulf and his henchmen. He brought the icy winter wind in with him, and through the open door I could see the snow coming down. We'd been sitting in our kitchen with the fire from the stove throwing out its heat. We'd been cocooned together, snug in our family home, until Wulf arrived to break the spell, '*Achtung*! I have received orders from Central Command. The German war effort is placing an enormous burden on our people. We need more Ostarbeiters*. We need more of you back in the Fatherland to work in our factories to support the war effort. You must realise that to keep the Bolsheviks at bay we must all pull together.'

Mother rose up out of her chair and moved towards Wulf, with her hands clasped together, 'Please, please! I beg of you! Don't take anyone from this house. We're a small family. We don't cause any trouble to anyone. Please Sir, just leave us alone!'

Wulf ignored her and stared hard at Father who responded by gathering Mother in his arms and placing her back down on her chair where she sat bent over with her face in her hands, quietly sobbing.

'Well, what's it to be?' said Wulf, his arms folded across his chest.

'Look,' replied Father, 'take me if you have to take anyone, but let these boys stay. They're too young . . .'

'Pah! Too young?' interrupted Wulf, 'When I was their age I was marching with the Hitler Youth. I took part in our youth camps, where we were treated just like men. We were given heavy work to do. But it made us stronger. So, tell me, how old are your boys?' Without hesitation, and with no expression on his face, Father replied,

'My eldest son is fifteen, and the little one is still only thirteen.'

Wulf's eyes narrowed. There was a moment's silence as he surveyed us all in front of him, 'Very well, we'll leave the young one here with you. For now. But the older one must come with us. Right now.'

'Please, Sir, please. I'm begging you. Take me. He's only a boy.' Father placed his palms on his chest as he spoke, offering himself.

'No. You are needed here. To run this smallholding. To provide food for our soldiers. So, young man. Get your hat and coat and put your boots on. You're coming with us.'

Mother looked up. She, Father and I watched in silence as Volodimir was dragged up out of his chair by two of the soldiers. He resisted a little but soon acquiesced when a third soldier stepped in front of him and pointed his rifle at him. The next two minutes passed by as if we were watching through a fog. We were helpless. Volodimir pulled on his coat and fastened his boots. Before he was led away he turned towards us one final time and, in a quiet low voice that echoed in my ears for a long time afterwards, said, 'Look after yourselves.'

He was led out of the door. As the last of the soldiers walked out we followed and stood just outside our front door. The snow was still coming down hard, and Volodimir and the soldiers tramped through it. He was bundled into the back of a truck. The engine roared as the driver clunked into gear and pulled away. Volodimir just gazed out from the back of the truck and we watched as he disappeared down our approach and away down the road. Mother dropped to her knees and, once again, began to sob.

Chapter 5

Ukrainian proverb: When one dog barks at nothing, a dozen will bark with him

It was as if I'd lost an arm or a leg. Volodimir was my big brother and he'd always looked out for me, we looked out for each other, but he'd been carted off by the Nazis, and I was left alone. I was like an orphan. The bedroom I'd shared with him was now more like a barn, it was too big. It was strange to be on my own in there. I had no one to talk to before I went to sleep. Consequently, I spent most nights half awake, wishing he was back with us. Sometimes, I'd find myself talking to the walls, as if he was still there. His bed was opposite mine in our room, and in the mornings I found myself walking over to it to wake him up, just like I'd always had to.

A week passed. Then two, and then three. We heard nothing. Would we hear anything from him ever again? We carried on living, day by day, but in something of a daze it has to be said. I carried on going to school, and my friends all asked me where Volodimir was. I had to choke back tears and be a Kozak as I told them. Then, they told me about their older brothers, cousins and neighbours. That very same evening, many of them had been hauled off by the Nazis.

It was systematic. The Nazis treated us as if we were nothing. Or less than nothing. We were just there to serve them. If we didn't do what they requested then we knew we'd be shot. Because, before long, we found out the extent of their wickedness.

As always, the information was passed on from house to house, whispered behind closed doors, through cupped hands into Ukrainian ears. The Nazis were committing mass murder. It was clear that they'd embarked on a programme to wipe out as many Jews as possible, but not only Jews. They were killing Ukrainians, and other nationalities. More than ever, our lives became about survival.

Living in a war zone carried so much uncertainty. Not only were we occupied by the Nazi invaders, but we had Ukrainian Resistance and Russian Partisans operating in the area. It was chaos. The Nazis took some of the produce from our smallholding, and then we had the Ukrainian Resistance approach us for supplies. By the time the

Russian Partisans came there was little left. There was one occasion, in the chill of an early evening, when a pair of Russians came into the village and walked up our approach. It wasn't the first time they'd come calling, but on this particular occasion, instead of giving them anything, Father got his shovel out and stood in the doorway of our house, 'Away with you! There's nothing here for you!'

I came outside with him and one of our neighbours also came out, with his shovel. The Russians didn't hang around. They fled back into the gloom, back into the murky outskirts of the village. For once we'd managed, in a small way, to defend ourselves and see off some of our adversaries. Okay, so we risked some retribution, but it was unlikely. The Russian Partisans had the Ukrainian Resistance to deal with if they did anything to us.

Our radio crackled away, and as the next few weeks and months passed we heard all about the Nazi drive to the east. They'd captured Kiev and were advancing into Russia, moving like a swarm of metal clad vipers towards Moscow. They seemed unstoppable. As the front moved further east, things calmed down in our village, and life became a little more settled. There were still plenty of soldiers around, but not quite as many as when the Nazis first arrived.

It was around the summer of that year, 1942, that the trains started running again, delivering goods, equipment and mail from the west, from across the border and beyond. These deliveries took place almost daily. Often, my friends and I would stop off near the train tracks on our way to school in the fuzzy haze of the summer mornings. We'd stand on top of an embankment, watching the sunrise, breathing in the warm air and drinking in that golden sun. We'd wait, with a misty silence swirling around our shoulders. We boys pierced through it by shouting, laughing and by fooling around in general. We collected big stones and threw them across to the other side, to see who could throw the farthest or hit one of the trees on the embankment opposite. We ran along into the orange glow of the rising sun. And then, after a while, we heard a rattle echoing from beyond. Thick black smoke poured over the horizon and then she came into view. It was a wonderful sight. With the funnel coughing out smoke, the wheels and connecting straps rotating furiously, the train roared around the bend, the bumpers and front plate of the engine gleaming. We jumped and cheered, and shouted down the bank. The driver leant out of the window of his cab and gave us a big wave.

We knew there was a cargo about to be unloaded, and that

meant we might get something good to eat. To us boys, who'd been through famine, through hardships, who'd walked past dead bodies in the road stripped of flesh and turned into skeletons because of the Soviets, this was a blessing and a gift from God.

Nazi soldiers ushered us away from the entrance of the train station because we were making a nuisance of ourselves as always, and with those rifles pointing at us, we didn't hang around. We continued our walk to school, but in my head I imagined all sorts of delicacies laden on a table. I hoped that, on those trains, would be food for us, endless supplies, with sumptuous aromas and flavours. To be able to sit at a feast and fill ourselves up like never before was a dream I'd had many times.

The Nazis employed local men to unload the trains, and those workers were paid in German Marks. It proved to be a great motivator. Some men got there in the early hours of the morning to secure such a position, others camped out overnight in often freezing conditions. Father never managed to get himself one of these jobs. Well, it was almost a fight to the death at times. There was more than one occasion when a pair of the men from the village would end up grappling with each other, while the Nazi soldiers looked on in amusement, as if they were watching a pair of dogs fighting for scraps.

Despite these petty wrangles, the fact the Marks came into circulation meant we could trade with each other for a wider range of goods. The trains were unloaded, and the goods transported over to the village hall. Father and some of our other neighbours went down there to see what was available, to see if they could exchange some of their own produce for tins of meat or fish. Many times Father came back with a bagful of assorted tins. Mother would pierce one of them with a knife and we'd have marinated herrings for dinner, with lovely fresh slices of buttered bread. I thought of Volodimir at times like these and I looked across at the empty space at the kitchen table. Sometimes I was sure I could feel him there, as if there was something in the air. It was strange. One evening, I sat in his place at the table and was surprised when the seat was warm. Other times, I thought about him sitting there with his big smile. I would've gladly given up my portion of herring to see his face again.

Then, one day, I came home from school, walked through the door and found Father sitting at the kitchen table with a strange expression on his face. A small smile was curling up at the edges of his mouth, but his eyes were reddening around the edges, and his eyebrows were furrowed as if he was struggling to contain himself. We looked at each other for a few seconds. Then he jumped straight up and walked towards me holding an envelope in his hand,

'We've got a letter, Stefan! It's from Volodimir! He's fine. Here, read it.'

He thrust the envelope into my outstretched hand. I stood there and looked at it. Mother was stood at her stove as usual, but she didn't move. She was looking at me, not taking her eyes off me, 'Open it, Stefan,' she finally said.

I pulled a small, flimsy sheet of paper out of the envelope and ran my eyes across it. It was from him! My big brother. My heart leapt inside me as I read those words:

Dear Mother, Father and Stefan,

I'm in a place called Bochum, in the western part of Germany. There are many young Ukrainians here, both men and women. The Germans look after us well, we have enough food, and our life is good. The Germans will win the war and then I can come home and work on our land again, with all of you. I hope to taste Mother's cooking soon and I hope you are all well.

Volodimir

It didn't say much, and the Nazi censors had run their eyes across it to make sure there were no negative words written about them; several sentences had been blacked out. At least we knew he was still alive! Once I'd read the letter, I ran up to Father and we embraced each other. Even though Volodimir was far away, at least I knew there was a chance I might see him again. My heart bounced around inside my chest like it was on a piece of elastic. It was a moment of pure joy, and, in those days, we had to make the most of such occasions. Father poured himself a large glass of *horilka*. Mother opened up one of the tins and we had slices of bread and ham, and she also placed a jar of home-made pickled cucumbers on the table. For an hour or two we chattered about Volodimir and how we hoped he'd be able to come home soon. I went to bed much happier that evening, happier than I'd been for some time.

Meanwhile, all around us things became a little calmer. The activities of the Resistance and the Partisans died off. We all speculated they were perhaps concentrating on targets nearer the front, or maybe on other more important strategic positions. We weren't complaining.

That summer of 1943 was a beautiful one, and, despite the Nazi occupation, we boys tore around the village going about our business. We'd get our chores done, and then in the afternoons we'd laze around the lake, and maybe try and catch some fish. All the usual things we'd always done, but it just wasn't the same without Volodimir. I'll never be able to explain fully how much of a hole he left behind him, and when I got home the mood was different. The thing is, two boys together make a lot of noise. I was on my own. I had no one to argue with, or to laugh and joke with. We always argued over everything and anything, which of us had the biggest portion of food, or who was the fastest or the strongest. Okay, I had the wooden aeroplanes and the tin soldiers to play with, but it wasn't much fun on my own.

Then, one morning during that summer, I got out of bed and went into the kitchen. Mother was there, as always, mixing and stirring in large ceramic bowls, always making sure there was enough bread, or kneading dough to make *varenyky*. Those small dumplings filled with mashed potato and cheese were simply delicious and I smiled to myself as I thought about how Volodimir and I always competed to see which of us could eat the most, until Mother would scold us,

'Boys, boys! That's enough now, you'll end up getting belly ache, you've had plenty.' We were growing boys and we loved our food.

I stood there, rubbing the sleep out of my eyes, still with thoughts of Volodimir lingering in my mind. Mother turned her head and gave me a small, sad smile. I caught my breath. It dawned on me that something was missing: Mother's singing. Those lovely, sweet melodies which always lifted my spirits were no longer floating around our house.

'Mother, why don't you sing anymore?' I blurted out.

She turned around and looked at me, 'I miss him so much, you know, Stefan. I can't sing when he's not here. It's like part of me has been torn away. When he comes back, then maybe I'll find my voice again.' I walked towards her. She pulled me closer and clasped me to her bosom. My beautiful Mother, she was so warm and loving. I wondered how Volodimir would be, without her near him. To be taken away from his family and sent to work as a slave labourer must have been so sorrowful for him, I really felt for him. However, we received several more letters from him over a period of months which were delivered to the village hall, and the tone of them was quite cheerful, but that was typical of him, he wouldn't have wanted us to worry about him and he would also have stayed defiant in the face of his Nazi overlords.

Meanwhile, life carried on. The area around the village hall became a buzzing area of trade, and pretty much the centre of village life. We boys became quite friendly with some of the soldiers who manned the communications room. Well, I guess it was quite boring for them sat in their office, sending and receiving messages. There were four of them, and they were all fanatical about football. During their breaks we'd often see them kicking a ball around. One day, they invited us to join in, and after a kick around, we challenged them to a game, using a combination of our clumsy German and making signs with our hands. It was to be four against four, and the first to five goals would win. We marked out a small pitch on a field next to the village hall, using jackets for the goalposts. As always, I kept goal. The Germans were young, fit soldiers, but their stiff uniforms hampered them to an extent. Even so, they expected to win, and they got off to a good start with two quick goals in succession, with some slick passing and a couple of darting runs from the back by the short stocky one with the shaved head, who grabbed both those goals. They were smiling and looking a little smug, obviously thinking they'd got the beating of us. But, they hadn't reckoned on Miron. Of all my friends, he was the most naturally sporty. He could swim the fastest and the furthest, and he could perform somersaults, cartwheels and flips. He was strong as a bullock, but, best of all, he was a shining star when it came to playing football. We knew our only hope of beating the soldiers was to get the ball to Miron. So that's what we did. He controlled it in a flash and set off on a weaving run with the ball seemingly attached to his feet. He glided past a couple of the soldiers, and then struck a low, hard shot into the goal. He repeated this move twice more and the soldiers stood scratching their heads. We had the lead, three goals to two. The next time Miron got the ball, three of the soldiers surrounded him. With a sly and silky touch he slipped the ball through one of the soldier's legs and the ball rolled to Taras who sent it screaming past the keeper for another goal. That was four two. The soldiers rolled up their sleeves and really got to work. They became a little more physical, barging into us to stop us getting the ball off them. They strung together a few passes and one of them cracked in a fierce shot from half way down the pitch. I was right behind it but fumbled my catch. The ball fell kindly for another of their team who swept it home. I was annoyed with myself, and perhaps a little downcast.

'Don't worry, Stefan,' said Miron, 'we're still in front. We'll beat them.'

But, the soldiers were fired up by then. They weren't about to let themselves become humiliated by a group of boys. They fought like madmen to keep the ball, they passed it around until one of them burst through a gap and was bearing down on goal. Suddenly, from nowhere, just as the soldier was about to blast a shot at me from about five yards out, Miron appeared and flung himself at the ball, just managing to get a toe to it and divert it away from the soldier. The soldier collapsed on top of Miron and the ball rolled towards me. I kicked it as hard as I could and it sailed the full length of the pitch. The soldier keeping goal at the other end lost the flight of the ball in the shimmering tangerine embers of that summer sky. Somehow, it whistled past his fingers. Goal! Five goals to three. We'd won! For a few seconds we went crazy. We jumped and cheered together, all four of us, and then we stopped, sensing that to bask in the soldiers' defeat was maybe not such a wise move. The soldiers just stood there, as if they couldn't believe it. Then, after the briefest of handshakes, three of them sloped back inside. The fourth one didn't rush off quite so quickly. He smiled at us, 'Well played boys. Come with me, I'll get you something to celebrate your win.'

He seemed a good hearted fellow, and we waited in the main hall next to the communications room, while he disappeared into a store room. While we were waiting, the other three walked past and nodded to us, offering congratulatory smiles.

'We'll beat you next time,' said one of them. The soldier returned and gave us each a handful of small chocolate bars. Of course, we were delighted.

We left the hall and I counted the chocolate bars. I'd got six. I hadn't eaten chocolate for a very long time and I was tempted to rip a wrapper off and guzzle down one of the bars there and then, but, I knew I couldn't do that. They were too precious. I knew I could trade them for food. So, on the way home I called into a neighbour's home, one where I was certain I could trade the chocolate. Mr Popovic lived at the bottom of our road, in the largest of the local smallholdings. Lord knows, through all the years of Soviet rule, somehow he'd managed to keep such a large amount of land. He'd most likely crossed some grasping Soviet palms with wads of roubles, and, under the Nazis, for some reason, he was allowed to keep a few hens for the eggs they produced. No doubt, the Soldiers were there most days to steal them, but, just like the rest of us, I also have no doubt that Mr Popovic scooped out as many as he dared in the early hours of the morning and kept them well hidden.

Mr Popovic lived with his wife. It was just the two of them. She was of Polish descent, and it was well known that she was just a little stuck up. She saw herself as the first lady of the village. Mr Popovic had made some considerable money over the years. Most of it had been spent on Mrs Popovic's taste for fine clothes, perfume, make-up and jewellery. The rest of us had always made do with rags, but she was always dressed up really fine. She and Mr Popovic always sat at the front in church, and she always held her hymn book aloft so everyone could see her fine, white silk, elbow length gloves. I was pretty confident I'd be able to trade some of the chocolate bars for some eggs with them, so I walked up their approach, up a set of steps to the front door and knocked. I waited. I was a little nervous, I must admit. The door opened. It was her,

'Hello. Oh. What is it? What do you want?' She stood with shoulders sagging. Her once golden hair was now faded, but I could see that, beneath the creases of time and the distortions of age, there had been a woman of great beauty. For a second or two I was mesmerised, but then I held up one of the chocolate bars and managed to mumble a few words, 'I . . . I'd like to trade some of these for eggs.'

She lowered her head and sniffed, 'Show me,' she said. So I handed it over to her. She peered at it and looked closely at the tiny letters on the packaging. Then she lifted her head up,

'Pavlo! Come here! Pavlo!' She continued to shout like this over and over again, only stopping briefly now and again to get her breath back. Eventually, there was a shuffling sound and he appeared. He too was hunched over, with thin wisps of greying hair plastered down over his head and a somewhat straggly orange moustache drooping down to his chin, 'What is it, my love?'

'This boy has some chocolate. He wishes to trade for some eggs.'

'Well, my love, do you think it's a worthwhile exchange?'

'It's fine Belgian chocolate. I don't know where this boy got it from, and I'm not going to ask him, most likely it's contraband. But Pavlo, you know how much I adore Belgian chocolate. I'd like some. I really would.'

With that she handed the chocolate bar back to me, twirled around and disappeared inside. Pavlo looked at me, 'Well, young man, how many of these have you got?'

I looked up at him, and with the practised deception of many years replied, 'Just two.'

He smiled at me, 'So, how many eggs would you like?'

'A dozen.'

He laughed softly, displaying his crooked, yellow teeth and furred tongue,

'Young man, the most I can give you for two small bars of chocolate such as these are six eggs.'

I hesitated. I didn't want to agree too quickly, but in the end I just nodded. He shuffled back inside and, after leaving me on the doorstep for an uncomfortable few minutes, returned with a box. He opened it, 'Here. Six lovely big ones for you.'

'Thank you, Mr Popovic.'

We made our exchange and I turned, danced down the steps, and ran all the way home. I burst into our kitchen, 'Mother! Mother! Look what I've got!'

She opened up the box, 'Where did you get these, Stefan.'

'I ran some errands for Mr Popovic and he paid me with these eggs.' I hated lying to my own Mother, but sometimes it was easier.

'Oh well, that's good. Well done, Stefan. These eggs look very fresh. Maybe I can do some baking.' She set to work right there and then, kneading and mixing flour with water, then adding one of the eggs and some sugar. I sat down at the kitchen table and watched her. She rolled out the rough dough on a large wooden board. Mother slapped, pummelled and worked the dough until she had it smooth and elastic. She broke off a piece. Then she pulled down her old battered rolling pin from a high shelf and rolled it until it was just the right thickness, about a quarter of an inch or so. Then she cut out her shapes. It was incredible to watch how she could make so much out of so little. She made tray after tray of *khrusty**. This was a dainty piece of sweet pastry cut into a pointed shape with the centre section folded back on itself. She slid tray after tray into the oven to bake them, and once they were done she dusted them with a fine sugar coating. Before long, I was biting into one of them. It melted in my mouth. I was allowed to have just two of them while they were still warm, the rest were to be sold at the village hall market.

The following day was a Sunday. We'd heard rumours that the Nazis were planning to reopen some of the churches, but were still waiting. So, instead, we woke up that morning and Father read from the Bible, and we said some prayers. Then, after breakfast, Father and I walked down to the village hall market to try and sell the *khrusty* which were wrapped in napkins and stacked into a pail which I carried. We knew it was a sin to work on a Sunday, but I'm sure the Lord would have recognised we needed to make the most of every day in every way and would have granted us permission.

We arrived quite early, about nine o'clock, and found an available space. The Nazis provided a few collapsible tables for the purposes of trade and there were only two or three of these left. We grabbed one, and Father laid out a tablecloth and some decorative plates. We arranged the *khrusty* on the plates.

'Well, Stefan, how much shall we sell them for?'

'I don't know.'

Father smiled, 'Well, we'll just see what happens, eh?' I smiled back.

Soon, the market was busy, with many people from the village wandering around it. Most of them saw the *khrusty* and walked on. It was the kind of thing they could have made themselves. A couple of elderly ladies tottered by and we sold them a couple each for a small sum, just a palmful of small change. It didn't look like we'd sell that many and Father started to pace around, 'I'm just going to have a look around, Stefan. You'll be okay on your own won't you?'

'Of course, Father. I'll be fine.'

He wandered off and I was left looking at the *khrusty*, my mouth watering. I thought that maybe I could slip a couple down, surely Father wouldn't notice. No. I didn't want to give in. They were very difficult to resist, if I started eating them I'd most likely end up eating at least half of them. They were really excellent. As I stood and looked at them I became aware of a shadow right in front of me. I looked up,

'Hello, young man, we meet again.'

It was the soldier. The one who'd given us the chocolate bars,

'H-hello.' I smiled at him weakly. He made me nervous, just like the other soldiers.

'I see you've been busy. These look very nice. How much are they?'

I was at a loss. I looked around to see if Father was nearby, but he wasn't anywhere around. The soldier saw my predicament, 'Okay, listen. I tell you what. Let me try one for free, and if I like it, I guarantee I'll buy the lot and I'll give you a good price.' I wasn't sure. I scanned around again and again. There was still no sign of Father. I had to do something, else the soldier could've turned nasty, and so I nodded in agreement. He picked up one of the *khrusty* and took a bite. His eyes widened and he chewed with obvious delight. He finished it in the time it would take for a butterfly to flutter its wings. 'That was beautiful. Just beautiful. Yes. I'll take all of them, if that's okay?'

'Of course.' I replied. What else could I say?

But I had a dilemma. I had no container in which to pack the *khrusty*. I stood there wondering what to do when the soldier said, 'Hang on. Just let me fetch a bowl.' He strode back into the village hall and returned with a large metal bowl, 'Here. Put them all in here. The other men and I will get through them before the day's out, I'm sure of that.'

After tipping all the *khrusty* into the bowl, I looked up at him expectantly. He smiled and reached into a pocket. He pulled out a bundle of notes, 'Here, young man. Take these.' He handed me the notes and picked up the bowl with a smile on his face. I thanked him and then he turned and walked back into the village hall.

I let out a big breath and I leant on the table in front of me. I was relieved, because he could have just taken everything from me without any payment whatsoever. I stood looking at the banknotes in my hand. I wasn't sure how much there was, but I hoped Father would be happy. Before long, he returned,

'Stefan, what's happened? Where are all our *khrusty*?'

I held out the banknotes. He took them. I watched him as he counted them, his eyes widening, 'Where did you get these, Stefan?''

'From a soldier. It was one of those we played football with yesterday. He tried one, and then he bought the lot.'

An expression of concern etched itself over Father's face and he turned just a touch pale, 'Stefan, you know, I really don't want you mixing with these soldiers. You never know what it might lead to. Just look at what happened to Volodimir. You need to make yourself invisible. So they don't know you even exist. This is quite a lot of money, much more than the *khrusty* are worth, but what's to stop that soldier informing on you and saying you cheated him, eh?'

'I know, Father. I know that. But there was nothing I could do, except maybe give him the *khrusty* for free.'

'All right. Well, let's not dwell on this any longer. We'll pack up and go home now.'

We rolled up our tablecloths and packed everything back into the pail. As we did this, I became aware of a hush that had descended on the market place. All around us, everyone had ceased going about their business and were looking across at the main door into the village hall. Wulf was standing there. He hadn't been around for a while, and we'd all assumed he'd been transferred elsewhere. Clearly, that was not the case. He was there, with his henchmen, looking every bit as powerful as always. Also alongside him were some of the men from the communications room. He stepped forward a few paces and looked around at the crowd,

'*Achtung!* We have in our midst a saboteur! We've granted you all the privilege of coming here to trade with us, but someone has taken the opportunity to commit an act of vandalism. I expect that person thinks that, by committing such acts, they will stop us or slow us down. They won't.' Wulf paused. He paced slowly into the middle of the market place. Everyone, all of us, just stood like statues, hardly daring to breathe.

Wulf continued, 'As part of our war against the cursed Bolsheviks, we require to be able to communicate with other battalions across this region and beyond. That's why we have facilities such as the ones here in this village hall. But just this morning, someone has cut through the cables leading to the generator. The radio equipment is no longer operational. Not until we can get more cables. That will take some time to organise, at least a week, maybe longer. I will not stand for this! Will you people never learn?' Then, he barked orders to his soldiers to assemble all the civilians in the immediate area onto the field, the one where we'd played our football match against the soldiers. There must have been about 200 of us, all lined up in four rows of 50 or so.

'This time the execution squad will require one hundred. That's right. One hundred of you will be shot for this act of insurgency.' Wulf hesitated and scanned across the faces of the people lined up. We all remained impassive. Expressionless. Soviet rule had numbed us and built up our tolerance to pain of all descriptions.

Wulf became more animated. He paced up and down, slapping his baton into a gloved hand. He approached the end of the first line, which, unfortunately, Father and I had been herded into. Slowly he walked along and then stopped. He placed a hand on someone's shoulder, and then stepped back while two of his men dragged the unfortunate off and bundled them into a covered truck, where they remained under armed guard. Father and I were right in the middle of the front row. I really hoped Wulf would just pass us by, but I had a bad feeling. He made another nine or ten selections as he approached us. My mouth was dry as a dirt track and my stomach was churning like crazy. There was no way he would pass without taking at least one of us, I knew that. I wanted to run, or collapse in tears, but I didn't. I carried on standing there. The stillness of the day made that moment seem like it was a dream, and I hoped it was, but the taste in my mouth was one of bitterness, like vinegar, stinging me back to reality. It was happening all right. It took every ounce of my energy not to shake and tremble.

An aroma of starch, leather and polish wafted closer as he stepped right in front of us. I watched out of the corner of my eye as he stood right in front of Father. A faint flicker of recognition played across his face as he stared into Father's eyes. Then he raised a gloved hand. He placed it firmly on Father's shoulder, his lips opening slightly in a yellow half smile.

Just then, there was the sound of a revving engine. It sounded like a motorbike. Sure enough, two seconds later, it appeared from around the back of the village hall. The rider and his pillion passenger both wore the colours of the Ukrainian Resistance: red and black. The passenger held aloft a glass bottle with a burning rag poking out of the top. As they passed by the village hall he threw the bottle through the windscreen of Wulf's Porsche staff truck. There was a small explosion, and then a whoosh as the seats caught fire. Everyone turned to look at the motorbike and its two passengers as they wobbled, then regained their balance and sped off into the distance. Wulf turned towards the inferno, holding his arm across his eyes. He stepped back a few paces and barked instructions at some soldiers. They jumped into a truck and one of them kick started a motorbike. They roared off after the Resistance riders.

The fire crackled and spat, and then, without warning, there was a thunderous boom as the fuel tank exploded. The fallout from this threw everybody to the ground and the flames spread and licked higher into the sky. There were other trucks either side of Wulf's and we watched with a delicious sense of horror as flaming debris floated into the air and landed on these other trucks. Within seconds they too were engulfed in flames. Wulf and his men ran around like demented rabbits trying to organise themselves. Of course, their communications equipment wasn't working so they couldn't radio to the town for a fire truck to come.

Amidst this chaos, all those condemned to the execution squad, and those waiting, managed to slip away from the market place. We scurried like ants, our legs a blur as we all followed an invisible line back to our homes. Father and I burst into our kitchen.

'What's happened? I heard some noises, some loud bangs. It sounded like they were nearby,' said Mother. Father and I looked at her. Neither of us could speak, I know my heart was pumping as if it was about to burst. Then Father said, 'Let's go through to the parlour.'

Mother fetched us both a glass of water and the three of us sat down. Father took a few sips of the water and told her what had happened, then he ran his hands through his hair, 'He'll track us down, Olha. He knows where we live, I don't know what we can do.'

Mother sat looking very calm, 'Mikola. You and Stefan must go west. To Stanislaviv, to see your sister Helena.' Father didn't respond, so Mother carried on, 'I was fetching water from the well today and I got talking to some of the other women there. Things are much calmer in the west. They are further from the front than we are, and so trade and business is starting up again. You might be able to get some work, who knows? But you can't stay here. Not with Wulf around.'

'But Olha, we can't leave you. How can we leave you here at the mercy of the soldiers?'

'I'll go and stay with my mother for a few days until things calm down, and then I'll come back. They'll still need someone to milk the cow and produce their food for them, so they won't touch me, I'm sure of that.'

'But we could all go to Stanislaviv.'

'Mikola, you know I can't leave my mother. She's old and frail and she hasn't got anyone else. I'll stay here and look after the house and our land, and everything we have left. Then, once the war's over, and they say it'll only be a few weeks before the Nazis win, you can come back. Things'll be better then. Wulf may not be here.'

'Olha, I don't want to leave you.'

'Mikola, if you stay, then Wulf will kill you, and Stefan. You know that. Please go, for Stefan's sake if nothing else.'

Well, Father and I knew she was right. Wulf had us in his sights. It was just a question of time. Father slowly stood up and said, 'Well Stefan, how do you feel about going to visit your Auntie Helena?' I nodded.

We packed a small suitcase each, put on our sturdiest boots and wrapped ourselves in our coats. Finally, we pulled on our caps. I didn't want to say goodbye to Mother. I didn't want to leave her all alone in our house. What would she do all on her own? But as always, we had to swallow down our pain and take this bitterest of medicine. It was another crooked step on the road to survival, but were we following the right path? I, for one, felt like I was heading into the unknown, towards a dark horizon, where the future was so uncertain I felt sick with fear.

Mother packed us up a parcel with some bread and cheese in it. I remember hugging her as hard as I could before we left, and exchanging kisses. Father did the same, but then we were gone. I followed Father blindly, not wanting to think about what was happening to me. We stayed away from the roads, but crossed over fields to get to the town. It was a two mile walk, and when I was younger it felt as if it went on forever, but this time the journey passed quickly. Too quickly. I didn't want to leave. We maintained a brisk pace, and before long we reached the outskirts of Vinnitsya. I could see the train station tower poking up into the sky. We were nearly there. We made our way through some of the smaller side streets, not even bothering to look at anything, until we stepped into a wide boulevard where the entrance of the station was. It was a grand old structure, with pointed, twisted, fine gilded turrets. The grand old clock above the entrance chimed as we approached. It was 12. Normally, I would have been ready for some lunch, but I wasn't a bit hungry. My stomach was all knotted up.

Father and I approached the revolving doors slowly. It was as if we were walking on silk, so lightly did we step. We clattered through the revolving doors a little too noisily, or so it seemed, but when we stepped out on the other side we could see no one was paying us any attention at all. It wasn't busy. There were groups of soldiers dotted around, and one or two civilians. There were a couple of armed guards positioned at strategic points, but they looked half asleep. Father pulled the bundle of Marks out of his pocket and said, 'Come on, Stefan, we'd better see if we can buy some tickets.'

When we got to the ticket office, we found the shutters down, the lights off, and no sign of life. Father looked at me, 'We'll just have to go down on the platform and see what's happening.' I nodded. It was a small station. There were only two platforms. So we went down the stone steps to platform number one, the one from which the trains travelled west. There were quite a few Nazi soldiers stood around in small groups. They were all talking together, smoking and some of them were drinking from metal flasks. Some of them had their arms in slings, others were on crutches. Father and I sat on a bench, 'Well, Stefan, let's wait and see. These soldiers must be expecting transport to arrive to take them home to Germany.'

I nodded. We sat quietly and waited.

We were lucky. Within a few minutes we heard a train approaching. Everyone on the platform looked up expectantly. A train pulled in, steam pouring into the air and with a thudding and a hissing of cranking machinery. The sign on the front of the train read 'Munchen'.

'Come on, Stefan,' said Father. We approached one of the doors. There was a group of Nazi soldiers congregated in the doorway. They were laughing and joking, and drinking bottles of beer. Father opened the door, 'Excuse me sir, would it be okay if my son and I board this train? We need to visit my sister who is very ill.'

One of the soldiers looked at him and then said, 'Of course, of course, climb aboard.'

That's how easy it was. Within a few minutes the train pulled away from the station. I sat next to Father, and I wondered how long it would be before we could come home again.

Chapter 6

Ukrainian proverb: To see a friend no road is too long.

'Here, take this, Stefan.' Father held out a piece of bread and cheese. I took it and chewed away at it, but I didn't feel hungry at all. We were in a compartment with eight seats in it. Somehow, we'd got ourselves two berths right next to the window. I was glad, because more and more people, mainly soldiers, were pouring into the train. I wouldn't have wanted to stand in the corridors in the middle of all those German soldiers. For them it was all a long party. They were going home. Some had their arms in slings, others were on crutches. They were drinking and smoking. Now and again they broke into song, and there was lots of laughter. The atmosphere was one of gentle celebration. Before too long they'd be back with their families, and so, they were happy.

Meanwhile, I was hurtling away from Mother. We'd left her behind and as we hurtled along, mile after mile, I began to feel uneasy, as if I had an itch. It wasn't right. I wanted to be with her, so she could put her arms around me, and watch out for me. So she could fill me up with her beautiful bread and delicious dinners. To leave her behind was like losing a part of myself. I knew Father would look after me as best he could, of course he would, but it just wasn't the same. As a 15-year-old boy, I didn't want to show how I felt. I just carried on, making out I was okay, but inside I was hurting.

The train rumbled down the track, with its unrelenting click clack rhythm. I tried to lose myself in this rhythm, to let it invade my head and my heart, so I couldn't feel anything else, but at the same time, through the window, I could see only too clearly the lush countryside we were leaving behind. The final glow of summer was filling the sky and, even though the sun was shining, you could sense that icy winds were on their way. The deep green was turning to a golden brown. These images would remain etched inside me and I hoped that I'd be able to return one day.

We stopped at several stations along the way and picked up more passengers. Mostly, they were more German soldiers on their way back home. Before long, their singing became more raucous. The corridor outside our compartment was overflowing with them, all smoking and drinking, with their arms around each other, swaying from side to side. So much so that, at times, I thought the train might topple onto its side. Their hats were tipped back, and they wore a smile that stretched right across each and every face.

Inside our compartment, the mood was more sombre. Father was very quiet. No doubt he was thinking similar thoughts to mine. Why should we have to leave our home? The invaders had forced us out, made us run, and abandon everything. Strangely, there were no soldiers in our compartment. There was an elderly couple who sat quietly by the doors, the man with a newspaper on his lap and the woman holding a cat basket on her knee. They reminded me of Mr and Mrs Popovic, they were well dressed and their clothes and luggage looked expensive. Every now and then the woman cooed and clucked into the basket. As the singing and general behaviour of the soldiers became more boisterous, with lots of booming voices and general commotion, I noticed the elderly man look a little worried. He took off his wrist watch and signalled to his wife to do the same. Then he stood up and stashed them into a holdall on the luggage rack above his head. The other passengers in the compartment were all men of a similar age to Father. It wasn't possible to tell whether they were Ukrainian or German or whether they were from one of our neighbouring countries. They could've been Soviets for all I knew. They all sat slumped in their seats with their hats pulled over their faces, either asleep or pretending to be so. I wondered why these men were on the train. Where had they come from and where were they heading?

Despite such distractions, it wasn't long before my thoughts turned once again to Mother. We'd left her all on her own. I hoped and prayed to God she'd be safe. I imagined all sorts of things in my head. Of Wulf arriving at our home to find we'd fled and summoning Mother to the execution squad instead. This thought trampled through me, leaving me battered and bruised inside, it was all I could do to stop myself from shaking and trembling. Father looked at me,

'Don't worry, Stefan, everything will be all right,' he whispered, 'I expect this war will come to a close soon.'

One of the men sitting next to us heard this and stirred briefly, he poked up a finger and raised his hat, using one eye to look us up and down. It scared me. After that, Father and I didn't speak to each other for the rest of the journey. We didn't know who could be listening.

I thought about Wulf, though. How I wished he'd left us alone.

Ever since he'd arrived as the chief of the occupying Nazi army, he'd given us nothing but trouble. I really hoped that one day a bullet would find its way to him and rid us of him for good. Surely, one day someone would put an end to his brutal ways.

The journey from Vinnitsya to Stanislaviv was about three hours long, covering a distance of just over 200 miles. We passed through many more stations and more passengers jumped aboard. Very few got off. The train became so crammed that for those in the corridors it was like being squashed into a goldfish bowl. More than once I saw a couple of the soldiers look into our compartment and then nod to each other in a discussion. I feared they might storm in and throw us out of our seats, but then more bottles of beer were passed down to them and they got caught up in the merriment once again.

I pressed my face up to the window and watched the world go by. We travelled through more countryside and the sun got lower in the sky. Shades of purple and pink layered themselves into our view. It was a typically beautiful early evening. Before long we arrived at our destination, Stanislaviv.

'Right then, Stefan, this is where we get off.' Father stood up and pulled our cases down from the shelf above. We squeezed past the legs of our fellow travellers. The men with hats over their faces didn't move, they didn't stir at all, even when we brushed against their knees. But the elderly man and his wife both looked up and smiled at us, and they both nodded a goodbye. I nodded back, but couldn't manage a smile. Father led the way as we virtually had to wrestle our way off the train, through a boiling mass of drunken, but happy, German soldiers. They had every reason to be happy. They were going home, but me, I was far away from my home. I could have been a million miles away, the world seemed so alien to me at that precise moment.

We stepped onto the platform, and then we looked up and down. There was a large clock suspended on an ornate overhead cast iron construction. It said five. Father passed me one of the cases and we made our way out of the station. Once out of the station we continued across a cobbled concourse. Then we were on a boulevard, heading away from the station, towards an area on the outskirts of the town. I suppose I could have said it was fortunate that Aunt Helena's house was within walking distance of the train station, but it most certainly didn't feel that way. We plodded on. We walked for about two miles and then Father lifted up an arm and pointed,

'That's it. Helena's house. Come on, Stefan.'

I'd been to Aunt Helena's house on more than one occasion. It was a house similar to our own, so that was some comfort for me. We walked up the approach, and I wondered what she'd say, since she wasn't expecting us. Father led the way and we climbed some steps to a side entrance. Father rapped on the door. Within a few seconds it opened and a face peered out from a gloomy interior,

'Hello?' It was Aunt Helena. She looked at us more closely and then her eyebrows jumped, and she stepped out of the doorway with a big smile,

'Mikola! Stefan! Oh, it's good to see you.' She pulled us both towards her in a big embrace, and I was comforted by her maternal arms.

'But what brings you here? And where is Olha?'

'Helena, can we come inside?' Father's face was drawn, he looked so weary.

'Of course, of course!' Aunt Helena ushered us into her kitchen, sat us down and made us a hot cup of tea. Father spoke at some length about how The Nazis arrived in Vinnitsya and why we'd travelled west to escape an execution squad.

'But what of Olha?' asked Aunt Helena.

Father's face dropped. 'I wanted her to come with us, Helena, but she wouldn't. She wouldn't leave her mother.' A wave of guilt washed over me, and I sensed that Father was churning inside in much the same way.

'Well, Mikola, you and Stefan can stay as long as you like. Don't you worry about that. We'll arrange things so there'll be room.'

We drank our tea and Aunt Helena made sandwiches with slices of meat. Father and I were hungry, and so we pushed them down like we'd never been fed. Before too long Uncle Yaroslav and my cousin, Oleg, returned from their toils in the fields of their smallholding. Oleg and I looked at each other and exchanged smiles. He and Yaroslav sat down and ate some dinner, and then Yaroslav pulled a bottle of *horilka* out of a cabinet. He and Father remained at the kitchen table and he poured the spirit into glasses. They both took heavy draughts and then Yaroslav topped up their glasses. He produced some cigarettes and he and Father lit up. Then they began to talk. All about everything. The war, the Nazis, the Soviets. Everything that had cut into our lives. Oleg raised his eyebrows and tilted his head towards a door. So, we both stood up and I followed him into his bedroom. Oleg was 12 years old, younger than me, but in his room he had more toys than I'd ever seen. He had many tin soldiers, and he had a wooden castle, which he'd made with help from Yaroslav. It was quite a release to play with Oleg and lose myself in such pursuits. We'd always got on well, and it reminded me of how I used to play with Volodimir.

With Oleg being an only child, it was relatively easy to rearrange things so that Father and I shared a bedroom, small though it was. We hadn't seen Aunt Helena or her family for some years so we stayed up quite late. It was midnight by the time we got to bed and I was very tired, so I fell asleep almost as soon as I lay down.

The following morning was a Monday and I opened up my eyes to see Father standing over me, 'Come on, Stefan, get up. It's late. We need to get ourselves up and about, and see what's happening in this town.'

'Yes, Father.'

'I'll see you in the kitchen.' He left me to pull my clothes on in the chill of the early morning. A couple of minutes later I followed him. We had a wash down and a bit of breakfast. Then Yaroslav left the house to get to work, and shortly afterwards Oleg also left for school. Aunt Helena poured Father another cup of tea. Steam rose from it and wafted in the air. I gulped down my milk.

'So, Mikola,' said Helena, 'what do you think, eh? About what Yaroslav said last night.'

'Well, if Yaroslav can get me some work on his building site, of course it would make sense for us to maybe stay here for a couple of months while there's some money to be made. I don't want to be away from Olha too long, though. I don't like to think of her back there all on her own. But you see, Helena, we had to leave. Wulf would have hunted us down. Maybe in a few weeks things will change. Maybe Wulf'll be posted somewhere else. But while we're here, I would like Stefan to get some schooling.'

'I don't see any problem there,' replied Helena, 'There are plenty of spaces in all the classes, in fact, more so in the older children's classes.'

'So, is that because the Nazis have cleared out all the Jews? This is what we've heard.'

'Well, that's right, Mikola. Lord knows how many they've slaughtered. Some have been shipped out of town, and many, many others have been shot. First of all, I prayed for all of us. I thought they would turn Stanislaviv into a ghost town. Then, it became clear that it was the Jews they wanted to be rid of. We've been lucky. Now, with so many gone, there is more work for the men. All we can do is work hard and keep praying to the Lord that we'll be spared.'

Despite everything, even with Wulf's murderous intentions towards us, I wished right then we'd stayed at home. I missed Mother, and, if what Aunt Helena said was true, Stanislaviv was no different. The people there lived day to day, always waiting for the next wave of brutal Nazi actions.

After finishing our drinks, Father and I slung on our coats and tied up our boots. We left the house and headed for the town. Father wanted to have a look around. We walked for about a mile without seeing a single soul. It was eerie. Monday mornings were usually busy, certainly back home in Vinnitsya, but, there was not a soul about. However, as we arrived in the town square we began to see more people going about their business. The market place was full of traders, and there were many shops open. We were careful to skirt the edges of the market place and we kept our eyes and ears open. On the way into town, Father had drilled into me the need to stay invisible. The last thing we wanted was to fall foul of the Nazis again.

Father still had the Marks left in his pocket so we had a quick browse around the stalls, and Father bought some meat. There wasn't so much available and we queued for almost an hour just to get a small cut. We made our way back to Aunt Helena's, and Father slapped the parcel of meat down on the kitchen table. Helena wasn't around, but she walked in a few minutes later, carrying a bucket of potatoes,

'Mikola, what's this?' She unwrapped the bundle. 'Oh, this looks lovely. Very fresh. Thank you, I can cook us up a nice stew for supper.'

That evening, the five of us had a lovely hot supper of stew and potatoes. It was really tasty, and for a minute or two things didn't seem so bad. Yaroslav told Father that he'd made enquiries and work was available if he wanted it. Father smiled broadly, wider than I'd seen for some time. He so wanted to work, to put bread on the table. It was also agreed that Helena would walk with Oleg and I to school in the morning to enrol me.

So, this is how we lived at that time. I soon settled in at the school and made some new friends, and then I'd come back and savour the warmth of Aunt Helena's home. After helping out with some of the chores on their smallholding, we'd have a hot drink and maybe a biscuit, and then Oleg and I would play together, or sometimes I'd read a book. A short time later, Father and Yaroslav would come back from work. They'd throw off their coats and take their boots off, and sit next to the stove in the kitchen. They'd warm their hands on the roaring flames and take big swigs of hot tea. It was chillier than usual for autumn time, the cold winds were biting and the sunshine was masked by a blanket of thick cloud. We wrapped ourselves up well before going out, but I was pleased to see Father a little happier. He was working hard and making some money. He tried to save as much of this as he could, to take home to Mother. Of course, he paid Helena for our upkeep.

We reached the month of October in the year of 1943. Even though I enjoyed playing with Oleg and with other children in the neighbourhood, I felt like I was in the wrong place. I belonged back home, in Vinnitsya, with Mother. One evening, I remember retiring with Father to our bedroom, perching myself on the edge of my bed, and saying to him, 'Will we be able to go back home soon?'

Father sat down at my side, 'Stefan, I've written to Mother. I've asked her to let us know as soon as it's safe for us to go back. I'm expecting a reply from her any time now. It should be here any day.'

His words warmed me. I longed for that moment when I knew we could return, 'Will we be able to go back before Christmas?'

'I hope so, Stefan, I really hope so.'

To be home for Christmas was something that I wanted very badly. Mother always made sure there was enough for us all to celebrate, even though we'd had times of real hardship. There'd be candles on the table and we'd all say our prayers before partaking of our Christmas supper.

Another month went by, and we became more settled than ever where we were with Aunt Helena, Yaroslav and Cousin Oleg. The evenings were dark and we usually all sat together in the kitchen. After dinner, Yaroslav and Father often sat and played chess together, or had a game of cards. Aunt Helena would be busy at clearing and tidying, and Oleg and I brought toys through from his bedroom so we could share the warmth while we played.

The radio was nearly always humming away in the background, with the voices of men talking about what was happening in the world. The war continued. We heard propaganda broadcasts by the Nazis where they claimed they were about to conquer Russia, and then, now and again, a crackly, very faint, Russian voice would proclaim a Soviet fight back. We didn't know what to believe, but we kept on listening, whenever we could.

Eventually, a letter arrived from Mother. I was overjoyed and I bounced up and down on my feet as I watched Father tear it open. I couldn't keep still. I was hopeful, so hopeful. Father scanned the letter, then he beamed at me, 'Stefan, it's good news. Mother says that Wulf has gone. He's been sent to the front. She thinks he may have got a promotion, because they had some sort of ceremony at the village hall. But that's not our concern. Now we know we can go back. We'll get a train first thing tomorrow.'

I threw myself around Father and he held me tight and ruffled my hair, 'Here, take a look for yourself.' He passed me the letter and I read it through three or four times. A great surge of utter joy overwhelmed me, and I felt light as a feather right then, as if I could just float right up into the stars. At last, we were going home! I was also relieved that Mother was well.

So that evening, Aunt Helena prepared us a hearty farewell meal, with slices of meat and cheese with lovely fresh bread. With lovely big tomatoes and jars of pickles. She baked a beautiful apple cake, and we sat and filled ourselves up with this delicious fare. We were in the middle of a war, but somehow, she put this feast together for us, from her own stores and from what Yaroslav could get hold of. Father and Yaroslav had a drop of *horilka*, Oleg and I had some apple juice. Helena sat with her hands round a cup of tea. We clinked our glasses together. After we'd eaten, the grown-ups sang a few folk songs, while Oleg and I watched and tried to join in whenever we could. I went to bed at about 11, and Father followed not long afterwards. I lay awake in bed for some time, just thinking about Mother. I would see her again the very next day and I could barely contain myself at the prospect. Eventually, I slid into sleep.

I woke up very early. It was still dark, so I lay there for a while imagining what it would be like to run up our approach and back into our family home. As soon as the first, very faint, flickers of light appeared at the window I leapt up from my bed and got dressed in that faint glow. Then I went to the kitchen where Aunt Helena was kneading dough on a workbench. I looked at the clock. It was six. Aunt Helena prepared me a mug of steamy hot milk and gave me bread and butter. I chewed into it and it was inside me in the space of a few seconds,

'Slow down, Stefan,' Aunt Helena smilingly scolded me. 'You'll get a belly ache if you're not careful. I know you want to get home and see your mother, but don't worry, you'll get there. Take each minute as it comes. That way you'll get things done. If you rush, you'll only end up making more work for yourself.'

She was right, I was in danger of wrecking our chances of getting back home. I could see myself doing something silly like barging into a Nazi soldier at the train station and getting us both arrested. I took a few deep breaths and sipped my milk slowly. It wasn't long before Father appeared. He had some breakfast and then we went back to our room to pack our cases. I folded all my clothes neatly, heeding what Aunt Helena said to me, I was trying not to rush. I needed to be calm. By seven we were ready to walk down to the train station. We said our goodbyes and thanked Aunt Helena, Yaroslav and Oleg for all they'd done. We walked down their approach waving as we walked out of sight. It was sad in a way, because they'd welcomed us into their home so willingly, and Oleg was a good kid, I enjoyed spending time with him.

The gloom of the morning lifted as we walked along. It was as if we were stepping into a brighter future. It was like walking on air but the walk seemed to go on forever and I had to steel myself inside, to try and not get so excited. We'd get there, I was sure of that. I just needed to accept that each minute would pass and we'd be getting closer as time ticked by.

We arrived at the cobbled concourse and approached the doors to the train station, but, something was different. On either side of the huge double doors were Nazi patrol cars, and a small company of armed guards. We slowed down. Father put an arm around my shoulders and we headed right towards the doors, trying to make ourselves look small and insignificant,

'Halt!' One of the armed guards stepped across our path, holding his rifle. 'Where are you going?'

'Please, Sir, we're going home, to Vinnitsya. We've been visiting my sister, who's been sick. Now we just want to get on a train and go home.'

'I'm afraid that won't be possible. Under current orders from High Command, the trains are strictly for military use only.'

'Please, I beg of you, Sir, we need to get home. My wife is waiting for us.'

'Enough! We have our orders. I must ask you to go now. Away from this area. Go!'

We hesitated, and the soldier lowered his rifle. We stood staring down the barrel for a second or two, and then we turned and walked away. We kept walking until we reached a shop doorway some distance away, 'Stefan, I wasn't expecting this. I don't know what's going on. This place is crawling with soldiers. I can't see any way through.' Frantically, we looked up and down the concourse to see if there was a wall to climb over, or a hole in a fence somewhere. There was nothing.

'Come on, Stefan!' Father set off at a brisk pace and headed towards a far corner of the station wall, and I followed him. We followed the boundary all the way round, slipping under a bridge, until we got to the other side of the station where there was a hill. We climbed to the top and stood there looking down onto the station. We could see both platforms. There were armed guards stationed at several positions on both platforms. We stood there, breathing hard, not wanting to believe what was in front of us. We both knew that, even if we managed to penetrate the boundary and get into the station, we'd be arrested immediately, or worse still shot. My heart was sinking into my boots as we made our way down the hill, and silently made our way back to Aunt Helena's. Well, what could we say to each other? I was completely stuck for words. Father said nothing. His face was like a mask as we trudged those two miles in the wrong direction. My footsteps were heavy, like I'd got lumps of lead on the end of my legs, and the small case I was carrying felt as if it was full of bricks, it dragged me down. My head was swimming, why did it have to happen like this? I said a silent prayer in my head. I just wanted to get back home.

We arrived back at Aunt Helena's to find that Yaroslav and Oleg had already left for work and for school. Helena listened as Father poured out our sorry tale and she made us hot mugs of tea. Father turned on the radio and we listened. As usual, the broadcasts were fuzzy, faint and crackly. I was filled with a sense of disbelief. For me, it was as if our trip down to the station had been a dream, and that I would wake up to find myself sat in a train compartment racing towards the east. I so wanted to hear the dull, metallic thud of the wheels and connecting straps as the train pulled into the station. I yearned to taste the sooty black smoke as it wafted around my ears on the platform. But most of all, I just wanted to be there, walking up that winding road that led to our house.

The radio spluttered and wheezed as usual. It was agony of a kind to sit and wait for it to tell us something, and then, after about an hour or so, we heard a deep voice boom out at us. It was clear, like it was right there in the room with us,

'*The glorious army of the Soviet Socialist Republic is advancing west. Many battles have been fought in this Great Patriotic War. The Nazi warmongers have invaded our republic and tried to steal it from us. But now we are fighting back, and we will crush the Nazi war machine! We are reclaiming our republic and, as each day passes, we take back more and more of what is rightfully ours. Join us in our battle. The Soviet Army needs you . . .'*

The voice faded, and with it our hopes of getting home began to fade also. My belly churned and twisted, it was as if I'd been kicked in the guts. I could hardly breathe, or was I just holding my breath as if I thought I could maybe stop time somehow? It was all just like a bad dream.

Father bent his head down and held it in his hands. Our whole world was falling apart. None of us said it, but the three of us knew it. The front was moving west and the Soviets were pushing the Nazis back. That was why the Nazi soldiers were guarding the station so closely and so strongly.

Of course, Yaroslav and Oleg were surprised to see us when they came home, and Yaroslav brought us more bad news, 'It's just the same on the roads. Our boss tried to get to a brickyard in the next village today but was stopped by a Nazi roadblock. They're not letting anyone in or out. Every single road to the east is blocked.'

As a family, they showed Father and me so much kindness and made us welcome in their home once again. Never for a second did I feel I wasn't welcome there with them. Luckily, Father managed to continue working with Yaroslav, and I resumed my place at the school. In many ways we were settled. We had somewhere to live, some work for Father and an education for me.

But it wasn't enough. It was like we were sleepwalking. For me, it was as if I were living in a dream. None of it seemed real, or perhaps I didn't want it to be real. I couldn't think about Mother. It ripped me apart to do so. I existed in a strange twilight world, as if I wasn't fully awake. I'd walk home from school with Oleg each day with the icy wind snapping around my ears and creeping through the holes in my boots, but I couldn't really feel it.

Winter was bearing down on us in that year of 1943. My old boots were beyond further repair, and most of my clothes were threadbare, but the purchase of some new clothes wasn't as simple as we'd have liked. Yaroslav gave us the name of a friend of his, who we met at the market. He then took us to a nearby house, where the clothing was available to buy, at inflated prices. Father haggled, but we still paid more than the clothes were worth, but it was either that or go barefoot. I got a brand new pair of boots and a big, warm coat for the winter, and also a hat and some gloves.

We bought a few groceries before heading home. As we walked

back that afternoon, we came across a group of about ten small children, they must have been about seven or eight years old. As we approached, we witnessed them playing a curious game. Half of them lined up along the edge of a ditch, while the rest stood in a line a few metres away, raised sticks up to their shoulders and shouted, 'Bang!' The boys along the edge of the ditch then fell into it. One of the boys saw us approaching, dropped his stick, and ran up to us. The others quickly followed him, they'd obviously seen our shopping bags.

'Hello, Mister!' The one at the front smiled up at Father, 'have you got anything for us, Mister? Any food? We're hungry.'

Father reached into one of the bags and pulled out a carton of biscuits. He handed it to the boy who uttered the swiftest of thanks before tearing it open. He, and the other boys, crammed the biscuits into their mouths and munched away, until they'd eaten the lot. It didn't take long.

'Tell me, boys,' said Father, 'What was that game you were playing?'

The leader of the boys looked up at Father with his eyes of deepest blue, and with the face of an angel. 'Shooting Jews.'

Then, the boys ran off, they picked up their sticks and carried on with their game. We picked up our bags and resumed our walk home. Just then, a woman came hurtling out from one of the nearby houses towards the group of boys, 'Hey, Andriy! What do you think you're doing? I've told you before haven't I? I don't want you playing that game! It's not right. Get inside!' She grabbed the boy and hauled him off by his collar, giving him one or two slaps around the head as they went. The boy let out a few howls, and then they were gone, with their door slammed shut behind them. The other boys carried on playing, and we walked on.

'You see what this war is doing to us, eh?' said Father, 'We're not a bad people, Stefan, but these Nazis are monsters and they spread their poison to all who come near them. Lord, help us get through this.' He looked up to the heavens as he spoke.

Father was right. We could have done with some divine intervention. Every night I prayed. For an end to the madness, and for everything to be back as it was. We'd stayed because we had to, and Father had earned some money but that didn't matter anymore. The money wouldn't last forever, even though Father tried to save as much as he could. Of course, he'd also just bought me new boots and a coat, for which I was grateful. I loved that coat. It had a large collar I could pull up to my ears and big, deep pockets to plunge my hands into when the frost began to bite at them. It was quite a severe winter that year and we spent most evenings huddled around the stove in the kitchen. Christmas came, and, although Aunt Helena put a good spread on, I couldn't really enjoy it. We didn't get any more letters from Mother through the whole of that winter, and I held onto a hope deep inside me that she was all right. The radio blared and spluttered, the signal struggled through the freezing winter air and sometimes we went for days with no reception at all. When we did, the news was not good. The Nazis were being pushed back by the Soviets. The Nazis would have struggled to cope with our winters, which were beyond belief sometimes. The snow would be so thick, sometimes as much as six feet of it, and then it froze creating an ice rink effect. Most of our terrain was flat with few landmarks, making it difficult to navigate across, and when the ice thawed it combined with the soil beneath to produce a thick sludge. On many occasions we saw Nazi trucks, and even tanks, abandoned at the side of the road where they'd got stuck, but, of course the Soviets were accustomed to these conditions. It seemed as if the advantage had swung their way again. We sat and kept warm, and waited to see what would happen.

Finally, all the snow melted and spring arrived. I stood outside Aunt Helena's home one fine morning; it must have been the first week of March 1944. The sun was beating down and I could feel the earth below me beginning to move again. Soon, the first shoots of flowers would be stretching through the soil to soak up those golden rays. It was a wonderful feeling. I looked across to the east. Back towards Vinnitsya. I pushed down an urge to run in that direction. I knew it was too far and also that I risked running into trouble, but what difference would it make? We knew the trouble was coming our way, in any case. It was like being a prisoner in your own land.

Later that same day, Aunt Helena, Yaroslav and Oleg all went together to a small neighbouring village to visit an elderly relative of Yaroslav's. Father and I stayed behind. We ate a supper and played cards into the evening while listening to the radio. We were sitting back in our chairs sipping at cups of tea, and I have to say, in that moment, I felt quite content.

Then something happened that made us sit up. There was a tremendous din in the distance, it sounded like an angry mob. It got louder. We heard some rumblings and some engines roaring. Then, there was a heavy clunk of boots that got nearer and nearer. We sat and listened in horror as the clunking came up the steps to the front door. It flew open. Nazi soldiers stormed in, waving their rifles around. The one in front yelled at us, 'Out! Get out of here now! We have orders to clear this town, to get everybody out!' Before we could even react or say anything we were grabbed and hauled to the doorway and ordered to put our boots on, with rifles pointing at us and with the same orders barked at us over and over again. We grabbed our coats, and our hats and gloves and we were pushed down the steps and down Aunt Helena's approach to the road. There were hundreds of townspeople there, all being shepherded down the road leading west, out of Stanislaviv.

It was getting dark. We had no idea where we were going. Some of those marching alongside us shouted out questions like 'Where are we going?' or 'What's going on?' They were told to shut up and keep moving. Anyone that was struggling, or too weak to keep up was hauled back up onto their feet and told to keep going, or those nearby were ordered to help them. I walked with Father. We said nothing to each other. We both knew we were heading in the wrong direction, but there was nothing we could do about it.

Chapter 7

> *Ukrainian proverb: Only three things in life are certain - birth, death and change*

It was dark when I woke up and my body was aching so badly I thought it would never stop, and then I realised I was lying on a wooden floor. Lord knows how many miles the Nazi soldiers had taken us, but we must have walked for many hours.

I sat up and rubbed my eyes. Within a minute, maybe two, I got accustomed to the darkness. All around me were sleeping people, many of them moaning and calling out as they slept. Some were thrashing around, restless in their slumber. I looked up to a window in that wooden hut and there was a moon sitting in the sky, watching over us. If only we could find some energy from somewhere, like the light from the moon, then maybe we could fight back, but we were powerless. All we'd been able to do was be herded along, like cattle. I cursed the Nazis; and the Soviets. They treated us as if we were less than human. I longed for the day when we could change things and reclaim Ukraine as a free country in its own right and drive the invaders out.

The ache in my muscles eased off a little as I stood up and stretched. In the dusty blackness I could just about see Father lying on the floor next to me, sleeping. Despite all our efforts, we hadn't managed to make it back home and we were further away than ever, but I didn't blame Father. Maybe it was meant to be that way somehow.

In the murkiness, I managed to make out the door to the hut and I moved towards it, taking care not to step on anyone. I opened the door and stepped outside. There was a Nazi guard right outside the door, he was smoking a cigarette. He turned towards me and his eyes gleamed, 'Halt. Where are you going?'

'Excuse me,' I replied, 'I've just woken up, and I need some air.'

'Well, we have our orders, and you must stay inside the hut.' He gestured with his rifle for me to go back inside. I looked over his shoulder and, on the horizon I saw an orange glow. It was unusual. It flickered and flared and I also heard some very faint bangs, like explosions in the distance. There was dust in the air, swirling in the early morning breeze, I could feel it on my face and I raised a hand up to shield myself. The soldier stepped forward, 'Back inside! Now!' He glared at me, and I stepped backwards into the hut. He slammed the door. I sat down next to Father who was still asleep and tried to get comfortable, with my coat wrapped around me to keep out the chill.

Before long, others around me began to wake up. I saw Father stirring and he pushed himself up into sitting, 'Stefan? Are you there? Stefan, is that you?'

'I'm here, Father. Right next to you. I put an arm around him.'

'Thank God. Thank God you're still here with me,' he whispered, 'but where are we?'

I couldn't really answer him. We could have been in Timbuktu for all I knew,

'It's all right, Father. We're okay in here. It's warm and dry.' I tried to reassure him, but was also trying to calm myself. I was scared. We all were. I could feel it in the air around me. Any minute the Nazi soldiers could line us up and slaughter us. That kind of thought was creeping into the head of every person in the hut, paralysing every nerve and every cell inside us. We were like statues, hardly daring to move or breathe. There we sat while the gloom turned into daylight outside. No one said very much to each other. Some people clasped their hands together and whispered prayers. Those people had a calm about them, like they'd accept whatever was to come, and be ready for it. Others, like Father and I, just sat very still. Inside my head I was praying too. The walls of the hut were closing in on us.

Eventually, after many long minutes and hours, I was sitting with my knees tucked into my chest with my arms around my knees, and with my face folded down, when the door burst open. I looked up. Several Nazi soldiers, armed with rifles, stormed in with one of them issuing orders at us, 'Right! Everybody out! Now!'

Everyone stood up slowly and straightened their clothes, and then we all wandered out into the lovely spring sunshine. It was a truly beautiful day, and such a relief to be out of that cramped wooden hut. The heat from the sun was mirrored by a wave of heat wafting across from the horizon. It was accompanied by particles of dust riding on a breeze that flew into our eyes and our noses, making us cough and splutter, and rub our eyes. Some of the soldiers had scarves tied around their faces and goggles covering their eyes; others simply pulled their helmets down over their eyes and walked with their heads down. They prodded us with their rifles and herded us away from the huts. Many hundreds of us were there, most likely from many different parts of Western Ukraine. I blinked away the dust and looked back at the huts. There were about 20 of them all in rows of five. We'd been staying in army barracks of some description. There were brick buildings nearby, but I didn't have time to look any closer because the Nazi troops were shoving all of us away from the huts. All around me, people were crossing themselves and muttering prayers. We were marched to the edge of a field and then the soldiers ordered us to stop. They all ran across to trucks that were waiting at the side of a road some 50 metres away. They clambered aboard. Then, from the opposite end of the field charged many more soldiers, some of them carrying large metal cylinders, others with bundles of sheets and blankets. They split up into smaller groups, and rushed into each of the barracks. They came out again without their bundles or the cylinders.

A roar and a crackle followed as all of the barracks burst into flames, with glass shattering and black smoke billowing skywards. The soldiers ran past us, some of them spitting and cursing at us. They jumped into the waiting trucks, and an exodus then began. All the trucks roared into life. They didn't hang around, in the space of a few seconds they were out of sight.

We were left looking into what resembled the jaws of Hell. An inferno blazed away right in front of us and, in the distance, an orange glow flickered, betraying the fact that the Nazis were retreating and laying waste to our land by burning it to the ground.

A man stepped out from the crowd. He was an older man, with wisps of greying hair on his head and a beard to match. He held his hands up, 'Listen! Listen to me, everybody! We must keep moving, and the only way we can go is west. We have to try to find water, and food. All we can do is head for the border, and hope that we can find some refuge somewhere.'

'What do you know, old man, eh?' shouted someone from the crowd.

'Well,' said the grey haired one, 'can we go back into that?'

He pointed at the eastern sky. There were balls of fire dotted around everywhere. The retreating Nazis had torched everything they could. I wondered about Aunt Helena, Yaroslav and Oleg. I wondered where they might be, and whether their house was still standing.

As one, the crowd of people turned away from the flames and the ferocious heat and walked. We found a road, one that was heading west and we streamed onto that dusty track as we faced the dreadful fact that we needed to flee our beloved Ukraine. Inside my heart I was feeling a fire of my own. The invaders had forced us to leave our home and now we were being driven further into the unknown. I wanted to lift my head up and yell. I wanted to turn around and charge headlong at the Nazi soldiers, if any were still around, and let them taste the fury of a Ukrainian fist. But, because we'd been so repressed over so many years, I knew I needed to keep my head down and be quiet. That was how we'd survived so many brutal years.

We walked about a mile or so and then the crowd began to break up into smaller groups. Some walked in gangs of 20 or so, Father and I found ourselves in such a group. We stumbled along, men, women and children, gliding across that terrain as if we were in a dream, as if we were floating. It didn't seem real. I thought about my home, my friends and most of all, my Mother. I really just wanted to be back home with her, all those miles away. But as we walked, I knew we were getting further away than ever.

The grey-haired one with the beard was at the front of our group. He seemed to have adopted us all, he was our leader. He strode purposefully on, and Father and I were drawn to him. We made our way through the crowd to be near him. We walked about a mile or so with the spring sun shining on us, but I couldn't really get warm, I had shivers running down me, which didn't leave me even when I pulled my coat tight around me.

Also, I was hungry and thirsty. Spending the night in a dusty old hut after walking so many miles had drained the life out of me, I was ready to drop. The grey- haired one, who we learnt went by the name of Peter, stopped at a part of the road where there was a dip. He looked across to the terrain at the side and waved an arm, 'Come on, this way, we need to find some water.' He led the way down into a wooded area and my ears pricked up as I heard a trickle of water. Many of us straightened up and broke into a trot as the sound of running water could be heard ever more clearly. It wasn't long before we were standing next to a small stream.

'Wait!' Peter held up his hand again as many of us threw ourselves down to take a drink. 'We must make sure this water is fit to drink before we take any.' He walked up and down, looking closely at the water, and the surrounding area, before nodding his head and waving us forward. We all plunged our hands in and took a good drink. I threw water over my face and freshened myself up.

Everyone spent a good few minutes enjoying the gift of that cool, clean water and then we all got back up onto our feet, refreshed and ready to walk on. We made our way back up to the road and carried on heading west. Behind us, in the distance, we could hear faint explosions. In front of us, a long winding road led to who knows where. It was a beautiful spring day, and the birds were singing in the trees all around us. Up ahead in the distance, towering above the horizon, were the Carpathian Mountains, with their jagged peaks running right across our view, jutting into the billowy clouds. They sparkled in the morning sun, and looked so beautiful that I wanted to reach out and touch them.

'That's where we need to get to,' Peter pointed at the mountains, 'we'll find more water, and maybe some food there.'

Nobody was arguing with him. Our empty stomachs spoke just as loudly, and Peter seemed so sure. He had a confidence like iron, an unshakeable belief. We simply couldn't doubt him, or maybe we just followed blindly because we didn't know what else to do?

Our weary footsteps dragged us along, and we kept our eyes down much of the time, so we didn't have to think how far we had to go. After a few miles, it could have been three or four, maybe five, none of us were counting, a fork in the road appeared. Peter held up an arm and we stopped. Heavy tyre trucks were evident on the right fork, while the fork to the left curved towards the mountains. Peter waved us to the left, and we carried on.

Before long, however, we reached a small village, where we weren't welcomed. Several village men came out armed with axes or hammers and stood glaring as we walked past. These people were barefoot and clothed in rags. Their houses were ramshackle and falling apart, with bundles of straw packed into some of the roof areas to plug the gaps. The local church had cracked window panes and crumbling walls right there before us. The graveyard next to it was like a bomb site. Gravestones had been knocked over and broken, clumps of grass sprouted up out of every available crack and crevice, and a soft breeze blew leaves around; they gathered in corners and crept over paths, making the graveyard look a shambles. Many of the fields and meadows in the area were overgrown and derelict. All we could do was keep walking and hope the villagers wouldn't try to rob us. We huddled closer together and followed Peter as he led us on, past the stares and the clenched fists.

A collective sigh of relief was exhaled as we made our exit from the other side of that village, but the mountains didn't seem to be getting any closer. Our trek towards nothing and nowhere continued, at least that's how it felt. We didn't count our steps, we just placed one boot after another as if it were the first step.

Around midday we stopped and found a shady area to cool down in. Peter took this opportunity to speak to us, 'Listen to me, my friends. The Lord is with us. He will guide us. We must be strong and keep our faith. The mountains are overflowing with life, and once we get there, we'll find food. I'm sure of that. We can find some shelter and survive. The Lord will provide for us.'

Peter led us in prayer, but I was becoming more and more desperate, I just wanted to find somewhere to stay until it was safe to go home, but that was becoming more and more uncertain, I could only see a long journey into darkness stretching out in front of me.

Like wounded soldiers, we staggered on, each step like walking through mud, each heartbeat like a hammer blow banging us backwards. Worn down, we finally arrived at the foot of the mountains. By then, it was early evening and the heat around us had lifted up and floated away. The sun was dropping down onto the horizon, its golden orange glow tracing a line all along the jutting mountain rocks. I pulled the collar of my coat up around my ears. The chill of the evening was creeping into my bones. We huddled together and gazed at the majestic splendour of the mountains, but the vision in front of us couldn't take away the hunger inside us.

Peter scanned the plateau. He paced up and down, and we watched him, wondering what he would suggest next. Suddenly, there was a rustle in the undergrowth, in several places. We looked again at the plateau, and I thought I saw some movement behind one of the bushes. It was moving. Then, another bush moved, and some twigs snapped, the echo of this cracked around our ears and I felt my whole body spring to attention. Were we about to be attacked by wolves, or some other mountain creature? I looked at Peter to see his reaction. He was perfectly still, just watching.

Then, some figures emerged from above us. There were four of them, clad in black and holding rifles. They clambered down the plateau with practised expertise, and every nerve inside me wanted to scream as I wondered whether they would try to rob us, or just cut us down where we stood. Peter stepped forward, 'Greetings to you. We come in peace. We're just ordinary people and we mean you no harm. Please, can you tell us where to find food and shelter?'

The four approached until they were right amongst us. They held their rifles at the ready. One of them was looking at me. I tried to avoid his gaze; I didn't want to annoy him. After all, he was holding a rifle.

'Stefan? It's you isn't it?'

I looked closer at him. He stood a good six feet tall and he had a woollen hat pulled down to his ears. He had a beard which was sprouting downwards, but when I looked into his eyes I saw something familiar. Those deep blue eyes got me thinking; got me wondering. Who was this in front of me? He lowered his rifle and held out a hand, and it was at that precise moment I knew who was standing in front of me,

'Sasha! Is it really you? I didn't recognise you. You look so different. So grown up.'

I took hold of his hand, and he pulled me towards him, we shared a warm embrace. It was so good to see someone I knew. Father stepped forward, 'Hello, Sasha.'

'Hello, Mr Szpuk.'

'Sasha, we're hungry, we've got nowhere to go. Can you help us?' Father looked at Sasha with desperation in his eyes. Sasha replied,

'I'd like to help you. I really would, but we can't take people in and give them food and shelter. We've hardly got enough for ourselves, never mind taking in all those who come past.'

'But Sasha, I've known you since you were a boy. You went to school with Stefan. Surely there's some way you can help us?'

Sasha frowned. The other three of his team had arranged themselves around Peter and the remainder of our group and were poised like panthers, with rifles at the ready.

'Wait here,' he said, and then he called to the other men, and they huddled together.

All we could do was stand and watch, and wait. Soon enough they broke out of their huddle and Sasha approached us once again,

'Okay, listen. There's no way we can take all of you in. We just haven't got enough provisions or places to stay, but what we can do is take you, Mr Szpuk, and Stefan. We can give you food and shelter and guide you across the border into Slovakia where you should be able to get taken in as refugees.'

'What if we volunteer to join the Resistance?' asked Father.

'Mr Szpuk, there are so many people passing through here right now. We have strict orders not to recruit any more. That's what we've been told, anyhow.' Father and I looked at each other. I wondered what the others in our group might think if we were to be given this special treatment, but my thoughts were interrupted by a voice from behind us. 'Of course you must accept this very generous offer, my friends,' it was the voice of Peter, 'if two of our group can get help here, then that can only be good. The rest of us will keep walking. Don't worry, we'll find what we need. We'll make a camp and build a fire in a sheltered position. There is life around here, we'll find some food.'

'He's right,' replied Sasha, 'You must come with us now, before it gets any darker.'

Father started to speak but Peter held up his hand, 'Please go with my blessing, Believe me, if you go then at least two of us will have found some sanctuary and some help.' He pulled us both towards him and held us briefly in a firm embrace. On releasing us he simply said, 'Goodbye.' He turned and walked away. I wished him and the others well and I'm sure Father did the same. I whispered a silent prayer, I hoped he and the others would be all right. Sasha extended his hand to me and helped me up onto the rocks, while one of his team did the same with Father. We clambered up until we were level with the tops of the trees opposite and we looked down at Peter and his group. Many of them dragged their feet with their heads bent, others needed an arm to hold onto. My heartfelt blessings were with them as they walked into the distance. For all I knew they could be walking right on into the heart of the Apocalypse, while I was lucky enough to find someone who could give me shelter. How long for I didn't know, but I didn't have time to think about it as Sasha urged us on. We climbed higher and deeper into the mountains and reached a densely wooded area. Sasha, with his men, led us to a small cave. Inside, it was cold and smelt damp, just like the inside of a well. I shivered and pulled my arms around me.

'Don't just stand there, Stefan,' said Sasha, 'you'd better get back out there and bring in some firewood.'

I was so tired I could barely stand up, and then I noticed a stack of wood in a recess at the back of the cave, 'Y-you already have some firewood here.' I pointed at the pile.

'That won't last long, Stefan,' replied Sasha, frowning at me, 'We always need to keep supplies topped up. Come on! If you're going to stay with us, you'll need to help out.' The light was fading fast as I trudged outside and, although I was sick with hunger and fatigue, I gathered up as many sticks as I could, as quickly as I could. I returned to the cave and stacked the sticks in the recess. Then I threw myself down on a bed of hay, next to Father. Sasha threw me a blanket and one to Father also. We lay down and tried to get comfortable while Sasha got a fire going. A blaze soon got the place warmed up and Sasha ignored us for a while as he searched through some boxes until he triumphantly pulled out a small carton. 'Eggs! Feeling hungry?' he looked across at us. We lifted up our heads and Father said, 'We're grateful for anything.'

Sasha poured some water into a battered and blackened pan and then positioned it on a specially constructed arrangement of stones that served as a stove. We waited. Sasha came and sat next to us, 'So. Strange that we should meet again after all this time, eh?'

'So much has happened,' began Father, 'you wouldn't believe me if I told you.'

'Many have journeyed through these mountains,' replied Sasha, 'all have a story to tell, some worse than others. I've heard so many different tales, of wives raped and murdered, of slaughtered children, of whole villages burned down. Believe me, I've heard it all.' Father and I sat silent for a moment. Well, what could we say? Sasha was right. Many of our fellow Ukrainians had fared much worse than us in many ways. Even so, that fact didn't ease my pain at all. Sasha continued, sensing our discomfort, 'But I can see you've both been through a rough time, and I've got a good idea how you're feeling. Remember what happened to my father?'

I remembered so well that night when Sasha came to tell me he was leaving after the Soviets took his father away. The memory was strong; his ashen-faced, wild-eyed look, the fire in his eyes and defiance in his soul showing through all too clear. He really hadn't changed very much. He'd grown into a man, of course, and he still spoke with the same intensity, 'That's why I'm here,' he continued, 'to stop that sort of thing happening, if I can. We're more organised now. We're not just the Resistance any more, we're the *Ukrayinska Povstanska Armiya**, or UPA for short. We're fighting for a free Ukraine. Anyone who's against that, be they Poles, Soviets or Nazis, then they are the enemy. It's as simple as that. If they pass through here, they risk death. This is our territory. They know that.' Sasha paused. The eggs were coming to the boil. He grabbed his rucksack and pulled out a paper parcel. He unwrapped it and inside it were a few slices of *razoviy**, a rye bread of delicious flavour and a staple of Ukrainians. That bread really filled you up. A few minutes later each of us in that cave bit into a slice of *razoviy* and a lovely hard boiled egg. We washed this down with half a cup of water each, from a bucket provided by one of Sasha's men. It wasn't the most substantial meal I'd ever had, but, at that point in time, it was a feast.

It was dark inside the cave, and I was tired. I lay back on my bed of straw and closed my eyes. I couldn't relax. I really wanted to sleep, but what would sleep bring? Dreams of home? Of Mother and Volodimir? I drifted off restlessly, fatigue eventually creeping into me.

I woke up the next day, in darkness once again, just like when I woke up in the hut. Father was still asleep, but Sasha's men were partaking of coffee and bread for breakfast, around that small fire. The smell of the coffee made my head spin a little, it reminded me, for a moment, of our kitchen back home. Blinking, as wiry shafts of sunlight found their way to me, I shook my head. I wanted my mind to be blank, to close doors on certain memories and thoughts. There were things I didn't want to think about. The embers of the fire were still glowing, and I gazed into them. For a few minutes I drifted into that make-believe world I visited as a child so many times. In my mind I conjured up the fire of the Kozaks as they rode the steppes. They were fearless and showed their enemies no mercy. They rode into battle side by side looking straight into the eyes of their foe. The Kozaks attacked like a hurricane. Swords clashed and much blood got spilt. Many times they fought to the last man. They were true warriors.

I was jolted from my thoughts by a rustling. I looked up to see Sasha entering the cave. He picked up a bundle of sticks. I watched him as he got the fire going again. With economy and grace he soon got a blaze up; Sasha was probably the only person I knew who was just like a Kozak. I was proud to know him. Maybe one day I would join him in the battle to free Ukraine. A quick calculation in my head said to me that he must have been about 21 just then. He was a man, and even though, at 17, I wasn't so far behind him, I felt like I was still only a boy compared to him.

Father woke up, and we breakfasted on black coffee and a slice of *razoviy*, 'Well,' said Father, 'what do you think we should do, Sasha?'

Sasha looked at us over the top of his tin mug. Then he set it down, 'It's difficult to say. As far as UPA is concerned we wanted the Nazis to win this war. That's what we thought at first, anyhow. But now, after seeing how they've treated us Ukrainians, we're not so certain. Both the Nazis and the Soviets are as bad as each other, that's for sure. But the Soviets are coming this way, and if they get this far and you're still here, you'll end up wearing a Red Army uniform and you'll get marched off to the front. Don't get me wrong, I'd like to say you can join us, but we've had strict orders right from the top not to take on any more recruits at the moment. On the other hand, if you keep walking west, eventually, you should be able to get refuge somewhere. The Allies will never concede control of Germany to the Soviets, so, if I were you, that's where I'd aim for.'

'So,' replied Father, 'how can you help us, Sasha?'

'I can take you as far as the Slovakian border. That's the best place for you to head right now, because it's away from the main areas of conflict, and we have contacts with their Resistance. It'll take a few days to get through the mountains and my men and I will need to keep our duties up as a patrol.'

So, over the next three days we travelled in much the same way. With meagre rations and with our hearts and souls scarred and stained. We stumbled over those mountains, dragging our feet and pushing down the pain inside us. The sun beat down on us, but no matter how warm it got, I didn't take my coat off. Even when I could feel beads of sweat forming on my forehead and a film of dampness on my chest and on my back, I never took that coat off. Well, anything worth anything, you hung on to. Simple really.

For two days and nights we continued on our mazy path and we survived on what we could find and what Sasha could spare us. At the end of the second day we stood on a peak overlooking some nearby settlements. It looked like several small villages grouped together. It was getting dark.

'Right,' said Sasha, 'we're near the end of our journey. Tomorrow morning we'll take you along the last couple of miles or so, and you'll be able to cross the border. Then you'll be able to get a good start.'

'Thank you, Sasha,' said Father, 'you've done so much for us.'

'It's been no trouble, but, before we say goodbye to you, we'll get you some good food to send you on your way. Follow me, Stefan. Mr Szpuk, you can wait here.'

Sasha and I climbed down the hill, stumbling now and again in the fading light. We reached the bottom of the mountains and he beckoned to me,

'Sit down here, Stefan.' We sat on some rocks and waited. I pulled the collar of my coat up. Within about ten minutes two figures approached. It was two girls, one aged about 16 and other little one would have been about six. They were carrying a pail. Sasha and I stood up and climbed down the final incline to meet them, 'Hello, girls. It's good to see you again.'

'Hello Sasha.' The older girl blushed, but the little one just looked up at us with wide eyes. 'We've brought you some *varenyky*.' The older one passed the pail to Sasha.

'Thank you, Slavka. We have some friends with us until tomorrow, so we'll get through this lot no problem. Listen. I've got nothing I can give you in return, but remember, if you and you families have any trouble then you know how to get hold of us. We'll always help you out.'

Slavka smiled shyly at Sasha and giggled. She walked up to him and stood very close to him. He put his arm around her, set the pail down, and they walked into a nearby glade, where they put their arms around each other. I sat back down on the rocks, with the pail at my feet, and the little one just kept looking on with her wide eyes, 'Why do you look so sad?' she said.

I tried to smile. 'I don't want to leave Ukraine.'

'Why do you have to?' she replied.

'Because the war is coming this way. We've got no choice.'

She pulled a bracelet off her wrist and passed it to me. It was constructed of small wooden beads.

'Keep this bracelet, so that wherever you are, you'll always have a piece of Ukraine with you. My uncle made it for me.'

I put the bracelet in my pocket just as Sasha came back. 'Come on, Stefan, we need to go.' After the swiftest of goodbyes to the two girls, Sasha and I clambered back up to our camp where we all feasted on those *varenyky*, those plump little pockets of dough filled with potato and cheese. They were still warm and had been doused with onions fried in butter. For once we ate well. We all went to sleep with our bellies full.

The following morning, we walked that last couple of miles or so, stopping now and again for Sasha and his men to peer through binoculars to see who was passing down below. We finally reached a peak where we looked down at some much larger settlements. It was a beautifully clear spring morning.

'Well,' said Sasha, 'what you see in the distance is the border between Ukraine and Slovakia. To the right is the Ukrainian town of Uzhorod. It's a big place and it's right on the border. To the far left is a small Slovakian village, Vysne Nemecke. It's a very small place, but the people around there are welcoming. You'll need to be careful, you know that, but with luck, from there, you can travel onwards towards Germany. That's probably the only place you'll definitely be safe from the Soviets You just need to climb down from here and then head towards the far side of the village. Here, take this,' he handed a piece of paper to Father, 'it's got the name of a contact in the Slovakian Resistance and an address where you can ask for him. His name's Ludvik. He's based in the mountains near the town of Presov. You'll need to get across the border, then go west for a while and then start heading north. He'll help you. Tell him I sent you.'

'Sasha,' replied Father, stuffing the piece of paper into his pocket, 'we can't thank you enough for everything you've done. I just wish we could join you. I know Stefan would like that.'

'If it was up to me, I'd take you straight away, just like that, of course I would, but we're under orders. But I've something else for you,' he signalled to one of the other men who walked across to us holding a shoulder bag, 'this bag's got a few things you might need. It's a basic mountain survival kit.'

The bag was passed to Father who looped it over a shoulder and said, 'Sasha, thank you. Are you sure you can spare this?'

'It's yours, Mr Szpuk. I hope it helps you. I really hope you make it through and get somewhere safe.'

Then I asked a question that was burning inside me, 'Do you think we'll ever be able to get back home, Sasha?' He looked at me, 'Stefan, one day we'll all go home. I can't say when that'll be. But I truly believe we will get back.'

Father shook Sasha's hand and slapped him on the shoulder. Then, I took Sasha's hand. He pulled me towards him, 'Take care of yourself, Stefan. You may not be able to join us now, but I know that inside your heart you'll be with us. And that counts. It drives us on, and makes us believe what we're doing is right. Promise me you'll never stop believing Ukraine will be free one day.'

'I promise, of course I do.' I had to steel myself. To stop the tears from flowing. To be strong. Because strength was needed right then. We said our final goodbyes to Sasha and his men. We turned away, and walked down that hill. We walked away from our beloved Ukraine.

Chapter 8

Ukrainian proverb: The fear of death takes away the joy of living

We climbed down that hill, our heavy footsteps kicking dust into the air behind us. Everything in our world was collapsing around us, that's how it seemed, I don't know how we managed to stay on our feet. At the bottom, we stopped and turned around to look back up towards the ridge. There was no sign of Sasha, or his men. It was just me and Father, on our own. Sasha had looked after us as if we were family. He'd shared the sparse provisions available to him and his men, he'd given us shelter, and now we'd said goodbye to him. I wondered if I'd ever see him again. The two of us turned around again and started walking.

The morning stretched out in front of us as we made our way across a layer of rugged foothills. The Carpathian Mountains towered beside us as we continued to head west, their majestic beauty occupying the horizon to the north. The bronze terrain of the foothills snaked and spread in front of us. I don't know exactly when we crossed the border into Slovakia, but I noticed something was different. An aroma of sweetness filled the air, a warm breeze blew around our ears, and the light was different somehow. This was how I knew we'd left Ukraine. I bowed my head. Every step was taking us further away from our home. My guts were twisting inside like water being sucked down a drain.

The next days passed by in something of a blur. We walked so far, so many miles, and I was so weary. My legs could hardly hold me up, they were like broken springs. Father led me through those foothills and deeper into Slovakian territory. Many days and nights passed with sunshine above us by day, and moonlight and stars twinkling above us in the night time. To this day, I don't know how Father kept the two of us going. Many times he pulled me back up when I'd stumbled. Other times, he placed a strong arm around my shoulders and walked alongside me. He found us food whenever he could, and more importantly, he was able to find running water almost at will. On many occasions, he'd stop walking, crane his neck to one side and say, 'Come on, Stefan, let's get ourselves some water.' Sure enough, there was always a stream nearby. We'd have a good drink and feel fresh again, even if only for a short time. Father could build a fire almost anywhere, from virtually nothing. The survival kit Sasha gave us had tinder, a flint and an army knife. That was all Father needed. In the cold darkness we'd huddle around the flickering flames and warm our bones.

There were many other lost souls wandering around, but Father and I kept ourselves away from the pack as much as we could, we tried to be invisible just as Father always said we should in the past. An endless search for food kept us occupied most of the time. By night we'd raid nearby farms and steal whatever we could, usually potatoes from storage sheds. They got roasted over a fire in the deep blackness of the night. It was never enough. I couldn't sleep so well because of the savage hunger that gnawed away inside me. So I lay awake under the stars and, with frightening regularity, heard explosions in the distance. I prayed they wouldn't come any closer. I saw flashes of orange and yellow dotted in the sky and a low drone from afar, sometimes closer, of what I guessed were bomber planes. I lay on the damp grass with a cocoon of black around me, with my coat collar pulled up and my hat right down over my ears, wondering when one of those bombs would land on us.

By day, we zigzagged across those mountains, Father managing to locate a route that took us north. By midday, the sun would be above us, and fortune shone down on us, because we had very little rainfall. Instead, I found myself, reluctantly, removing my coat, the heat from the sun threatening to boil me should I keep it on. I slung it over my shoulder or tied it round my waist, but in many ways was relieved when the weather cooled in the evenings, and I could put it back on. I didn't want to lose that coat, or for it to be stolen.

Many nights were spent tucked into those cold rocks, shivering away, just waiting for morning to come. The days got warmer, and now and again we'd stop at a stream to try and catch fish with a hook and line from the bag Sasha gave us. Sometimes we caught one and I have to say that fish tasted so good when roasted over an open fire.

Our lack of proper washing facilities caused us to be covered in fleas and lice, it was impossible not to scratch ourselves as we walked along. The same clothes had been on our backs for many days, how I wished I could be back home taking a hot bath in that old tin tub in our warm kitchen, and then changing into clean clothes. I felt so grubby, but there was nothing we could do, apart from the most basic of washing in the mountain streams around us.

It was taking forever to get to Presov, until one evening, when the light was just turning, we found ourselves on the brow of a hill gazing down at a big city below us, 'We've made it!' said Father, 'This must be Presov.'

To describe the joy I felt just then was impossible, I could have cried with laughter as we trotted down that hill. The trek through those mountains had been tough. The terrain levelled out and there were numerous smallholdings dotted around the landscape on the approach into Presov. We passed close by to one of them. A middle-aged woman stood at the front of the house, tidying her garden. Her eyes widened as she saw us coming, 'Oh dear Lord, what have we here? You look like you've been crawling through a bog. Come in, come in.' She opened that gate, and we walked in without even thinking. We slumped down on a bench at the front of the house. She brought us each a large glass of milk, 'Dear, oh dear. You look like you've been to Hell and back. Well, my daughter's visiting her grandmother in the town and is staying there until tomorrow, so you're welcome to sleep in her room tonight. You look as though you need a good night's sleep. Tell me, where are you from?'

'We're from Ukraine,' replied Father, 'I'm Mikola and this is Stefan, my son. The Soviets were driving towards the west so the Nazis threw us all out into the streets as they retreated. They destroyed whole villages; Ukraine is like a burnt-out shell. It's been blasted to pieces by both the Soviets and the Nazis. We've walked so many miles since then, so many I can't begin to think how far we've come.'

'Well, I'm Sara. Come inside and meet my husband and son.'

We followed her into the house and exchanged handshakes with her husband, Kazimir, and her son, Tomas. They'd been out at work on their smallholding and were getting cleaned up in the kitchen. There was a large stove, similar to our own back home and a large wooden table with chairs arranged around it. It was warm, and there was an aroma of cooking. I was reminded of my Mother. In the flickering shadows on the wall next to the stove I could see her. Moving in flowing, graceful curves, standing over a steaming pan, stirring. That's what I missed.

Sara took us upstairs to her daughter's bedroom. She swung the door open and a dazzling sight was there before us. The room was like a palace. There was a double bed with sumptuous, wine coloured, satin sheets. The floor was covered with a thick, brown carpet that looked good enough to sleep on. The windows were framed by luscious curtains of a golden hue. There was a beautiful dressing table and stool, constructed of a deep mahogany. There were cushions of a bewildering range of colours strewn across the bed. I stepped forward, but Father raised an arm to stop me,

'Sara, we can't sleep in this room. Just look at us. We're filthy; we've got lice and fleas all over us. We haven't washed for days. Please, just let us sleep in your barn. That'll be fine for us.'

Sara nodded, her cheeks reddening a little, 'Yes, yes. Well, maybe you're right. Okay, you two rest up in the barn for a while and then I'll heat up some water so you can get yourselves cleaned up. I'm making some soup for supper. You're welcome to have some with us once you've both had a rest and got yourselves cleaned up.'

The hay in the barn was fresh and we lay down on it. Before long I was in my own land of dreams. I stirred a short time later that evening, feeling refreshed, but with an emptiness inside – I was hungry. Father woke up at the same time and, after a good scrub down in the yard, we joined Sara and her family in their farmhouse. Kazimir poured Father glass after glass of *samohonka**, a powerful home brewed spirit. There was buttered bread and a delicious bowl of *borsch**. There were pickles, there was cheese and a few slices of ham. We ate well, and sang a few songs. Father looked so much better having had a good wash. It was good to feel clean. To rejoice in our freedom and in life itself at that moment was only right, I couldn't think about the future. I marvelled at Sara and Kazimir. They could've let us pass by their home without a word. They didn't know who we were, we could've been bandits or thieves. They showed us so much warmth and kindness, and welcomed us into their home and fed us. It showed me there was some good in the world despite the terrors heaped on us by the Soviets and the Nazis.

Father told them of our lives. About all manner of things. The war, life in general, all about how our life had been in Ukraine. They listened to him attentively, Father always had the gift to tell a story. They laughed as he told them tales about the absurdity of the Soviet collective farming scheme. But then, their jaws dropped when he gave them his account of the famine in the early thirties.

We slept in the barn again that night. It was warm and dry, much better than sleeping in fields or hedgerows, or in between the cold, hard rocks in the mountains. Father nodded off quickly, the effects of the drink maybe. I lay awake for a while, listening to booms and whistles in the distance. Now and again, there were flashes of light. It was raging all around us, and getting closer, or so it seemed.

The next morning, we had a good wash down again and I felt

much better. Sara cooked up some eggs for our breakfast. As we ate, Father showed Sara the piece of paper with the address on it.

'Ah, yes. I know this place,' she said, 'it's right on the other side of the town, just as it starts to get mountainous again.'

Over a final steaming cup of coffee, Father told them more about our life back home, all about our smallholding and the land we had. Kazimir and Father entered into a lengthy discussion about crop rotation, while I sat and thought about Mother. Would I see her again? Sara reminded me so much of her. I longed for that touch. That softness. There is no love like that of one's mother.

It was soon time to leave, we needed to make an early start to continue our search for Ludvik, the leader of the Slovakian Resistance. Sara packed us up with some buttered bread and some slices of *kovbasa**. Kazimir and Father shook hands firmly. Sara gave me a big hug, and once again I was reminded of Mother.

We thanked her for her hospitality and said our goodbyes, to her, and to Kazimir and Tomas. They were truly like rays of light in a dark hole. For an evening, and those few hours in the morning we found an oasis that gave us life and fresh hope.

Feeling much stronger we made our way into the town, with a spring sun throwing ripples of warmth upon us. The main street was lined with the most magnificent churches. There were so many twisted spires and elegant turrets, and so many simply beautiful stained glass windows. We gazed in wonder at them as we passed, and I could have sworn I felt a presence walking with us through that street. Now and again, I felt an icy cold grip on my arm. It happened two or three times, and it scared me. It made me keep my wits about me. We walked right through those streets. Neither of us wanted to stop.

'Stefan, I really hope Ludvik can help us get safe passage to Germany,' he looked once again at the piece of paper given to us by Sasha, 'we need to find this tavern, called Slavia.' I marvelled at the way Father navigated his way through those streets. He stopped to ask people directions when he needed to and struck up many conversations. Father spoke a few different languages, and consequently he could make himself understood to anyone, or so it seemed. He had an ability to connect with people, and an instinct which he used so well. Somehow he knew who to speak to, and who to avoid. Eventually, without too much trouble, we found the place.

It was a three storey building with a cream-coloured frontage, with elegant, arched windows and a roof pitched at a low angle. It looked inviting. Father and I crossed the road and pushed the door open. Inside was a bar area with tables and chairs on one side and an open area to the other. A man sat in a corner of the room with an accordion, playing a slow melody, while a lone couple waltzed across the floor. There was an array of mirrors behind the bar, and shelves full of polished glasses. There were one or two bottles dotted around on the shelves, and not much else. The landlord looked across at us and came out from behind the bar, pressing his greased black hair over his scalp and smoothing down his moustache, 'Hello, welcome to Slavia.' He wiped a hand on his apron before extending it to Father. They shook hands.

'Can I get you anything?' Before we could reply, two men stepped from behind a pillar and pushed the landlord out of the way. One of them, a thick set fellow with a wide face and beard growth, and with a cap pulled down low over his dark eyes, looked us up and down, 'You're strangers, what do you want here?'

'W-we're looking for a man called Ludvik,' replied Father.

The man cuffed Father with the back of his hand sending him sprawling against the entrance door, 'Ludvik, eh? What do you want with him?'

Father staggered forward rubbing the side of his face with one hand and pulling the piece of paper from his pocket with the other, 'Here, we've got an introduction from a mutual friend.'

The man snatched it and ran his eyes across it. Then, he screwed it up and threw it to one side, 'Ukrainian Resistance eh? Pah. Weren't much use to us last week when we needed them. Some of our boys got killed. We got caught in a skirmish with the Nazis, they had too much for us. We lost quite a few that day. Including Ludvik. He's dead. Won't be coming back. So . . . understand me, this is not a good place for Ukrainians right now, because we're about to send the Nazis off to Hell. We're going to bomb them and blast them and shoot them up. We don't want them here. And if there are any Ukrainians in Nazi uniform then they'll get it. They'll get it good!'

He stepped forward with murder in his eyes, but was held back by his companion. We didn't hang around. I pushed the door open and we bundled through it back into the street, and walked back the way we came, but slowly, so as not to attract attention. I looked back several times and we weren't followed. A few hundred yards later we stopped at the fountain in the town square. There was no water running from it, just a pool of scummy water sitting in the base. Father and I stood and looked at it.

'Stefan, it looks like things are going to get dangerous around here, I don't know what to do for the best.'

'Father, I want to go home. I want to see Mother. Please . . . can we go home?'

I collapsed onto my knees, and I'm not ashamed to say it, I cried. Tears flowed from me like a heavy rainfall. Father put his arms around me, 'Stefan . . . Stefan, my boy, we'll get home. Of course we will. Don't worry, son, I'll get you home.'

He pulled me up and sat me down next to him on the side of the fountain.

'Come on, Stefan, I need you to be a Kozak. I need you to be strong, just like you were back there when you got me out of that tavern.' I knew he was right. There was no use in sitting around weeping, we needed to keep moving. I dried my eyes on the sleeve of my coat and stood up.

We headed south. To go east would have led us right into the arms of the Soviets, while to the west and the north were battle zones. Father and I were not equipped to be in such places. So sure enough, we went south. To get away from the guns, the bombs, and the sounds of war; the explosions, the thudding of nearby hits; the flashes of fire on the horizon.

The sky and the stars above us became our blanket once again as we slept beneath them, night after night. The days passed by without much in the way of food and, despite Sara's efforts to feed us up for our journey, we got weaker as we trudged along. I turned into a shadow. Father constantly beseeched me to carry on. I remember his voice saying to me, 'Keep going, Stefan, keep going.'

But I was ragged, I was sick with hunger and fear. I remember being in a train carriage, in the hold with other peasants, I can't even remember getting on or off that train, I just recall the inside of the carriage. I sipped at a cup of water held for me by Father, warm gritty water, it tasted like soil. It revived me, poured some life back into me. And so, this is how we went. By train some of the time, the rest of time we trod the land in our worn out shoes. Until we reached the border. Once again, the clouds were kind to us as we made our journey, they held the rain inside them, and parted to let a glorious late spring sun shine down on us. My thoughts often returned to those years when I'd run around our village back home with Volodimir and our friends in such sunshine. Even though we were hungry boys with bare feet, we were happy enough, but we'd all been ripped away from there by the dark forces around us.

So, there we stood, with Hungary just in front of us. What would we find there? It was another step into the unknown. Would we find further hostility towards Ukrainians? Father and I were like vagabonds, with wild hair and unkempt, dirty clothes upon us. How would we be received by the Hungarians? Well, we didn't have much choice, there was no turning back. So we crossed that border, together with many others, and prayed we would find something or somewhere, a place to lay down our heads and get some rest. By day, we dragged our feet over grassland and fields. Insects buzzed around us, crickets chattered, birds sang. I was dizzy with hunger. All this food around me, and yet I couldn't catch it, couldn't grasp it in my hand, and then cook it and eat it.

We stopped several times to fish in a stream, pretty much whenever we passed one by and got a bite once or twice. Every time we did, the fish thrashed around as we tried to land it. We were so weak, so feeble, it was a hard battle. The fish was strong, flapping madly, with an eye staring at us, furious in its desire to get back in the water. Father got hold of a rock and bashed it. Then it was still. We cooked it and ate it, but it was never enough.

Many times I'd lie awake at night shivering. The stars twinkled above and many times I saw them transform into fish and swim towards me. They gathered around above my head and, one by one, they dropped into my mouth. On those occasions I got a warm feeling inside and eventually drifted off to sleep.

I lost track of time. I lost myself. I was like a sack, a hollow shell just drifting aimlessly. With guiding hands around me, Father's hands, somehow I kept moving. Now and again, I got a trickle of water down my throat, but I wanted food.

I remember sitting around a fire, sniffing the air, with my mouth watering. A hot potato burned me as I gulped it down. Where it came from I couldn't say, but I didn't care, I just wanted more, but there was none. We walked some more. All around us, early summer was beginning to bloom. The trees were sprouting leaves. The grass underneath our feet was lush. There was birdsong all around. It was maddening.

Without Father I would have surely perished. What little food we found was because of him. He led the way, across field and track, through meadows and mountains. I followed him. He kept me safe. We slept in open spaces, in between boulders, or beneath a tree. Father woke himself many times through the night to tend the fire, to keep it burning, to stop the wolves from coming to us. The days passed in a haze.

Then one evening, just as it was getting dark, we found ourselves walking into a town. The lights dazzled as we approached. What would we find? A line of men with guns ready to shoot us down? Or an angry mob armed with clubs and sticks, ready to run us back out the way we came?

We glided in. As if we were just a flicker in the shadows, like a tree root growing beneath the ground, weaving our way into those streets almost without breathing, without making a sound.

And then we saw it. It made our eyes widen and sent a shiver of expectation down us. There was a large church, and just in front of it was a group of people, just ordinary people, civilians like us. They'd set up some tables and brought out some extravagantly sized pots and placed them on those tables, which creaked under the strain. Steam drifted from the top of those pots. The aroma was good. I licked my lips.

'Come on, Stefan, Father put an arm around me, looks like we've found a meal.' We stood in the queue for many minutes until we reached the front and were given a bowl of steaming hot stew and a hunk of bread. We sat on the church steps and ate. It was wonderful. I licked my bowl clean. With the blessing of the priest, we took sanctuary in the church and, for a couple of nights, we slept there. The priest and his helpers gave us blankets. We were fed well during those two days and got ourselves cleaned up a little. The food was good, if a little spicy for us, we got a touch of the runs, but we still went back for more. On the third morning, the priest approached us, 'Well, Mikola and Stefan. You've been here a couple of nights and it's been gratifying to see you both in the chapel, joining us for prayers. But can I ask you what your plans are?' It was clear from his tone that we'd stayed the two nights maximum allowed there and needed to move on. I could see it troubled him to say these things, but it was part of his job, so that was that.

'We are weary,' replied Father, 'we've travelled far. Our feet are blistered and sore. We're grateful to you, and your people, for feeding us and giving us shelter. But we have to keep moving, to stay ahead of the Soviet Army.'

The priest nodded and looked a little relieved. Food was scarce everywhere. The church was doing its Christian duty as best it could and we'd got lucky on this occasion. From somewhere they'd got hold of a quantity of food and were prepared to distribute it to those like us; the driftwood floating through the land, bent and broken, sometimes drifting without direction or purpose. But as it was, we couldn't hang around. It was common knowledge the Soviets were pressing on the Hungarian border, it was whispered on the breeze from all corners, we couldn't stay around to see what they'd do to us.

We travelled on, towards the west, caught in a pincer grip of advancing Soviets and desperate retreating Nazis. We kept our heads down and walked in the shadows, like many others around us. There were hundreds and thousands of people lurking in those shadows. Like us, they'd been forced out of their homes and left to wander the earth, scavenging for what they could find.

Germany was our destination. The Soviet war machine would trample over everything in its way and take whatever it could, but we were pretty sure the Allies would hold onto Germany. Late at night, we'd sit around a fire with other travellers and it was believed by everyone that Germany would never become Soviet controlled. Those early summer nights were balmy, we began to feel more hopeful. After all, we'd lived for several weeks on the road, and we'd walked hundreds of miles. Okay, we were bedraggled, filthy and hungry for much of the time, but with the summer sun beating down on us, it revived us. The nights weren't so cold. Belief was building inside us. Belief that we might somehow survive.

It was decided by Father, the best way to get to Germany was to continue through the northern part of Hungary and then head back up into Slovakia. From there we'd be able to get across the border into the southern part of Germany. It was many, many miles and all we could do was take it one step at a time, and so we continued like this day after day.

We scrabbled around in fields to get food, sometimes we even loitered near to army encampments to see if we could find some scraps, anything, but we didn't get too close and always stayed downwind.

Somehow, we floated along that summer breeze and arrived at the capital, Budapest. A fine old town it was, with the Danube running through it and so many bridges. I counted eight. It was a magnificent place, but we couldn't stop to admire it. Our search for food was never ending. Father dropped a fishing line into the river, but we couldn't get a bite. In the end, we were forced to give up and keep on walking. The relentless trudging, together with so little food, turned us into sticks. We were like dead men.

I had visions. Many times I had them. Of platefuls of hams and sliced sausage. Of thick slices of buttered bread. Of ripe, luscious tomatoes and fresh smelling cucumber. That's all I wanted. Nothing fancy. As we walked through the town, my head spinning and my legs dragging, I saw a man approaching. He was eating an apple. He finished it and threw the core into the gutter. Without hesitation, I dived forward, and before the core had even settled in the gutter I'd scooped it up and eaten it. All of it. The man turned and watched me as I did this, with an expression of shock on his face. I didn't care. Not right then.

On empty stomachs, somehow we made our way north, by following the river. There were hordes of people just like us, trying to get somewhere, but we could have been going nowhere for all we knew. We trekked on, through roads and plains, through the day and often, through the darkness of night. Back towards Slovakia. Across the border and towards the capital, Bratislava. Father urged me on,

'Come on, Stefan, we've got to keep moving. The Soviets aren't far behind us.' I wanted to make him proud, so I walked. Tried to walk like a Kozak, even though the fear inside was filling every thought and every move I made. War was all around. Rockets flew back and forth. Both towards us and from behind us. Many times we threw ourselves onto the ground and covered our heads with our hands. We soon learned to recognise that familiar whistle. It started slowly, but as soon as you heard the faintest sound, you knew you had just a few seconds. We ran like rabbits to get shelter. Behind a rock, or in a ditch. Anywhere. On one occasion, we were caught by surprise as a rocket flew overhead. It came from nowhere, and looked as if it was coming right at us. I stood there, looking up at the sky with my mouth open. Next thing I knew, Father had thrown himself at me and I was lying on the ground with him on top of me. The rocket exploded about a hundred yards away, covering us with soil and stones. Father took the worst of it. He stood up, rubbing his back. Smoke swirled around us. It was raging hard all right.

Many more days passed by and turned into weeks. The summer began to fade and the cool evening breezes told us that autumn would soon be with us. The nights were starting to get colder.

Finally, we reached Bratislava, and made our way through the city, looking for food and water wherever we could. The streets were full of people just like us, rooting around in bins, being chased away by patrons of kerbside cafes, sniffing around for a crust of bread, or some potato peelings, anything.

On the north side of Bratislava, we ran into some partisans. They offered to feed us if we would work for them. We weren't in a position to say no, we hadn't eaten anything much for a few days. They fed us, and gave us shelter. Then, the following morning we were sent on a task. To help dig trenches to stop the Nazis from advancing east. We didn't question the wisdom of this, but were just grateful to be fed and sheltered. Weakened as we were, we couldn't dig as hard or fast as the other men, but we did as much as we could. And after a few days, and a few more meals, we grew stronger. Summer was now behind us and the winds were really starting to bite as they swirled through the mountains. We'd got lucky once again, in finding sanctuary, even though it was with the Slovak partisans. Their leader was Leo, there was fire in his soul. 'This land belongs to the Slovak people, no one else.' He fixed his expression on ours as we sat around a camp fire late one evening, 'They shouldn't be here. Any of them. Neither the Nazis nor the Soviets. We live a simple life here in Slovakia. The Nazis have come and taken whatever they can get their thieving hands on. We want them out. So tomorrow I'll need you both to work with different work details. Mikola, you'll be with the work party at the north side of the city. It's heavy work, digging a whole new set of trenches, the ground is very rocky there. So, Stefan, you'll go with the party working to the east. Work there is nearly complete.'

We retired to our beds but on the way Father spoke to me, 'Don't worry, Stefan, we'll head on from here soon, just as soon as we get our strength up for another few days on the road. This isn't our war, we shouldn't be getting involved.'

We bedded down for the night in our tent, amidst the crashes and the bangs around us, accompanied by flashes of light. This was a cauldron of war and we were right in the heart of it, but at least we had some shelter from the elements. Winter was creeping up, and the cold would be biting at us, so we were grateful. But we still wanted to move on.

The following day, we woke up and separated off to our work details. It was strange to be without Father, but the other men were friendly enough towards me. It was an easy morning, with just some general clearing up and checking to do. We stopped early for some lunch, just a couple of slices of bread and butter with some cheese and pickles. I was getting my strength back.

The constant sound of bombing was shredding my nerves. It was wrecking me. The sounds seemed to be getting louder and nearer by the day. Okay, we had shelter with Leo and his men in the mountains, but there was an air of defiance around that threatened to boil over at any moment. They were getting themselves organised. There were many hushed conversations late at night with fists banging and fingers pointing. It was all about to go crazy, we had to get away. As Father had pointed out, it wasn't our war. I know it doesn't sound very heroic, but we knew that we Ukrainians could never win. Whether the Nazis or the Soviets won, we'd be persecuted, tortured, killed, or sent to death camps in barren places. I just wished the Soviets and Nazis would blow each other to smithereens and into oblivion. Then maybe we'd get some peace.

With the other men I made my way back to the camp in the middle of the afternoon. I scanned across the camp from side to side to see if I could spot Father. There was no sign of him. Maybe his work detail hadn't returned yet. Or maybe he was getting cleaned up.

As we got closer I saw Leo. He was standing at the edge of the camp looking up towards us with his hands clasped in front of him. We took a few steps further and I could see he was looking straight at me. He was quite still, which was unusual for him. Something wasn't right. We reached the camp and he signalled for the other men to keep on walking, while he stood in front of me and placed a hand on my shoulder,

'Stefan . . . I don't quite know how to say this. I have some very bad news. Your Father has been killed. He was working with some other men, when a bomb landed nearby and a wall collapsed on him . . . he was killed instantly . . . we lost three other men too. I'm sorry, Stefan.'

I looked up at him. I didn't want to believe him. I wanted him to take those words away. I looked over his shoulder, hoping to see Father standing there, wiping his hands on a towel and smiling at me, but I could see from Leo's expression he was telling the truth. I crumpled onto the ground, threw my face into my hands and wept.

Chapter 9

Ukrainian proverb: The earth will cover the doctor's mistakes

I sobbed so much I thought I'd never stop. Leo stayed with me, and tried to comfort me; he lifted me up and held me in his arms. I was still only a boy. He took me to the place where Father was. It was a walk of dread. I didn't want to believe he was gone. I kept hoping he'd just appear in front of me with his usual expression. He was always so serious. That was the face I wanted to see so badly. Leo led me on, without many words. We arrived at our destination. It could have been anywhere as far as I was concerned, I could barely make sense of where I was, my head was so full of dark clouds, and my heart was beating hard, so hard I was ready to burst.

Father was laid out alongside three other victims. A woman was mopping the faces and hands of the bodies, and tidying them up. I recognised him straight away, just by the shape of his body. I knew it so well. I threw myself onto him. He was cold, but I didn't care, I was next to him, and didn't want to leave him. I couldn't even venture to say how long it was before I felt arms on me. Those arms prised me away from Father. I'd never be near him again.

Leo and one of his men took me back to their camp. It was early evening,

'Stefan,' Leo spoke to me in a hush, 'if you like, we can go to the village nearby and see the priest, and ask him to give your father a Christian burial.'

'Yes . . . yes, he would have wanted that.'

'Fine then. Let's get ourselves cleaned up a little and we'll take a walk down there.'

Leo got me a bucket of water and I threw some on my face. It stung as it mixed with my dried, salty tears, but it refreshed me. We tidied ourselves up and tried to look a little more respectable and then we made our way to the village. The autumn wind was biting into us as we walked, but it couldn't take away my numbness. Leaves swirled around our feet, and the crunch of them beneath our feet pierced a sheet of silence that hung between Leo and me.

There was a track leading into the centre where we found the church. It was a small wooden construction, of typical design. Leo found a door at the back of the church which looked like it led to living quarters. He rapped on the door. A sound of shuffling came from the other side. A key turned in the lock, the door opened and a face peered out at us, 'Yes?'

Leo wasn't slow in making our case, 'Father, please. We need your help. I've got Stefan here with me; he's walked many miles. He's come from the east, from Ukraine; he's been travelling with his father, Mikola. But . . . Mikola's been killed. A bomb caused his death. Please, can you come with us? To give Mikola a Christian burial. He deserves that, surely?'

The priest looked us up and down. He opened the door wider still and stood there fastening up his topcoat. His fingers were shaking as he fumbled his buttons. He cleared his throat and spoke, 'I'm afraid I have many people to visit in the village this evening. I can't help you.' He shut the door and locked it, and walked right past us,

'Good night to you.'

I couldn't believe what I was hearing. I ran up to him and grabbed his arm, 'How can you just walk away like this? My father was a Christian. You can't let him be buried without the last rites! You just can't!'

The priest snatched his arm away, and from the surrounding houses a group of villagers appeared, as if they knew something was happening, they must have been stirred by the commotion. They were a group of solid-looking farmhands. There were a dozen of them. One of them spoke, 'Is everything all right, Father?'

'Yes, yes. These people are just leaving.'

The villagers escorted the priest towards the houses nearby while Leo and I stood and watched them walk away, taking any last hope of a Christian burial for Father with them. I wanted to run up to the priest and tell him, insist to him that he should give a Christian a decent burial. All I could do was watch as he disappeared into the dusky charcoal of the early evening.

'Come on Stefan,' said Leo placing an arm around me, 'I don't think we're going to get anywhere here. We'll have to go back to the camp.'

So, we returned as supper was being dished up, but, I couldn't eat, and I couldn't sleep. All I had left to remind me of Father was the bag given to us by Sasha. I kept it next to me through the night.

Just when the sun was beginning to creep over the horizon, I stood up. I wrapped my coat around me and pulled on my cap. I picked up the bag and made my way to the north side of the camp. A guard posted there asked me what I was doing. I told him I was taking a walk. He let me pass. The truth is I could not accept Father's death. I was running away. I didn't want to see Father's corpse again, or see him lowered into a hole in the ground without a priest in attendance to bless him on his way. One thing I knew for sure though, I'd never trust a priest again.

I walked away from the camp and kept heading north, along the bank of the river. The black, shimmering surface of the water bounced the first rays of sunshine up into the air and they died in sparks of yellow in front of my eyes. The water looked inviting. How would it be if I should plunge in and sink to the bottom? Down into the soft mud, to sit with the weeds and watch the fish swim around me. At least down there I'd get some peace, away from the madness and the mayhem. I walked down to the water's edge and stood there with the water slopping around my threadbare shoes. Ice-cold water trickled into my shoes and the shock of it made me gasp and shiver. I clambered back up the bank and carried on walking.

I didn't know where I was going and didn't really care. Father was all I could think about, and it troubled me that, very soon, his cold body would be buried beneath a mound of soil, without a priest to give him his last rites. That was something I didn't want to hang around and see. Never would I understand why that priest refused. He was a holy man, that was his job. I'd tried my best, but the priest had simply waved me away as if I were a just an insect annoying him. Suppose I ran back down to his church and kicked away at the door until it fell off its hinges? Then maybe he'd talk to me properly, but I knew it would end in trouble for me if I did that, I'd end up getting locked up, then the Red Army would most likely come and recruit me. There was nothing I could do. A cloak of shame hung over me.

I walked all day, stopping for a drink of water from wherever I could, I didn't stay still for long, and walked as fast as possible, to fill my senses up. Fractured stabs of sunlight flickered between the branches of trees all around me and I breathed in aromas of delicate flowers. Best of all, the birds sang to me. Even though the autumn was almost upon us, some of them still chirped away, marking their territories for the winter. They helped to drown out the thoughts in my head. Even so, I found it hard not to think about Father. At times, I could have sworn he was next to me, walking alongside me, but when I turned to face him there was nothing there. I swear I heard a voice at times. His voice. Telling me not to worry and that everything would be all right. I'd spin around to see where he was, but of course he wasn't there. I pulled my collar up, put my head down and marched along that river bank. For miles and miles.

Eventually, I stopped, breathing hard with near-exhaustion. It was getting dark and there was a chill in the air. I just wanted to fall down somewhere, go to sleep and never wake up. I found a place along the river bank; it was just a shrub with a hollowed out pocket beneath it. I threw myself into that pocket and lay there. My mind wouldn't stop. I kept going through it all over and over again. Why? We'd never been any trouble to anyone. Why did this happen to us? I cursed Leo. If he'd let us stay together, then maybe Father would still be alive. Or maybe we'd both be dead. Maybe that would have been better. Eventually, I drifted into sleep.

Many more days passed that were just like that one. Not many morsels of food were to be found. I knew I needed to eat to keep my strength up, Father had always hammered that into me, but I wasn't hungry at that time. I had things on my mind, I'd lost my Father, and was far away from home with no way of getting back. The coldness of the nights numbed me, much of the time I couldn't feel my feet, and I kept my hands deep in my coat pockets. I thanked the Lord I had that coat, if it were not for that I would have frozen.

Day blurred into night and back. Many times, I fell and lay down to rest. Or to die. If I were to be crushed by a Nazi tank then at least it would all be over and I wouldn't have to endure the pain that stabbed in my head and in my heart.

One day, I can't recall exactly when it would have been, I was walking down a road, swaying from side to side when I heard the sound of something, horses' hooves and the rumble of a wagon. It was a familiar sound from my childhood. It was right behind me. A voice penetrated the fuzziness that filled my head,

'Hey you! You, boy! Where are you heading! There's marshland up ahead, you'll never make it through there. It'll suck all the life out of you and pull you under!'

I turned around and saw a horse and cart, with a man sitting above, holding onto the reins. He jumped down, he was of a stocky build, with a sun burnt face and a mop of curly black hair. He wore a dark blue shirt and matching trousers held up with braces,

'Let's have a look at you, boy,' he placed his hands on my shoulders, and I didn't resist, 'My my, you've been through some rough times. You're just skin and bone. You look as if you could do with a hot bath. Come with me. My wife'll feed you and run you a bath so you can get yourself cleaned up. You'll need to pay me back though; I need a pair of hands on my farm for a week or two. What do you say?'

I nodded, too weak to speak. He helped me to climb up onto the wagon and, before too long, we were on a long approach, with fields either side of it, heading towards a farmhouse of generous proportions.

'I'm Ivan,' he said as he helped me down off the wagon, 'come inside and meet my wife.'

'I'm Stefan.' I managed to mumble my name to him somehow. He guided me into his home and into a warm kitchen that reminded me of home. I held back a tear. A woman stood in front of a stove, busy cooking something that smelled good,

'This is Stefan,' said Ivan as the woman turned around, 'I found him near the marshes. Brought him back here before he got lost in there.' He turned his head towards me, 'This is my wife, Marina. We're just about to have some dinner, so sit yourself down and join us.'

I slumped down onto a chair. The warmth of that room soon spread through my bones and, in the space of a few minutes, my cheeks burned as if they were about to catch fire. I stood up and took my coat off, then sat back down again. It was good to be under a roof and in the warm. A plate of fried potatoes and cabbage was placed down in front of me. The aroma of it was tantalising. I didn't waste any time. I shovelled it into my mouth and savoured the taste of the butter and the vegetables as they dissolved in my mouth and slid inside me.

Once I finished I sat back and looked up. I wiped my mouth with the back of my hand. The kitchen was of a substantial proportion, and the fittings and furniture looked solid and well made. Above the table was a religious picture of the Father, the Son and the Holy Ghost. I swallowed as I thought about my home, back in Ukraine. Would it still be standing? Or had the Nazis burned it down as they ran from the Soviets. And what of Mother? Would she have survived? Those questions nagged away at me. They tormented me.

During the course of my wanderings across these lands, I'd wanted to just crawl into a hole, close my eyes and sleep forever. The way I saw it, the world was a bad place, with cruelty and pain the common currency of every day. I wasn't sure whether I wanted to live in that world, but there I was, saved once again by the kindness of these people. Ivan poured me a glass of water and I sipped it, I carried on looking around, naturally curious. Either side of the religious picture were framed photographs, portraits of what looked like boys. They were a little faded, and I strained my eyes to look closer.

'Stefan,' Ivan placed a hand on mine, 'those photographs you see up there on the wall are of our two sons, Theodore and Nikolai. Some weeks ago they ran away to join the Resistance, We haven't seen or heard from them since . . .'

At that point Marina, who had stopped eating and was sitting motionless, threw her face into her hands and wept uncontrollably. Ivan placed his arms around her.

I didn't know what to say or do. I just sat there, frozen. A few minutes passed. Marina managed to compose herself and she busied herself heating some water, pausing now and again to wipe her eyes with her apron. I had a bath in a small room off the kitchen. Some of my pain and the misery soaked away for a few minutes as I scrubbed myself clean. The heat spread through me and chased the cold from my bones. Marina got me some clean clothes and I was shown to a bedroom. Before too long, I was asleep in a warm bed, in a room, under a roof. Something I hadn't known for a while. Sleep came to me quickly.

The next morning, after breakfast, Ivan showed me around their land, 'Here's our cowshed,' he pushed the wooden door open and Marina was right there in front of us, squatting on a small stool, milking away. 'We have just three cows, but we get a good yield from them. I've milked the other two myself, earlier this morning. Look.'

He walked over to a large metal pail which was standing in a corner. 'We store it in these containers, and then take them down into our cellar until market day. You're welcome to help yourself to the milk, whenever you feel like it. There's plenty. But I must insist you do not waste it. No throwing it around or drinking so much that you get bellyache. Just take as much as you need, but treat it with respect. It's our livelihood. Understood?' I nodded. He reached up to a rack above the pail where there was a ladle and some tin cups. He poured me a drink of the lovely, frothy, fresh milk. It settled inside me and I felt a warmth inside as it flowed into my stomach.

Ivan showed me around the rest of his land. He had fields just next to the perimeter of the farmyard, big enough to plant wheat or corn to keep a family in bread for a whole year. Beyond those fields was lush green pasture. To one side of the farm, near the kitchen, was a walled area. Ivan opened a door and we stepped inside. We were inside an orchard; there were about two dozen apple trees, some with fruit that was ripe, others were bare, but there also two big storage crates overflowing with apples in a corner of the orchard. I breathed in an aroma of acid sweetness that made my mouth water.

'You see, Stefan, we have everything here.' He waved me across to a door on the far side of the orchard and opened it, revealing an impressive expanse of land, which had separate plots, each dug over, and some with green shoots bursting through from a late crop. Ivan handed me a spade and grabbed one himself. We made our way over to the far side of the plot and spent an hour or so digging over a plot ready for more planting, for crops that would be harvested before the frosts came. After that, Ivan asked me to take his cows over to the pasture land. I was happy to do so, because I loved cows. They never ceased to amaze me. They were so big, so ungainly, but my, what wonders they produced! All that creamy milk, which could be churned for butter, or made into cheese. And all that just by eating grass. Incredible.

Next to the farmhouse was a pig pen and a chicken shed also. Ivan and Marina had plenty to keep them busy, and I was only too happy to help them out.

One day stretched into another and then a week went by, and then another. I settled into living with Ivan and Marina, and they treated me like a son.

We filled a need in each other, and plugged something of a hole. A big hole in my case. I still couldn't quite believe that Father was dead. Many times I lay awake at night and, as I dozed, I'd hear him. I saw him. He was in my head, as clear as day. It was like watching a film: The flints would strike each other and then there were sparks. One, two and then a third strike, sometimes more, and then came flames and a feeling of warmth. I'd wake up with sweat pouring off me. Without Father, I'd have been dead long ago.

So, I'd get up in the mornings, having slept badly, but restless, wanting to get out of the house and do something. I'd shuffle and fidget over breakfast. I'd rock in my chair as I bit into my bread and butter and gulped down my milk. Ivan got me out in the fields. They needed their soil turning over for the winter crop of potatoes, cabbages and other vegetables. I'd never used a plough before. I stood with him and looked at it as he explained to me its workings. Next thing I knew I was there with two horses in front of me, trying to get the plough running straight. It was hard work, but that suited me. I wanted to work myself hard, so that I'd just drop. I ran that plough up and down, in wavy lines, in straight lines sometimes. It didn't matter, as long as the ground got turned over. Once finished, I handed the plough over to Ivan and I stood, dripping with sweat. He patted me on the back, 'Well done, Stefan! You're a good worker, come on, that's enough for today, let's go and get cleaned up.'

That's how I lived at that time. I worked like a madman. It was a wonder my arms and legs didn't drop off. At the end of each day, Ivan put an arm around my shoulders and we walked back to the farmhouse with the autumn sun blazing gold on the horizon. A glass of cool milk later and I was refreshed. Marina's cooking was wholesome and I ate plenty.

In the evenings we listened to the radio. It was just like being back home, it was exactly the same model as Father's. It coughed and spluttered as it tried to catch a signal. Whenever we did manage to tune into a station, the news was always the same.

War was raging all around us. Millions had died, and hundreds more every day. Somehow, right there, in that part of Slovakia, we seemed to be in something of a cocoon. There was very little bombing around there, and not much of a military presence. Ivan drummed his fingers on the table as he listened to the broadcasts. Marina clasped her hands together. I could feel the tension. After all, they had a lot to lose. And they had their sons to think about. I often caught Marina looking at those pictures on the wall with an expression on her face that betrayed her longing to see her boys back home. Marina was never still. Even when the dinner was simmering gently on the stove she'd be pacing about, muttering to herself. This is what the war did to all of us, it tore our hearts and our souls to shreds, it drove a bloody wedge through families, caught between fighting for different causes. Caught between trying to fight a battle or just to survive.

It was a miracle that Ivan and Marina took me in. They saved me. Lord knows, I would have ended up in a ditch somewhere, with just the worms for company if Ivan hadn't rescued me. That was why I worked so hard for them. And the work suited me, it stopped me from thinking too much.

One day, I got up after another unsettled night of dreams. I breakfasted and tore around the smallholding, busying myself with feeding the chickens and the pigs. When I came back inside to see where Ivan was, things were different. He was wearing a suit, his hair was combed into a neat parting, and he was standing in front of a mirror, fastening a necktie, 'Stefan, it's market day today. I'm going into the village, and you can come with me. Get yourself cleaned up and Marina will find you some clean clothes.'

I scrubbed myself down and put on a crisp white shirt that was just a touch too big for me. I threw on a black jacket that was, again, for someone of greater proportions, but I didn't care. I liked to look smart. Marina handed me a pair of pressed grey trousers, they were a good fit, but I slipped braces onto them anyway to make sure they stayed up. A quick wash down, a comb through my hair and I was all ready. Ivan had already loaded up a small wagon with milk, butter, eggs, cheese and a few boxes of apples that were ripe, so we set off.

It was a crisp, autumn morning. Birds sang and the trees on the leaves shimmered and billowed in the breeze, with lush shades of red and gold around us. The click clack of the horses' hooves on the road, and the rumble of the wheels as they turned on that uneven track combined together to make a background rhythm that somehow felt just right. It was good to be moving, to be going somewhere. The breeze blew my hair back, and I enjoyed that wind on my face. I listened as Ivan chattered away next to me, telling me all about his family and his friends in the village, but, in some ways, it was hard for me to take in. I missed my own family and friends so much. I drifted off into my own daydreams. The Kozaks came into my mind. They always did when I needed to feed some fire into my soul. A swirling, heady melody played in my head as the Kozaks charged at their enemy. They must have been a fearsome sight, hurtling at their enemy on their horses with their *sharivari** tucked into their boots, billowing wildly in the breeze like the sails of a ship, with their *hohol** flowing from their shaved heads and with whiskers like those of a beast. They fixed their eyes on the quivering soldiers that had been sent to face them and roared as they charged. No wonder many of the enemy turned and fled. But the Kozaks weren't around anymore. We Ukrainians needed to find another way to fight our battles.

About half an hour later, Ivan and I arrived at the village square which was overflowing with people. We parked up next to an empty stall and climbed down from the wagon. We looked around at the market which was already busy. All manner of items were being traded. Many different foods were available, some of them still alive, like plump, fine looking chickens. There were various jars of pickles and jams. And some fresh vegetables also. There was fine, embroidered cloth, and religious paintings. There were tea sets and trinkets from faraway lands. Even with bombs crashing down to earth nearby and bomber planes droning in the distance, people still met up to trade with each other.

Ivan and I were kept busy. Everyone wanted the goods we were selling, they were basic foodstuffs after all. Within an hour or so, we'd sold everything and Ivan counted up. He slipped me a couple of *korunas*, which was generous. 'You've been a great help to us these past two weeks, so you deserve that. Come on, let's have a look around, you might want to get something for yourself.'

We wandered around, and the two *korunas* jangled in my pocket. Ivan stopped to look at some tools, so I carried on walking. I reached a stall where an elderly woman was selling wooden carvings and painted eggs. On one of the higher shelves I spotted something and I picked it up. It was a wooden cross, about eight inches in length, and four inches across. It was beautifully engraved with a traditional pattern. The woman accepted my two *korunas* for it and I slipped it into my bag before Ivan should see it. My intention was to give it to him and Marina for looking after me.

'Stefan, come on.' Ivan appeared from a corner of the stall and beckoned me towards him. 'There's some entertainment being put on by a good friend of mine in a field near here.'

I followed him out of the market and we walked a few streets until we reached a narrow track. There were several large barns either side of us as we walked along a well trodden path to a gate. A man stood at the entrance. Ivan handed him some coins as admission for the two of us and we walked into the field. There was a large crowd in the middle, all men, and as we got closer to them, we were hit by waves of noise, by a burning intensity, by the smell of money and by a buzz of anticipation.

Two stalls were set out. One sold shots of home-made plum *horilka*, the other was taking bets. I stood back as Ivan quickly carried out a transaction with the man who was taking bets, I didn't know what he was betting on, I didn't really know what was happening, but it was a party atmosphere and I could feel myself melting into the energy and euphoria around me. Ivan bought us each a shot of the plum *horilka*. I threw it back and it stung on the way down. We had another one and then Ivan said,

'Well, Stefan, now you're really going to see how we live here in Slovakia!'

The crowd of men all turned and rushed towards an adjoining field, Ivan and I joined them. There were two paddocks on opposite sides of the field and I swallowed hard when I saw what was in them. There were a pair of full grown bulls, stamping and scraping the ground in front of them with their hooves. They were like mountains of muscle on four legs, with horns that could cut a man in half. Each of those bulls had two men handling it, trying to control it.

Someone waved a white handkerchief in the air and a pair of men rushed to each of the paddocks and pulled the gates open. The bulls charged out into the field and stopped. They stared at each other and paced in semi-circles. The sun was setting and a chill wind was whipping across the plain, but none of us felt that. With the plum *horilka* inside us and a pair of mighty bulls facing each other, about to do battle, we were full of fire.

One of the bulls reared up, thrust its horns forward and charged. The other one did the same and we watched as they pounded towards each other, dust kicking up in the air as they charged. Seconds later, there was a thud that vibrated through the ground right underneath us all, as the bulls locked horns. They slammed into each other, over and over again. Each time they smashed into each other the crowd roared. The force of each hit was like a bomb blast. It reverberated all around us. We watched as one of the bulls began to buckle, with its knees wobbling and its head sagging. The dominant one sensed this quickly and surged forward, its horns powering into its foe, digging in, sending its opponent crashing to the floor with a resounding whack that juddered through the earth. We all felt it. Several men sprang forward to get the winner away. They herded it back to its paddock. Meanwhile, the defeated bull was revived and soon up on its feet.

Ivan collected his winnings. We stayed around for a few more drinks, and then staggered and swayed back to where we'd left our horse and cart. We meandered home in the little light that was left. We woke up the next day feeling a little sore in the head. Over breakfast I gave the wooden cross to Marina to thank her and Ivan for everything they'd done for me. Marina was delighted and the cross was soon mounted in a suitable position in the kitchen.

We reached the middle of October 1944, and winter was getting closer by the day. The work on Ivan's farm became heavier, we worked from early dawn to dusk, but Marina fed us well, and I began to get my strength back. In the evenings we listened to the radio. The Soviets were still pushing west, driving the Nazis back. Surely it wouldn't be long before they crossed over the border into Slovakia to take what they needed for their war machine. There was a tension in the air as the three of us listened to the broadcasts.

A week or so later I was in the orchard after breakfast. I plucked an apple from a tree and pulled my pocket knife from my bag to cut slices from it. The crisp, sweet flesh just about dissolved in my mouth. It was a slice of Heaven.

Suddenly, there was the sound of an engine and the skid of rubber on dewy grass. I peered through the crack in the door and saw a Slovak police car parked outside the farmhouse. A pair of armed policemen jumped out and ran up to the door. Ivan was already there, 'What is the problem, officers? How can I help you?'

One of them pushed past him and went into the farmhouse while the other looked Ivan up and down, 'We're looking for vagrants! Anyone who's travelling without papers. We've been ordered to arrest them and keep them at the police station.'

'Whose orders are those?'

'That is not your concern! Now, have you seen any vagrants around?'

'No . . .'

'You don't mind if we take a look around then?'

'No . . . of course not . . .'

'Good! We'll need to conduct a thorough search of your land, just to be completely sure. Those are our orders.'

The other policeman came back out of the farmhouse and reported that he'd found nothing. The three of them turned and started walking towards the door to the orchard. I saw Ivan pointing in the opposite direction, but the policeman shook his head and continued towards me. I crept back from the door, turned and ran towards the far end of the orchard. I reached the biggest and tallest of the trees; the one with the densest foliage. I climbed like a cat, faster than I'd ever climbed. Until I was right at the top. I curled myself around one of the thicker branches and hid my face in some leaves, watching below me with just one eye. The door opened and I stayed still, not daring to breathe. The men marched up and down, and had a quick scout around. One of them kicked the apple I'd been eating. Ivan watched them. I saw him look up. I don't know if he saw me.

The men marched out of the orchard, ordering Ivan to follow them. I waited a few minutes, and then I climbed down. With my heart beating hard, I hitched myself up onto the top of the wall and looked over. Ivan and the policemen were some way in the distance, heading towards the pastures. I saw Ivan look over his shoulder, back towards where I was, but he was too far away for me to see the expression on his face.

I didn't understand why the policemen were rounding up people like me, vagrants as they called them. I feared it would not be a good reason. Most likely, they were planning to hand us all over to the Soviets to be used as fodder for their army. I didn't want Ivan to get into trouble on my account either, so I knew what I had to do.

I plucked a few apples from the trees and put them in my bag. Then I climbed over the wall at the far end of the orchard, and I ran. Like I'd never run before. Right into the nearest area of woodland I could see. I concealed myself in between some trees and took some breaths. Then I turned and walked away from Ivan's land, taking care to stay under cover, weaving myself into the landscape around me. I wondered if a day would ever come when I'd be able to stop running.

Chapter 10

Ukrainian proverb: God is looking for those who come to Him

From that point on, it was just me and my coat. I didn't have much else. Ivan and Marina were good people and they'd saved me from Lord knows what fate. I whispered a blessing upon them as I walked, for them to stay safe from any harm should the Red Army arrive on their doorstep. Marina's home cooking had filled me out again, and the farm work had strengthened me up. The land swallowed up my steps as I followed the river once again, with my coat pulled around me to keep out the cold.

Ivan had been like a father to me. I knew I'd miss him, but he was Theodore and Nikolai's father, and they could return any day and in that circumstance, I may have been expected to leave anyway. In any event, from what we'd heard on the radio and from the recent visit by the Slovak police to the farmhouse, it sounded like the Soviets might not be too far away. I'd be horsemeat if they caught up with me. A Soviet citizen in German territory? Why hadn't I volunteered to join the glorious Red Army as it advanced? That was just one of the many questions they'd ask me. Then there would be the terrors they'd inflict on me. I had to stay out of their reach. As far away from them as possible.

Of course, I also had the bag with me. Father's bag, with the basic survival kit given to us by Sasha. I unfastened it, took out one of the apples I'd taken from the orchard, and crunched into it. There were about a dozen in there. I knew they wouldn't last me long, so I ate it slowly. In one of my pockets was the wooden bracelet given to me by the young girl just as we were leaving Ukraine, I'd forgotten it was even there and when my fingers happened upon it, I wondered what it was. I pulled it out and held it up in front of me, and then I rubbed the beads between my fingers. It gave me a strange kind of comfort, and the girl was right, it gave me a connection with the land that was my home.

The nights were cold as I wandered westward. Once again, I was sleeping out in the open, beneath trees, in fields, getting shelter wherever I could find it, sometimes in an old abandoned barn. Most nights, I got a fire going, thanks to my observations of Father's fire lighting skills. The fire kicked out heat, and I watched the flames dance in front of me as I tried to sleep. They hypnotised me, but it wasn't enough to really keep me warm. By morning, I was like a block of ice. I swear I creaked because of the cold, and I stamped my feet, blew on my hands, and tried to keep moving. My stiff legs soon loosened up and I got a little warmer.

Days and nights passed. I don't recall the name of the river that I walked beside, but it gave me hope, because where there is water, there is life. There were many others travelling along that same stretch of water, and, at times, I walked with them. Other times I was alone, but whether in company or alone, I stayed close to that river.

Every now and then, I got out my fishing line and a hook, and I'd find a spot where I couldn't be seen. I'd sit, for as long as I could, trying to get a bite. I hooked one or two in, but I needed to be careful. There were many people around just like me. Hungry people who wouldn't hesitate to whack you over the head to get whatever you'd got. I only fished where it was away from the main flow of people, and then roasted the fish slowly over a small fire, fanning the smoke towards the water. But there weren't so many fish to be caught around that time, maybe they'd all swum off to a better place.

Within a week or so, my strength was waning. To exist like that, to try and survive on the road was so hard. On many occasions, I found myself stopping to rest my body and my aching heart. I'd been through so much and was still only a boy, just 17 years old. There were times when, after stopping to sit beneath a tree to ease the aching in my legs, I was unable to move again. I was in a strange state of paralysis, but it wasn't because of a lack of physical ability to move myself, it was the clouds that were blowing around my head that rendered me lifeless. There was a storm inside me. My heart was crying, and my head was heavy. So many of my memories brought me pain, so much so that I had to keep trying to close the door on them, but to shut them out was to deny who I was, and where I'd come from. I wrapped my coat around me and pulled my hat down over my face. I buried my face in the collar of that coat. It was as if I was trying to hide, like a creature with a shell, I wanted to curl up inside it, safe and warm, with nothing to worry me.

It was a terrible state to be in, and, at times, I wondered how much longer I might last. I could easily have just rolled into a ditch, closed my eyes, and gone into a good, long sleep, and never woken up again.

One morning, I stirred from a bitter autumn night, with my body screaming from the cold. I jumped up and tried to ignore my stomach's noises. I thrust my hands in the pockets of my coat and made my way around a big curve in the river. The morning sun was dazzling me as I walked that bend, but it seemed different. It was more intense, but I paid it no heed, dismissing it as a quirk of Mother Nature, and I covered my brow with an arm as I walked on.

As I came around another bend onto a straight stretch of river, I walked into a blinding light. I stopped. It was too powerful. I sank down onto my knees, with my head bowed. The light was surrounding me. I didn't understand what was happening. Then I heard a voice, 'Stefan, stand up.'

As soon as these words were spoken, the glare of the light receded. I stood up, my legs wobbling a little. There was a man standing in front of me. He looked familiar.

'Take my hands.' He reached out to me.

I looked up at him. The light was fading, but still touching him somehow. I blinked a few times and I was able to see again. I held out my hands. As we connected, I felt a surge of something, a rush of belief, and a sense of life. I cast my eyes upon this person stood in front of me and I recognised him from a time before, from a time when I was still with Father. 'Peter . . . is it really you?'

'Yes, it's me. Peter. Come and join us. There are many of us. We travel together, and we look out for each other.' He squeezed my hands and I felt a surge of energy enter me. I followed him to an encampment close by. There was a fire still burning from the previous night and Peter sat me down next to it. I stared into the embers. All around me were Peter's travelling companions. They were busying themselves with a variety of tasks. One of them, a middle aged woman dressed in a black skirt, grey cardigan and embroidered headscarf, came over to the fire and stacked a few small batons of wood against it. Flames soon licked onto them and the fire kicked back into life.

'Hello Stefan, I'm Martha. Peter's asked me to make you some breakfast, so I'll heat some water and boil an egg for you. We've got some bread too, so that should fill you up and give you a good start to the day.' She smiled at me. I smiled back, and it wasn't too long before the food was ready. As soon as the plate was in front of me I shovelled it all down.

As soon as breakfast was done, the camp was packed up. There were 12 people with Peter, five men and six women, and then there was me. The group congregated around Peter to say a prayer, and I joined them. Then we started to walk. We headed towards the west, as I had before. It was a blustery morning and I pulled my collar right up and pulled my hat down tight. After a mile or so, I found myself at Peter's side. 'So, Stefan, what happened to your father?'

I hesitated and a lump formed in my throat. Peter seemed to sense this and put an arm around me. He led me to one side of the group as we walked. 'He's not with us any more, is he?'

'N-no.'

'I'm sorry to hear that. He was a good man.'

'I miss him, and I miss my family. I don't know what to do, or where to go. I'm heading for Germany, to stay out of reach of the Red Army, but I don't know what I'll find when I get there.'

'Just do what you think is best. Follow your heart.'

'Where are you all heading?'

'I've travelled with these people for some time now. We pick up one or two strays such as you, and we help them find the right path. The one for them. Most of them are like you, escaping from the Soviets. They've all left their homes behind, not because they want to, but because they had no choice. Most of their lives, they've lived in fear of the Soviets. So, they run and they hide. Just like you.'

My cheeks burned as I spun away from Peter, 'I don't want to run anymore! I'm sick of running!' He stood and looked at me, and I stared right back. 'I've had enough of this, I'm going home!' I turned around and headed in the opposite direction.

I took long strides and marched away, my head down and my arms swinging, but no matter how fast I walked, Peter was right there next to me. I was about to break into a run when he spoke to me once again, 'Stefan, I know you're angry, and you're hurting, but I don't really think you have any choice right now. Look.' He pointed at the eastern horizon. It was glowing shades of red, orange and pink, and there were clouds of smoke dotted around. In fact, there were groups of big clouds above us, like giant balls of cotton. They were all racing away from the east as fast as they could.

'It's a war zone. You'll never make it back home. All you can do is come with us, and then one day, when things have settled down, maybe you'll be able to return.'

I stopped. In the distance I could hear a faint booming sound. Bombs ripping into towns and villages causing untold devastation and bringing death. Peter was right. To walk back home was to walk right into the heart of an apocalypse. I had no doubt in my mind, the eastern front was like a scene from Hell. I turned around once again, and it tormented me to do so, but Peter was there to guide me and we rejoined the rest of the group.

We walked through the days and the nights, just as I had done before with Father, and on my own. We scavenged from the land around us, although with it being autumn time, there was little to find. Somehow, by day we made progress, we crossed over into Czech territory. By the time the evenings came we were all ready to just wilt and drop. After several days of wandering, Peter turned towards me, 'Stefan, can you catch us some fish?'

'I can try.' I dug out the fishing line and hook from my bag and headed to the bank of the river, with a bucket and a pocketful of worms. It was getting late and I didn't think I'd get a catch. I squashed a worm onto my hook and cast my line, using a stick as a rod, just as I'd done when I was a boy. I sat down and gazed into the shimmering water but didn't have much time to daydream before the line tightened and I grabbed the stick. I hauled in a big one. It was a beauty! I bashed it with a rock and laid it next to me, once it had stopped wriggling. I cast again. Before I'd even had time to sit back down again, I felt a pull on the line and I hauled in another one. It slid up the bank, wriggling like crazy, but I once I'd whacked it with the rock, it was still. That was two of them, lying at my side, plump and juicy. I had a mind to pack up then, thinking that two was more than I'd ever caught at one attempt, and so quickly, but, with so many of us, I felt obliged to try for another. Within the next half an hour I caught another three! I had to blink at the sight of those five fish tails sticking out of the top of the bucket. Maybe I was dreaming. I hauled the bucket back to the small camp that Peter and the others had made. It was getting late, the sun had just about set, and I was grateful for the fire that Peter had built, it guided me.

'Bless my soul, look what the boy's brought back for us!' Martha approached me and took the bucket. She prepared the fish and roasted them over the fire. I sat down, and several of the others said 'well done' and 'thank you' to me.

It wasn't long before the fish were cooked and then, somehow, from nowhere, Peter produced two small loaves of bread. We all ate well that evening. It was a blessing from the Lord above, I have no doubt about that. That night we slept with full bellies.

The next day, we walked on. The days flew by. We stuck together and we fed on what we could find. There was little. I tried to catch more fish, but wasn't so successful. Winter was almost upon us and there were less of them around.

We headed north west, hoping to stay away from any trouble and from the bombs that were flying back and forth. Somehow, Peter navigated us through, until we were deeper inside Czech territory. We managed to stay ahead of the advancing Soviets and out of sight of any Nazis that were around.

And so, the winter came, and the days were shrouded in darkness. The nights were so cold. We spent long hours huddled around a fire. Somehow, Peter always managed to find firewood, and many times I'd wake up in the middle of the night and see him stacking more logs against it to keep it going. I wondered if he ever slept.

At that time, we were approaching the border into Germany, that's what Peter told us anyway and we had no reason to disbelieve him. I wondered what would become of us once we crossed that border.

By this time, it must have been close to Christmas. I know this because the prayers that Peter chose when he led us in worship were all about the birth of Christ. The time of our Lord was close, and we needed to be faithful to him, no matter what happened to us. Our Lord guided us, I was sure of that, through those bleak winter days, when it got so cold, we sometimes woke up frozen solid and glued to the ground beneath us. Because there were many of us, we huddled together for warmth, and we collected whatever we could find to keep us warm, mainly sticks to build fires. It was a bitter winter and we spent much of our time huddled around a fire, taking the opportunity, whenever we could, of any brief bursts of sun and good weather to walk a few miles further.

In my head, and in my heart, I struggled to answer questions that were consuming me. In the sky, clouds loomed over me, and I felt suffocated by them, as if they were stopping something inside me. I followed Peter and his group, all the while as if I were walking through a fog, but, there was no fog, only the one which swirled inside me. My coat wrapped itself around me, it comforted me, and kept me warm, until such a time came when I found myself unfastening the top two buttons and folding down the collar. It was getting a little warmer and the days began to stretch in length, we had more light. I hoped the worst of the winter was over.

One night, we were eating some potatoes which one of us had found nearby, Martha baked them over a fire, they smelt delicious as they were cooking, and they melted inside us. Whilst with Peter's group I was safe, warm and ate quite well considering our circumstances. Okay, every so often, we went hungry for a day or two, but somehow, Peter always got us through and we found something. My admiration for Peter grew like a sunflower in the heat of summer for the way he looked out for us. We looked out for him too, but he didn't seem to need it so much. He was a great leader, and had a quality about him that I couldn't work out.

Despite this, as we sat around the camp fire that night, a rage grew inside me. I'd been through so much, forced out of my home, out of my country and left to wander or to lie down and die. Father had been killed by a bomb. I didn't know whether Mother was still alive, or the whereabouts of my brother, Volodimir. I wanted to lift my head up and scream. Instead I looked at Peter, 'So! This is what God provides for his flock, eh? Thousands dead, and many more just like us, wandering, going nowhere. Walking like the blind. Towards who knows what? My Father's dead, my village has most likely been burned down or bombed. I've got nowhere to go.' I covered my face with my hands. I wanted to jump up and shout, to punch someone or something, but I couldn't. I was like a sack of potatoes, just like a lump of nothing. Years of ill treatment had turned me into a shadow. Both the Nazis and the Soviets had treated me and many others like dirt. We'd been ground down. There was no fight left in us. Peter was sitting just opposite me. I lowered my hands from my face and shouted, 'So Peter, tell me. Where is God? He's not here, is he? How can he be? He shouldn't let this happen. So many people have died. Why? God should have stopped all this. Why hasn't he stopped it?'

Peter looked at me, his gaze was unwavering. 'The Lord performs many wonders. He is with us now, I can feel him . . . '

'How can you say that? All I can feel is death and fear. All around us. That's what we've got here. We're in a living Hell!'

'That's right, and you know why that is, don't you? It's because there are forces of darkness at work in the world. The Devil is among us. There is a great battle going on between good and evil. But, we must always remember that the world is God's creation. It's a beautiful creation.'

'God has forsaken us. If He made this world, then why do we have bombs and weapons that can blast a village or town to pieces? People are being murdered every day. That is not beautiful.'

'Sometimes things happen that test our faith. But how can we truly see what is beautiful if we do not know what is ugly, or if we do not experience hardship?'

I hesitated, still burning inside, but the flames weren't roaring so hard. 'This is more than just hardship, this is a catastrophe. I'm all alone in the world. I fear what is to come for me.'

'With the Lord at your side you will find a way. You will find a path. You must place your trust in the Lord. Remember the tale of the merchant who sold everything so he could have just one pearl? That pearl is like the kingdom of Heaven. Whatever happens to you in life, whatever losses you may have, the kingdom of Heaven is always there for you. You must never forget that. I understand you've been through difficult times, enough to break any man's heart twice over, but you must stay strong, Stefan, and keep your faith.'

I didn't know what to say to that, because I knew there was truth in his words. Above us the moon threw its beams down at us. There were no clouds above us anymore. In the space of a few minutes the sky had cleared. I felt a strange sensation. As if I could just float up into the air and fly into the heavens. I shook my head to free myself of that strangeness, and then, feeling very tired, I lay down next to the fire and drifted into sleep. The following day, I woke up and the sun was shining. It threw out brilliant yellow rays as it simmered on the horizon. Spring was on its way, and not only was the sun in the sky, it was in my heart. I don't know whether it was Peter's words or the sunshine that made me feel so much better, but the clouds inside me had disappeared. I felt as if I was floating.

We soldiered on, and of course with the spring came a wider choice of food. We were able to get a range of vegetables from the countryside and farmland around us as we continued on our trek. The fish returned, they became more plentiful, and every few days I pulled enough in to feed our group.

'We're close to the border now,' one morning Peter spoke to us following prayers, 'Germany is just the other side of this village. Soon we'll be safe, away from the danger of the Red Army. Refuge is there waiting for us.'

I wondered how Peter knew so much, but did not question him. How could I? He'd led us through a wilderness, through some dark days, and provided for us, both physically and spiritually. He was, in my eyes, a superman.

That morning, we'd got no provisions for breakfast, so I wandered along the river bank, savouring the spring sunshine and looking for a spot where I could cast my line to maybe get a bite. I sat down beside the river in a secluded spot and opened up my bag. I had a good rummage through to find my line, and to choose a hook that was still in good enough condition. Whilst doing so, I pulled out a bunch of scrunched-up paper. I unfolded the crumpled mess and saw they were German Marks! The ones issued by the Nazis in war time. Of course! Father had got them when working back in Stanislaviv. These were the last few, which had been hidden away in the bottom of the bag all that time.

Jumping up, I strode away from the river bank and down an embankment. It was just a short walk to the nearest village. The first few houses were soon in sight, and I broke into a run, hoping to buy something with my money.

Nervously, I made my way down onto the rough track that divided the dwellings. I looked at the first house, and the one opposite. Which one to approach? The one on the left was well kept, and the gate was open. I found myself drawn towards it, went through the gate and walked up the path. I knocked on the door, timidly at first, then a little bit harder, I was hungry and there was nothing to lose.

Within a minute or so, the door opened and a well worn, stoutish woman stood, filling the doorway. 'Yes?'

'I . . . I have some money,' I spluttered, 'and I wish to buy some food. Do you have anything to spare? I can pay. Look.' I waved the notes.

Her expression didn't change. 'Wait there,' she replied.

Another couple of minutes crawled by and then she returned holding a box.

'Here,' she opened up the box and there were six lovely eggs sitting in there.

She passed the box to me and I gave her the German War Marks. She unfolded them and then held them up in front of her. Then, she tore them up, into little pieces, and they fluttered away on the breeze.

Well, I didn't wait around to ask her why she did that. I turned and ran back down the path, clutching the box of eggs, and kept running until I got back to where Peter and the rest of our group had been camped. At least I tried to, but I couldn't find them. I stood there scratching my head. It was definitely the right spot. I looked around. The landscape was the same, but there were no ashes from where our fire had been, no patches of flattened grass where we'd camped. I thought I must have made a mistake and was in the wrong place, so I scouted around, and must have covered every blade of glass within a square mile, trying to find Peter and the others. I found nothing.

Eventually I stopped. I was so confused. Where could they be? Meanwhile, my stomach was rumbling. I was still holding the eggs in my hand. Beneath a nearby bush I found an old discarded burnt-out tin. I tapped the bottom of it. It was flimsy, but still just about intact. I scraped out the bottom, there was some burnt-out food debris in there, and then I got some water from a nearby stream and cooked those eggs up. I ate three of them and put the others in my bag.

I was at a loss what to do next. It must have been about midday, the sun was overhead. I decided to keep heading north west. Maybe Peter and the others had gone ahead, maybe they hadn't realised I'd gone missing. That seemed unlike Peter, but what else could have happened? Maybe they'd decided to walk around the outside of the village, rather than into the middle of it as I had done. It was likely they would have done this to avoid any confrontations.

With the bag slung over my shoulder I strode off in that direction. If I hurried along, I might catch up with them. I skirted around the left side of the village, giving it a wide berth, following the borders of the freshly ploughed fields, using walls and hedgerows for cover. Flowers were coming into bloom once again, the earth was ready for nature to spring its bounties and the sun up above me was feeding the land. Within a week or two it would all begin to burst up from the ground.

Before too long I'd passed by the village. It was a quiet kind of place anyhow, and I was grateful for that. As I walked I scanned the horizon constantly, and on one occasion I saw what I thought might be a group of people, but as I got closer I realised it was just a group of saplings. I walked on and reached the bottom of a hill. It was a steep one. Surely this would have slowed them down. Some of the older members of the group, such as Martha, couldn't walk so well. I was certain that, once I'd got to the top I'd be able to look down and see them somewhere. I'd be able to shout down to them.

I flew up that hill, breathing hard and breaking into a sweat. I stopped halfway to take off my coat and threw it over my shoulder. I pulled the peak of my hat down to keep out the sun and carried on. When I was near the top I stopped once again. I turned around and had a good look around. It was a beautiful morning and I could see villages dotted here and there all over the landscape, but there was no sign of Peter and the others. For a second or two I wondered to myself whether they were real or whether I'd just dreamt them up. How could they just vanish like this? I turned back around, and carried on walking. I finally reached the top and stood there taking a good few deep breaths. Then I looked down.

I drew my breath in. Down in the valley below was a convoy of trucks and armoured vehicles. They'd all stopped and some soldiers were wandering around smoking cigarettes. Others were looking at maps. There were soldiers with rifles and guns, there were anti-aircraft guns mounted on some of the trucks. They hadn't seen me, so I threw myself down onto the ground. I examined them more closely. They weren't Nazis, nor were they Soviets. The uniforms weren't the right shape or colour. I strained my eyes to make out the markings on the vehicles and was able to just about make out an oblong shape on one or two of the bigger trucks. There were a few faint stripes and a blur of small stars dotted onto those oblongs. Americans! I stood up and straightened my clothes, and put my coat back on. I clambered down that hill, holding my hands up. It was a descent towards safety, or so I hoped. Once I'd surrendered myself to the Americans, the Soviets would never get hold of me.

When I was half way down, some of them saw me and lifted up their rifles, so I lifted my hands higher. On reaching the bottom, a soldier rushed up to me and snatched my bag from me, 'Don't move a goddam muscle! This is the US army! Stay right where you are and don't say nothing!'

He ran his hands around my body, and rummaged through my coat pockets. Then he stepped away. He emptied the contents of my bag onto the grass, squatted down, and picked through what was there. He walked up to me. 'Okay kid, where are you from?'

'I . . . I'm from Ukraine.'

He frowned. 'Yeah? What the hell are you doing out here, all on your lonesome?'

'I'm running from the Soviet Army.'

He frowned again, and looked me up and down. 'Okay, kid, get your things and follow me.'

I scooped up my belongings and stuffed them back in the bag, and he took me to one of the trucks.

'Wait here, kid.'

He spoke briefly with what looked like a senior officer. The officer looked at me and then nodded to the soldier, who approached me once again. 'Okay, kid. Get in this truck, we're gonna get you outta here, until we can figure out what to do with you.'

I climbed into the back of the truck. There were two other boys in there, both of them a year or two younger than me. We nodded to each other. I reached into my bag and got the three remaining eggs out. They were a little cracked after being thrown on the grass, but were still all in one piece. I handed one to each of the boys, who both smiled and accepted them. We all peeled off the shells. I bit into my egg. The truck started up and pulled away.

Chapter 11

Ukrainian proverb: He is guilty who is not at home

So there I was, in a town called Regensburg, that's where the Americans took me. I was registered into a Displaced Persons Camp. There were thousands of us there, of many different nationalities. There were lots of Ukrainians, and there were also Poles, Czechs, Latvians, and others from neighbouring countries.

I was given a bed in a wooden barrack. There were 12 of us in there, Ukrainians mostly, but, before I could settle in I was taken to a medical point and sprayed with powder to clear the lice off me. I was pushed into a shower where I was able to scrub myself down properly for the first time in many months. The water turned almost black as it collected on the floor of the shower. It swirled around as it disappeared down the drainage hole, leaving a layer of grit and scum. I washed my hair and scraped the soft bristles from my chin with a clean razor. It felt good to be clean. I was given a new set of clothes. My old ones were incinerated, including my beloved coat. I felt a twist of pain inside me when they took that coat. It was more than just an item of clothing to me, it was more like a second skin. I wanted to reach out and pull it back. For quite some time, I mourned the loss of it. The new clothes given to me by the Americans were decent enough, including a brand new overcoat. It wasn't quite as good as my old one, but I took it gratefully. For the first time in a long time, I felt human again.

The Americans were good-hearted and the camp was well run. There were plenty of blankets, pillows and clean sheets available. We kept warm, and ate well. Every day I queued up in a long line to get my meals. The camp was positioned on an old army base, it covered a huge area of land, completely flat, with a variety of buildings. There were a large number of barracks assigned just for use by the male population of the camp, and a separate, similar sized area for the women. Right next to the female quarters were several dozen more barracks, which were assigned to children, so that they could be cared for either by relatives or by the womenfolk. When I first arrived at the camp, I wandered into this area and was shocked to see how many children had washed up there in the aftermath of the storm that was the War. Many of them were outside their huts, wide-eyed and scrawny, one or two were running around, but most of them looked painfully thin and just stood looking forlorn. There were dozens of them, some of them were so small, I was amazed at how they could have survived the endless carnage we'd all been through.

There were six shower blocks with adjacent toilets at each one, and in the middle of all this was a large hall with a kitchen at one end. This was where I ate my first meal at the camp, a dish of potatoes and cabbage with gravy. It tasted so good, I could have eaten it twice. It was the summer of 1945, the weather was good; no rain and lots of warm sunshine stabbing through a cool breeze, so the Americans organised tables for us to eat our meals outside.

At the far end of the camp was a group of brick buildings, about seven or eight separate units, some used for storage, others for cooking and others as workshops. In the middle of them all was a large two-storey mansion house. This was where the Americans based themselves, it was from there that the regular patrols and guards came from.

The day after our arrival, we were interviewed by a clerk and allocated to our work details. I was assigned to work in the barber shop. A group of us got marched over there and we were greeted by Victor, who was in charge. He was a Latvian, stoutish, with big bushy eyebrows and what seemed like a permanent grin on his face.

'So, young man, we're going to teach you how to cut hair.' Seeing the expression on my face he chuckled, his shoulders shaking, 'Don't worry, we'll start you off slowly.'

Victor was good to me. He was good to all the young men and women who worked for him. Within a week or two, I was snipping away, just basic haircuts, nothing too fancy, but it gave me a little bit of confidence. It made me think that maybe I could be my own man one day and make a living. I got into a good daily routine. Up early and, after a quick breakfast of coffee and bread, I'd start work around eight. Those of us who worked there began the day by scrubbing the whole place down. We'd clean all the cutting tools, the razors and the wash basins, and then mop the floor down. And then the first customers would begin to arrive. Many were new arrivals at the camp, a dishevelled-looking lot, all with wild hair and whiskers. They all looked in need of some attention, and there were hundreds of them. We were kept busy every hour of every day, and I got quite good at cutting hair. I enjoyed the feel of the metal clippers in my hand, and once they'd done their work, it was time for the scissors. I'd snip away and then comb, and then snip some more. Finally, I'd scrape with the razor, just to finish off. The men would then stand up out of the chair, I'd give them a napkin to wipe their necks down and they'd walk out looking like new.

It was good, solid, steady work, and many months passed by. We reached the winter, and I was so glad to be working inside, in the warm. It was a small barber shop and Victor had an electric heater which he switched on in the mornings to warm the place up. Often, some of the new arrivals would sit in there after their haircut just because it was warm, but Victor soon shooed them out.

The barracks weren't quite so warm however, but we were issued with extra blankets to get us through the cold nights. I had a bed in the barrack which was up against a side wall. I liked that. It gave me just a little bit of privacy. I still, somehow, had kept the bag. It was strange to have that with me, as if I'd existed in another life. Now and again I'd empty the contents out onto the bed. The fishing line was there, the mangled hooks, and the few tins with fire lighting equipment, and also the wooden bracelet given to me by that young girl on the border of Ukraine and Slovakia. That seemed like a lifetime ago, rather than just a few months. I rolled those beads between my fingers and it lifted my heart up a little to hold those small wooden beads carved from Ukrainian oak. All I'd got in the world was there before me on my bed. It wasn't much, but at least I was safe and dry, clean and well fed.

At night, many of the young men, and women, would sit around outside their barracks, all through the year, whatever the weather. If it rained we crowded into one of the barracks, and during that first winter I found myself wrapping my new coat around me to keep out the chill. In the fading light of evening, cigarettes were smoked, tea and coffee were brewed up and we talked until it was late. Hitler was dead and the Nazis were defeated, we all praised the Lord for that. We swapped stories, each one as tragic as the last. We had a lot of laughs too. There was horseplay; the young men arm-wrestled and had all sorts of competitions to see who was the strongest or the most acrobatic. All to impress the girls of course, who sat in a group giggling as they watched us young men showing off.

As those evenings turned into night, the girls drifted off to their own barracks and the conversation took on a more serious tone. There was one topic that dominated: going home. That was what most people were looking forward to. Getting back to their old way of life, back with friends and family. Of course, there were those who may have lost loved ones and didn't even know. That caused a lot of anxiety, but in general, the feeling around the camp for many was one of relief that the war was over, and we could go back to where we'd come from and start living our lives again. I was settled at the camp, it wasn't such as bad place to be, and I'd pushed thoughts of going home to the back of my mind. Living in the Soviet Union still gripped me with fear.

'What about you, Stefan?' Asked Jan, one of the Poles, 'Are you looking forward to getting home?'

I looked at him carefully.

'Well, Jan,' I replied, 'It's like this. We've just spent most of the last year running away from the Red Army, right?

He nodded and took another long pull on his cigarette.

'So, do you really think we want to go running back into Stalin's arms?'

He looked a little taken aback. 'But Stefan, surely you want to get back home just like the rest of us?'

'What do you think the Soviets will do to me? In their eyes, I'm a traitor. I ran away when I could have joined their Red Army. Maybe they'll shoot me, maybe they'll hang me. I don't know. But even if I did get back home alive, I'm scared what I might find. I don't know where my brother is, he was taken to Germany to work as a slave labourer. My father's dead. I'm afraid to even wonder what might have happened to my mother. You see, the Red Army were advancing and my father and I had to make a run for it. We left her all on her own. Lord knows what's become of her. I don't like to think about it.'

Jan nodded, 'I know. It's the same for all of us. None of us knows what we'll find when we get back.'

'Before the war started, we were systematically persecuted by the Soviets. We never knew what would happen from one day to the next. People just disappeared. Some of my best friends lost their fathers and brothers. They were either shot in the back of the head or shipped off to Siberia. That's what they do.'

Jan shook his head and a frown etched itself over his face. 'It's not just Ukraine that's suffered though, is it? Millions of Poles have been butchered, by the Nazis and the Soviets! We'll probably never know how many.'

And so we talked, on into the night, just about every night. Not just Jan and I, but all the men. Each one had a different story to tell.

There were frequent arguments, and sometimes even punches were thrown.

Sure enough, everyone had to face demons of one sort or another, and I don't, for one minute, think it was any different for our neighbours in many ways, but those of us who had fled from Soviet rule faced a dilemma that was difficult. We'd been there before and it was brutal.

1946 arrived and we were all still at the camp, those first few months whistled past like a falcon chasing a field mouse. The daily routine of work and regular meals meant we were all regaining our health after our struggle to survive. Of course, we all wondered what our future might be, and it wasn't long before whispers weaved their way to us. The camp had ears everywhere. Of course, you didn't know how accurate the information was, but it was all we had. The word was that Stalin had issued a decree. He wanted all Soviet citizens to return, wherever they were. He'd officially asked the Allies to round up all of those who had, for whatever reason, left the Soviet Union. This news created tension around the camp. A group of us Ukrainians sat around, whenever we had the time, and talked about what might happen, 'We can't let them take us. It'll mean certain death for us.' Ivan rubbed the side of his head and lines popped out on his forehead as he spoke in hushed tones, 'I was a guard at Janowska. It was terrible. They killed thousands of Jews there, just shot them as they were walking along, sometimes for no reason. I came close to getting shot myself, so, one day, I made a run for it. I really don't know how I survived, but I'm here now, praise the Lord, but the Soviets aren't any better than the Nazis. I'm afraid to go back.'

One of the older ones, a man called Oleksa, lifted a finger up to his lips, 'We must be careful,' he hissed, 'we have to make sure we don't end up in the hands of those communist sons of bitches. Right now, we must give the Americans as little information as possible. Until we know more. Until we can work out the best thing to do. Understood?'

We all nodded. And he was right. So, we went about our daily business, with our mouths tightly shut, but with our ears close to the wind. We needed to know what was happening.

Before long, the spring was with us once again, and things were changing. Oleksa was getting us all organised. He'd set up a number of facilities for us Ukrainians: a church service on a Sunday morning, cultural afternoons once a week on a Wednesday where we sang traditional songs and organised dancing with the younger boys and girls. Many of the people joined in these activities with much enthusiasm and heart, but there were also those who tried to use them as a diversion. One or two of the young men decided they'd try to make themselves some money by robbing nearby houses, or by hanging around the cookhouse to catch a moment when they could sneak in and steal food to sell. A network of criminal activity and black market dealings quickly established itself, but the Americans didn't stand for any of that. They clamped down hard on these individuals and they were arrested and locked up. The relationship between the governing American army and the people in the camp grew a little more distant.

It wasn't long before summer was upon us. I watched as Oleksa and a couple of the other men ran those young boys and girls through some traditional dance routines in the sunshine. There was one boy, he must have been about seven years of age, who was able to jump higher than the others, he could spin around faster, and leap around like a lion cub. Many afternoons I stood and watched him, and the others. One day, he came up to me and said, 'Can you get me a drink, please? I'm thirsty.' So I fetched him a cup of water.

'What's your name?' he asked before drinking down the water.

'Stefan,' I replied, 'what's yours?'

'Taras. I love to dance, I've always liked it, as long as I can remember. My father taught me. He's dead now.'

When I looked at that young boy, I saw a great future for Ukrainians. He had fire inside him and he wasn't afraid to show it to the world or whoever was watching. Like him, we all needed to stand proud and lose the fear that had eaten into us after years of Soviet persecution, and that period of Nazi terror. To watch Taras and the other boys and girls as they danced and sang raised my spirits and locked my heritage deep into my heart. No one would ever take that away from me again, I was determined to uphold our traditions.

As well as organising all the activities at the camp, somehow, Oleksa managed to compile a small library. Only about 20 or 30 books and pamphlets. They were all a bit battered and stained, which wasn't surprising. After all, they'd been through the same journey as their owners.

I browsed through them one evening and, as if propelled by magnetism, my fingers plucked out a volume of poetry by Ivan Franko, one of my favourite writers. I flicked through it, and there they were! Wonderfully woven words lined up across the page. I closed the book and nodded to Oleksa. I signed the book he used as a loan record and the book was mine for a week.

The work at the barber shop eased off to some extent, because the camp was just about full. We were all given extra time off, a couple of afternoons a week, to engage in cultural activities, and sometimes, on such occasions, I'd take myself off to the edge of the camp. The camp was on a hill overlooking the old town and, once I'd walked through our perimeter, I saw some beautiful buildings dotted around. Some were wrecked by bombing, but many still stood with their majestic turrets and spires puncturing the clouds above them. I sat for an hour or two reading those poems, losing myself in the passion and the power of Franko's words. *Kotlyarevsky* described the power and the force of the eagle and how the Ukrainian language was the same. My mother tongue always sang to me, with a grace and a beauty, but also with a burning flame. Franko's words leapt off the page and flew into my heart like sparks from a fire. They were like medicine; they healed my mind and caressed my soul. By reading his works, I was reminded of the need for humanity, but also for boldness and courage. I felt a hurricane stir inside me. I'd never known freedom, but I'd read about those who'd battled for a free Ukraine, those fearsome Kozaks! They, and only they, filled the pages of our Ukrainian history with glory, but that was long ago. Since then, we'd become downtrodden and mistreated by our neighbours. Ukraine was like a shadow, like a man in fear of his own reflection. To be righteous, as Franko wrote, was the only way we Ukrainians would ever find our way to real freedom. Our time would come, I was sure of that.

I walked back to the camp thinking about those people who, like my good friend Sasha, still battled our enemies. I looked across to the East and I knew that, over there, the insurgents would be hiding in the mountains, stockpiling weapons and ambushing our enemies. My heart and my soul were with them. Not a day would pass without thinking what the future might bring.

One day, after reading that book on that hill, I returned to the camp just as a convoy of trucks roared in through the main gates, and I watched as soldiers unloaded boxes of supplies. I watched them and waited. They usually filled the trucks up with bags of rubbish and then roared off again. This time it was different. The soldiers left the tails down on the trucks and we were all marched out of our barracks and lined up. A Sergeant paced up and down in front of us with a soldier by his side carrying a notebook. The roll was called to make sure all were present, and a few stray persons were rounded up by the soldiers. Once we were all there, the Sergeant cleared his throat, 'Right! We have an order here. The first group of Displaced Persons from this camp have been selected to return to the USSR. Due to limited resources, we have to take you guys home little by little. So, I have a list. When your name is called, step forward and climb into the back of one of the trucks. We'll take you to get official travel documents, and you can then return here to get any possessions that you may have. Your journey home will begin from there.' He beamed at us, flashing his big smile side to side. No one responded. In fact, we all stood there, stony faced. It was obvious no one wanted to hear their name called out. The Sergeant frowned. Maybe he sensed some unease from us. He cleared his throat again and proceeded to call out names. As I listened I breathed inside, and I breathed freely, because the names he called out were all from the first half of the alphabet. Some of those men took a small step forward and betrayed their identity. Others stood right where they were, and were pulled out of the line by soldiers who were able to identify them with the help of a clerk who held all the information on us in a large black file. The men were escorted into the trucks and driven away to the far side of the camp, to the large manor house used by the Americans as their base. The rest of us stood around, gazing over at it.

'It's started,' said Oleksa, 'damn it, the Soviets are coming for us. We have to do something.'

'But what can we do?' asked Jan.

'I don't know, I really don't know. Let's wait and see what happens.'

So that's what we did. The minutes passed so slowly. It was like waiting for milk to turn sour. Oleksa paced about, smoking cigarettes, and cursing the Soviets. Two long hours passed and then the trucks returned. We gathered around and watched as the men climbed out and were escorted into their barracks to get their personal belongings. One or two of the men struggled and tried to break free of the military escort, but were shoved back into line. Oleksa and some other men rushed over to them, 'Hey! Hey!' bellowed Oleksa. 'Let these men go! They'll be shot by Stalin's men! You can't let this happen!'

A Sergeant turned towards Oleksa and snarled, 'Back off! We have our orders! Step back right now!' He lowered his rifle and pointed it at Oleksa and the other men, and the soldiers did the same.

Oleksa and the men backed away, merging into the larger crowd where I was standing. From there, several of the men around me raised their fists and shouted at the Sergeant, desperate for their friends to be freed. One or two stones were thrown, and the soldiers dodged them. The crowd began to surge forward despite the fact the soldiers were all pointing their rifles.

One of those soldiers stepped forward clumsily. He was a youngster, he couldn't have been more than 16. He was shaking and beads of sweat trickled down his cheeks. He was trying to hold his rifle steady, but was trembling all over. We watched as he placed a finger on the trigger of his rifle. I half closed my eyes and tensed all my muscles. The whole crowd stood so still it was as if we were in a photograph, but then, in a blur of motion, the Sergeant stepped forward. 'Step back Private!' he roared, and he shoved the soldier's rifle down so it pointed at the ground. The soldier stiffened at the sudden sound in his ear and reacted by stumbling forward, firing the rifle into the ground. The boom of the rifle and the aftershock caused us all to take few steps backwards, and it was like watching a film as the soldier screamed and blood spurted everywhere. He'd shot himself in the foot. The soldier threw himself to the ground writhing and crying out. The Sergeant barked orders to his men and some of them rushed off to get medical aid. One of the soldiers took off his jacket and wrapped it around the foot to stem the flow of blood. Another cradled the injured soldier and spoke to him to reassure him, to let him know that help was on its way. Before too long, a team of medical personnel came running across from the farmhouse and gave first aid to the wounded soldier, whose screams had subsided into whimpers.

In the middle of all this chaos, I noticed a group of men, six of them, break away from the escort. They ran off, unnoticed, and plunged into the cover offered by a group of trees at the side of the camp. Those of us who were onlookers saw all this and tried to remain impassive, to betray nothing with our faces. We all stood still, like bags of sand.

The Sergeant charged up and down issuing orders to his men, and order was restored in the space of minutes, but those minutes were enough for six to flee. I wondered what would become of them. Within a day or two, news filtered through. The Americans had quickly realised that some of their escort were missing and launched a manhunt. They found four of the escapees the next day, but two were never found despite strenuous efforts by the Americans. Day after day for a week, maybe two, search parties were seen to leave the camp early morning, returning empty handed as the sun set.

Oleksa got to work, as did all of us. We infiltrated every part of that camp. We had to know what was going on. The fear inside us was strong, it was something that crawled into every cell. We knew that Stalin would either kill us, or send us off to Siberia, to work in the salt mines. That knowledge was enough to keep us all sharp with our eyes and our ears. We saw everything, nothing passed us by. Anytime we saw soldiers or officers talking, we'd find a reason to get closer. Whether it was to take a bag of rubbish to the bins, or to collect something from stores. We were everywhere. Collecting scraps of information, little snatches of sentences, anything. And we remembered them; we held onto them like they were gold.

At least two of us had escaped and I hoped they'd got themselves onto the right road; away from the Soviets. At least they had the summer weather in which to travel. Often, I wondered what became of those two.

That summer was very hot and I spent as much time as I could outdoors. I'd read poetry, or join in some of the sporting activities. At least once a week we'd have a game of football, and on one occasion I remember a couple of fellows charging right across the pitch with half a dozen American soldiers in pursuit. No doubt, some misdemeanour had been committed and an arrest was about to take place. The Americans ran the base well, but were beginning to come down hard on the criminal fraternity. Keeping control of several thousand people who had been through Hell was no easy task.

Summer faded, autumn rustled past and then the winter was with us once again, as we waited to see what would become of us. To keep our spirits up, Oleksa organised a full programme of Christmas activities, including a show. The boys and girls were to perform their dances, a couple of the guys were lined up to tell jokes and there was much more entertainment planned.

One day, around that time, I was sitting outside my barrack with my nose in a book when a shadow loomed over me, it was Oleksa. 'Stefan, you love your poetry don't you?'

'Yes, I've always loved to read the work of our great Ukrainian poets. Doesn't everyone?'

'Yes, but not as much as you. How do you feel about reading a poem for us at our Christmas show? It'll be really good for everyone's morale.'

'I-I don't know. I've never read to an audience before.'

152

Oleksa fixed me with a look, 'You know you have to do this, don't you?'

Then he walked away. I knew I had no choice. To deliver an oration to inspire my fellow countrymen was something I could not turn away from. The show was scheduled to take place on 4th January, 1947, I had two weeks in which to prepare. Oleksa lent me half a dozen books from his library and, whenever I had a spare moment, I flicked through them. Eventually, I decided to read a section of Taras Shevchenko's epic poem *Haidamaki*. I chose the first section of the epilogue; it wasn't so long but it was a powerful part of the poem, with lines that needed to be delivered with passion. For the next ten days, in the early moonlit nights, I crept down to that spot down by the river and practised, pacing up and down.

The evening of the show arrived and I stood at the side of the stage in the big hall and ruffled Taras's hair as he went onstage to perform his dance with the other boys and girls. He leapt around with his usual enthusiasm and vitality and, when they finished, I clapped along with the rest of the crowd. There were some loud cheers and whistles for those dancers.

'Good luck,' said Taras as he came off the stage, because he knew I was onstage next. Oleksa introduced me with a few words and I stepped onto that stage. The poem I was about to read out was on sheets of paper I held in my hands, but to be honest, I didn't really need them, each of those words were seared into my brain:

Much time has gone by, since a child a poor orphan,
In sacking and coatless, without any bread,
I roamed that Ukraine where Zaliznyak and Gonta
With sanctified sabres had wreaked vengeance dread.
Much time has gone by since, along those same highways
Where rode Haidamaki, exhausted and sore
I tramped through the country, its high roads and byways,
And weeping, sought people to teach me good lore.
As now I recall them, my youthful misfortunes,
I grieve that they're past! I would trade present fortune
If only those days could be brought back again.
Those evils, the steppes that seem stretching forever,
My father and grandfather old I remember
My father is gone, but my grand-dad remains.
On Sundays, on closing the book about martyrs
And drinking a glass with the neighbours, my father

Would beg of my grand-dad to tell us the story
Of the Haidamaki revolt long ago,
How Gonta, Zaliznyak once punishment gory
Inflicted on Poles.
And the ancient eyes glowed
Like stars in the night as the old man related
How gentry folk perished and how Simla burned
The neighbours from horror and pity near fainted.
And I, a wee fellow, the churchwarden mourned,
Yet, nobody noticed, all gripped by the horror,
The child that was weeping alone in the corner.
I thank you, my grand-dad, 'twas you that preserved
The story I've told of the old Kozak glory:
And by the grandchildren it now will be heard.

The crowd of about 200 people clapped and a few cheered as I finished my oration. There were men and women in that audience who needed a shred of hope to cling onto, and maybe that's what they got from me. That evening gave us more than just a Christmas show, it gave us a little piece of Ukraine right there in Germany.

It was in those early weeks of January 1947 that one or two convoys left the camp, carrying their human cargo of people returning home, but none of them were Ukrainians. The difference was that the Poles and the Czechs may have found tragedies on returning home, but they didn't have to face a murderous dog like Stalin.

However, it wasn't long before the Americans began, once again, to prepare some of us Ukrainians for our journey home. The group of men to be chosen on this occasion looked so downcast. They dragged their feet and their heads hung low. They were loaded into the back of one of the trucks and off they went. Some of them struggled and became violent, screaming and begging not to be sent back. The Americans used force to get them into the trucks and they roared away. Oleksa stubbed a cigarette out beneath his boot, 'Okay, after work we all meet up, okay? I've got a plan. We've got to stop this.'

We all nodded and then went off to our respective workplaces. By this time I was well into my second year at the camp. Time had passed quickly. At lunchtime, I grabbed a sandwich and stepped outside to get some fresh air, even though the winter chill nipped away at me. I sat down on some upturned crates with a group of other men and we huddled together to talk and eat our lunch. All around the camp you could see others doing the same, a murmur of voices floated over us from all directions. Our calm was broken by the roar of a truck arriving at the main gate. We watched as they checked in at the guardhouse. Something about the driver and his mate seemed different. There was a lot of arm-waving and their faces were set hard, like they'd seen something that had unnerved them. The arm-waving was no different to normal, the Americans did a lot of that, but it was their faces that made some of us stand up. Something wasn't right. Some of us younger boys raced after the truck. All the way to the farmhouse, which was just a small dot in the distance. We'd recovered from our war experience and were getting stronger by the day. Some of us ran over there without stopping. By the time we'd got across there, the soldiers had lowered the tail of the truck. We stood getting our breath back, the steam billowing in the cold wash of winter.

A pair of familiar looking men stepped out, two of the men who had left the camp earlier, destined for home. Why were they back? They jumped down and straightened their clothes. One of them turned and looked inside the truck, and then he turned around and covered his face with his hands. The other one pulled a pack of cigarettes from his pocket with trembling hands, but at that point, one of the soldiers bellowed at him, 'Hey! Put those goddam smokes away! We haven't got time for that. Now both of you, jump back up there and get to work. Move!'

The man put the packet away, and he and his partner climbed back into the truck. There was a great deal of grunting as a wooden box was pushed out and the two soldiers took the load while the two men clambered out of the truck. The four of them carried the box into the farmhouse. We watched them, and it was clear to all of us that the box was exactly the right size and shape to contain a human body. We didn't even have to say it to each other, it was as if the information flowed through all our heads at the same time.

The soldiers scowled at us as they carried the box, and they scowled again as they returned and, with their two helpers, hauled a second box of similar dimensions out of the truck. One of them waved his arms at us and tried to shoo us away, but we stood firm. We knew it was our own people inside those boxes. Don't ask me how, we just knew, and we needed to know what had happened to them.

Later that evening, Oleksa's meeting took place as he'd

suggested earlier that day. Several of us gathered in the usual place, on a pile of crates and tea chests in a secluded corner near our barracks. This was where we regularly met to discuss plans for our futures. Ten o'clock was the usual time and we were all there, the usual gang, Jan, Ivan, several other young men and I, but there was one person missing. Oleksa. We sat and waited, we lit cigarettes and chatted. It was unlike him to be late. Eventually, he arrived, his shadow looming large in the moonlight, but he was not alone, another shadow walked beside him.

'Apologies for my late arrival, I've brought a guest.' Oleksa and the other fellow sat down, and we all peered through the dimness until we could make out this man's features. It was one of the men who had returned on the truck that afternoon with the two boxes! He sat fidgeting and swaying, like he had an itch inside him.

This was typical of Oleksa. The Americans would have taken steps to keep the two men apart from the rest of the camp, at least for a while, but through his contacts, Oleksa had managed to get to one of them and bring him to us. 'This is Yanik. He's come to talk to us. We need to welcome him. Has anyone got a smoke for him, and a drink, maybe?'

We all rustled through our pockets and several of us thrust cigarette packets at him. There was a glug glug from somewhere within that dark circle and a tin mug with *horilka* or something resembling the same was handed to him. He took a long pull on his cigarette and a swig from the mug, and then he didn't look so nervous.

'So, can you tell us all what happened today?' said Oleksa.

'I-I'll try,' replied Yanik. He took another long pull on his cigarette and exhaled, 'it was terrible. Really terrible. You see, none of us really wanted to be on that truck. It was like sitting in a tomb on wheels. We sat and smoked all the while. No-one really had much to say. Well, what could we say? It was like we all knew we were on our way to either a bullet in the head, or years and years of hard labour in Siberia. But there was nothing we could do. There were soldiers with guns in those trucks with us. We were trapped. Anyway, we stopped after about two hours for a toilet break and a stretch. I think it was one of the American soldiers who wanted to stop.' He paused to take another swig from the tin mug and to ask for another cigarette. He lit up and continued. 'We were all standing around in a wooded area, and there were two youths with us who had been very quiet in the truck. They were both pacing up and down and trembling. They looked scared. There was terror in their eyes. So much that one of the Americans kept a close eye on them, I guess for fear they might make a run for it.'

Yanik paused again, 'Then, we heard a roar in the distance. It was a truck heading towards us. It got closer, and we could see it was one of the American trucks coming down the road towards us, probably with supplies on board. All the soldiers turned and waved at the driver, and he waved back and grinned. Then it happened.' He stubbed out his cigarette and ran his hands over his head. 'We all watched as the driver stopped smiling and his expression switched to one of shock. There was a squeal of brakes as he tried to stop, but it was too late. You see, the two boys just threw themselves in front of the truck, and he smashed into them, and ran over them. They got flattened.' Yanik sat there shaking his head, with pain showing on his face.

'Some of the guys turned away and threw up. I just stood there. Miroslav was right next to me, and we watched as the truck reversed. The two boys were squashed into the mud, with their bones poking through their skin. It was horrible. The soldiers got me and Miroslav to help with digging the bodies out, and they radioed for another truck to come and pick us up. The soldiers ordered me and Miroslav to go with them and help them. That's why we're back. At least we don't have to go home now, not just yet anyhow, but I didn't want to come back here like this, not as a coffin bearer for two young boys.'

As I listened to Yanik, and as his story unfolded, I found myself clenching my fists and breathing hard. Not only did Stalin butcher our people at will, he created such a fear inside people that they were driven to do thing like this. If I could have got hold of him there and then, I'd have throttled him with my bare hands, but I knew I would have been in a long queue of people who wanted to do the same.

We all mourned the passing of those two boys, they were both only 17 years old. From that time on, the Americans started to see things differently. They interviewed all of us. It was quite a lengthy process, but by this time we all knew what to say to them. Oleksa's infiltration of the whole camp had been so slick and so polished, that we found out just about everything that was going on. We all said we were from the Western part of Ukraine, because we had inside information suggesting that was the best thing to say. I told them I was from Stanislaviv. They noted it on their records. So many of us went through that process, and we hoped and prayed we wouldn't have to return to face Stalin's jurisdiction, to be delivered to the people that carried out his murderous directives.

It took the Americans just over a year to plan everything, right through to the summer of 1948, but then my prayers were answered when they took me in for a final briefing.

'Well, Stefan, your documents are ready.' said a man in plain clothes whose name I cannot recall. 'Now, you have a choice. As a refugee of the War and also because you originate from Stanislaviv, you can take up residence in a number of different countries, as you know. You've seen the list?' I nodded. 'Good, then what is your chosen destination?'

I hesitated. I'd been given a list to choose from a few days before, and I reckoned I'd made my mind up, but was it the right one? There was Belgium, the United Kingdom, Canada, Australia, Israel, France, Venezuela, Brazil, Argentina and the United States. I'd done a lot of thinking. I didn't want to go as far as Australia or Canada, and although I liked the Americans, the United States was also too far. I still held onto a faint hope that one day I would be able to return home, to my beloved Ukraine. I didn't want to be too far away. The South American countries were also too far. I reasoned to myself that, because I'd been in the camp nearly four years and picked up a bit of English, maybe the United Kingdom would be the best place to go. Many others in the camp were making the same choice.

'Well?' said the man, tapping his pen on his clipboard.

'United Kingdom.' I replied, and that was that. He made a note on a sheet of paper,

'Fine. Okay, you'll need to inform Victor at the barber's shop, and make sure you're ready to go. We'll provide you with a few essentials, like some extra clothes and a bag, and you'll leave in two days, okay?'

'Okay.'

I went straight from there to the barber shop and told Victor. He gave me a big bear hug and said he'd miss me. He said it would be like losing a son. He gave me a small holdall with a set of clippers, scissors and such-like, for cutting hair,

'Stefan, you've been a good worker. Take these, and if you get short of money, you can cut hair and earn for yourself. Take care and best of luck.' As I walked away, he still had that huge grin spread over his face. I'd miss Victor, but the time had come to leave. It didn't take long to pack, so I just had to say goodbye to my friends.

'The rest of us will be leaving soon, Stefan.' Oleksa had an arm around my shoulders. 'I know this place has been good to you, but it's just a temporary camp. In the end, we'll all be transported away from here, but there is one thing that will always unite us. Our Ukrainian blood. One day, Ukraine will be free. We may not live to see that day, but we must fight to keep our traditions alive.'

As always, Oleksa was right. The battle wasn't over. It would never be over. On the morning of my departure, almost three years after arriving, I climbed into a truck and left. To another foreign land, and to a new life.

Chapter 12

Ukrainian proverb: Our boots will find their way

I'd walked about a thousand miles to stay out of the Soviets' reach, most of it with the violent sounds of the War ringing in my ears. There were no more booms of distant bombs exploding anymore; or whistles of rockets flying past. There was just the steady drone of trucks, driving up and down the roads, moving people from place to place, trying to establish some order from the chaos.

Some of the men, in the back of the truck I was in, chattered with excitement,

'England. I reckon it'll be a good place,' said a young man called Marko, 'it's one of the richest countries in the world. I reckon we'll all make a pile of money there, if we work hard.'

'I don't know about that, my friend,' replied an older man, Yarema. 'They'll want to look after their own first. We'll be getting the worst jobs, the dirtiest work. Just you wait and see. And they won't be paying us in gold bars, so you can forget about getting yourself dressed up in any fancy clothes or fine silks.'

Others in the back of the truck sat quietly, it was to be a long journey. The excitable ones, such as Marko, settled down after we'd been on the road for a couple of hours. Yarema reckoned it was about a thousand miles or so to the United Kingdom. I smiled when he said that. At least this time, I'd be transported in relative comfort, whether by road, rail or boat, with a roof over my head and enough to eat.

Even so, I was hurtling further and further away from my home, towards the unknown, into a new world, where the language would be different. I had to thank Father for at least teaching me some basic English. When I was just a boy he'd say to me, in English, 'Come on, John.'

That phrase meant an English lesson was coming my way. He taught me how to count from one to ten, how to say yes and no, please and thank you. That was about all. But, when you're in a camp like we'd been, you became a good observer and a good listener. I'd also picked up a quite a few phrases from the Americans.

Wherever I was and whatever language was spoken, my heart

and soul would always be Ukrainian. Inside, I was torn apart, because a large part of me wanted to go home. I missed Mother, but I didn't know what might have happened to her. Father and I had left her at the mercy of the marauding Soviets. It turned me cold just thinking what those barbarians might have done with her. A veil of great shame hung over me to think that we'd left her behind, even though she'd refused to come with us. I tried to convince myself she was a clever one, one that would be able to either hide herself, or tackle the marauders face-to-face and, somehow, send them away, but deep inside I was in turmoil. At times I feared the worst and had to shut out images in my head of Soviet soldiers barging into our home and making Mother scream and struggle. The thought of it made me sick. It turned me into a statue. I couldn't move or breathe and just sat in the back of that truck, with the pain of those thoughts entering every inch of my body, rendering me lifeless. If someone was to dig a grave right then, I'd have jumped into it and gladly let the soil cover me, until I was so far below ground I could escape the thoughts that threatened me.

'Everybody out!' A sergeant hollered at us, as the tail of the truck was lowered. Our journey had reached its first stop. We clambered out with our meagre belongings, which we grasped in small bundles or in fraying bags. We'd arrived at a train station.

We looked up in wonder at the twisted turrets and the gilded glass, and climbed aboard a train to continue our journey. It was like a fairy tale, the whole thousand miles was like a dream. We jumped onto another train further down the line, until we arrived at the French coast. A night boat took us across the Channel to the shores of England. We walked off that boat at around six in the morning. A warm summer breeze curled itself around us as we tramped down the gangway. A blazing sun threw streaks of gold at us, and above us flocks of huge white birds screeched away,

'Hey!' Marko tried to reach up towards one of them and seize back the hunk of bread that had been expertly plucked from his fingers. I found out, not long afterwards, that these birds were seagulls, and masters of scavenging from unsuspecting visitors. Their piercing squawks were our welcome to the United Kingdom.

We were registered in a wooden cabin. There were two tables with clerks to check us through. We queued up, our papers were scrutinised, and they waved us through. I looked down at the document as it was placed back in my hand, I saw the date. It was the 1st August 1948. I was just a few weeks away from my 21st birthday.

Each of us was given a shilling as our papers were handed back to us. Marko held up his coin and looked at it, turning it to see both sides. Yarema laughed, 'Marko, so this is your first step to that fortune you were talking about, eh?'

'It doesn't look like it's worth much, how long do you think it'll last us?' replied Marko.

'I really don't know,' smiled Yarema, 'but don't spend it too quickly, will you?'

We all held up the coins to get a closer look. There was the King's head on one side, and a lion above a crown on the other, images of a royal kingdom. It felt like we'd arrived in a whole different world to the one we'd come from. The way we'd been treated by the Allies made me think that life in the west would be considerably more civilised than under the communists.

Another group of escort trucks was waiting on the other side of the wooden cabin, and we were marched across to them. It was to be yet another two or three hours on the road, and I, like most of the others, was wearying of life in the back of a truck. I wanted to be somewhere, get settled, and start living some kind of life. Just sitting around thinking wasn't good for me.

Eventually, we arrived at a small town called Market Drayton. There was a camp there, which looked just like any other army base. As we climbed out of the truck, there was a warm and sticky breeze, as if the air was tinged with the stale sweat of a punch drunk boxer knocked out in the last round of a prize-fight. Our escort took us across to a group of barracks, and we saw a group of them hanging around. Nazi prisoners. They must have been the last few left, waiting to go back. They walked past us, dragging their feet and looking down at their boots. I turned towards them as they passed, and felt myself tensing up. I drew a fist back.

'Stefan,' a heavy arm wrapped itself around me and pulled me away, 'you don't need to do this. It's over. Let the war tribunals deal with these men. You'll only end up getting yourself in trouble.'

Yarema was right. I was so angry though. The fires of my rage were burning inside. The war had, first of all, taken me away from everything and then snatched away whatever was left. Inside me, my Kozak blood was boiling. I swear I could have killed those Germans there and then, crushed them underneath my boot, just like their nation had crushed our nation. The German soldiers passed us by, and I pushed Yarema away and scowled at him. He was right, I knew he was, but would never have admitted it to him. He continued, 'We have to find another way, war isn't the answer. Surely we know that now?'

There was nothing I could say to that, I just turned and walked off. Those words stuck inside my head though. His observation had a truth about it. If there was one thing I'd learned through the last few years, it was the ugliness of war.

The base at Market Drayton was our home for a brief period until we were assigned our final destination. As with many of the countries in Europe, Britain had a shortage of manpower, a shortage of food and lots of rebuilding to do. Clearly, as refugees we would play our part in that. The youngsters, such as Marko, were keen to get going. 'I wonder where we'll end up,' he speculated as he paced up and down in our wooden barrack, which was our accommodation during our stay there. The rest of us sat around smoking and drinking watery tea from tin mugs. He sent us dizzy with his pacing, 'London, that's where I'd like to go. That's where the big money'll be. It's the capital, after all.' He was so full of hope, his eyes were wide open all the time, like a bright-eyed puppy's.

'Relax, kid.' Yarema was frowning, and that was unusual, he rarely got flustered. 'You're giving me a headache. I've already told you, we'll all have to work hard to make any real money here. From what I've heard, Britain took a beating from the Nazis. Some of their towns and cities are wrecked. There will not be a lot of money around for you to get your hands on.'

Marko carried on pacing, almost as if he hadn't heard Yarema. All of us breathed easier as he stepped outside for some air.

Finally, a couple of days later, we got the news we'd been waiting for. A line of us formed once again in front of a table in the mess hall. An official informed me that I was to go to work on farms in a nearby county called Worcestershire. My shoulders dropped. Marko's enthusiasm had infected me. I guess I'd have liked to be in the excitement of a city, with all its busy noise and big buildings. Of course, I accepted my fate, as a good Ukrainian always does, and braced myself to make the best of it. After all, I had plenty of experience in farm work.

The next day I took my place in the back of yet another truck, it was to be my final journey in the back of those army trucks. My destination was to be a place called Clifton on Teme. There were a dozen of us all headed there, and it was in the back of that truck I made friends with a couple of fellows who would become part of my life for many years. I didn't know it at the time, but Mikola, Fedor and I would become good friends.

Six of us were dropped at a hostel in Clifton on Teme, Mikola, Fedor, myself and three Poles, Pawel, Otto and Karel. It was basic accommodation, the six of us shared a room. There was a small kitchen and bathroom and breakfast was provided for us at seven o'clock, before we went to work.

There were a number of farms in the area, and transport came daily to take us to them. The first one we went to was the Robinson farm. Mr Robinson lived there with his wife. They were both around the same age as my own mother and father. There was a sadness about them, and many times I wondered what their story was, but we were only ever allowed into the kitchen for our lunchtime meal, never into the other rooms in the farmhouse, so I never ever saw very much, certainly nothing that would give any clues to their life, past or present.

Mr Robinson was friendly to us, but firm from the start. He had cows, sheep and pigs, as well as several acres of crops. The six of us worked from dawn to dusk every day. To keep us going, Mrs Robinson kept us well fed, her generous lunches were the best I'd had for some time. Sometimes we'd be sent off to other farms for a week or two, but most of the time we were at the Robinsons.

Our wages weren't much, as Yarema predicted. Each week we were paid a small amount, I can't recall how much it was, but I guess it reflected the fact that we got free board at the hostel, and some free meals at the farms. It was right at the peak of a beautiful English summer when we first arrived, with golden fields all around us, dotted with lush, green pastureland. One of our first jobs was to bring in the harvest. It was back-breaking work. There was an occasion, on the second day of our stay there, in the blistering heat of the afternoon, when our spirits rose as we saw Mrs Robinson approaching with a tray of drinks. Each of us picked up a glass full of a pale, yellow liquid. We all took several big gulps, and then stood gasping, with our eyes beginning to water. It was so sour! Very different to the sweet fruit compote we had back home. We forced it down though, so as not to offend Mrs Robinson. Over time, we found out this was lemonade, English style, and I grew to like it.

Now and again, the three of us, Mikola, Fedor and I, would walk on down to the village. Sometimes our three Polish friends would join us, but that made us more conspicuous, walking around in a big gang. The village people would stare at us. Some would cross the road if they saw us approaching, so we quickly realised it was better to get around in smaller groups. There wasn't a great deal in the village: a Post Office, a Village Store and a Garage. We bought cigarettes at the Store. Of course, at first, we didn't have much of a clue about the money so just held out a handful of coins. The Storekeeper squinted at us suspiciously and then picked out a few. Lord knows whether he took the right amount or just helped himself to however much he wanted. Towards the far end of the village were a church and a small schoolhouse. There the village ended. After we'd been there a few times the villagers soon worked out who we were and some even greeted us as we passed them by.

There was an inn in the village called the Lion. We got into the habit of going there at the end of the week, usually on a Saturday night. The first time we went there, we walked through the door and were met with a silence and all eyes upon us. We walked up to the bar. It was busy. The three of us waited until our turn came and then the barman looked at Mikola, 'Yes?'

'Beer?' replied Mikola

The barman then listed all the different beers available there, far too many for us to make any sense of. Mikola was a clever one though, he tapped his hand on one of the pumps, just as he'd seen one of the locals do, and we ended up with three pints of a dark ale with a foamy head.

Ignoring the whispers and sly glances from around us, we found a quiet corner and sat down. We were beginning to understand more and more of the language, but at times it paid to pretend you didn't understand, particularly when you heard whispered phrases such as *bloody foreigners* slipping through the smoky haze.

The beer was very bitter and heavy. It settled in my stomach and swirled around in there like sour treacle. We got used to it though, just like the lemonade. The Lion was the place where I celebrated my 21st birthday, in the company of Mikola and Fedor. We drank a few glasses of the beer, and as ever the talk came around to going home. 'You know that old Ukrainian proverb don't you, eh, Stefan?' Mikola fixed his eyes on me, '*A dream is sweeter than honey.* Never stop believing, Stefan. *Nazdorovya!**'

Three glasses crashed together and we drank to health and long life. There wasn't much more we could say about our longing to go back. All we could do was live day by day, and cling on to those dreams.

Our first year working on the farms passed by like butter melting in a hot pan, but there were times when I wished I wasn't there. Our first winter in England was such a cold one. I remember, on one occasion, Mikola and I were on the Robinsons' farm and he'd asked us to go and gather in some manglewurzels for cattle feed. It was so cold that day as we trudged up that field. On reaching the top Mikola turned to me,

'Stefan, how about we build ourselves a fire to keep warm?'

I nodded, and we gathered together a heap of firewood and twigs. Several attempts later and after a lot of thick smoke had poured into the sky, we managed to tease a few flames out. They grew into a good blaze, and we stood there getting warm. The manglewurzels could wait.

Without warning, he was there next to us. It was Mr Robinson. Luckily, we'd just extinguished our cigarettes and were warming our hands in front of that fire.

'What are you doing?' He fixed us with a firm stare.

'Mr Robinson,' replied Mikola, 'we're just drying our aprons and our gloves.'

'But you are going to pick the manglewurzels aren't you?'

'Of course, of course. Yes, as soon as we dry off we'll pick them.'

Mr Robinson nodded, seemingly happy at this reply, and he walked off towards the farmhouse, but we didn't rush to start work, it was such a cold day. Eventually, we picked a few, but I guess it was something that went against our whole way of thinking. We'd always had our smallholdings back home, so working for someone else and getting paid a few pennies was too similar to the way we'd been treated by the Soviets.

The summer arrived again, and we were faced with another mountain of work. The six of us were doing enough for twelve. During those gruelling summer months we'd work until it was getting dark, get fed and then the transport would pick us up and take us back to our hostel, where we got ourselves cleaned up and collapsed into our beds.

I got to know Mikola and Fedor well over the course of that year. Mikola was a tall fellow, and well built, like a bull. A fold of tight curls sat on his head, swept back and held in place by a handful of hair wax. Mikola didn't like to rush around, he took things steady, but he was so strong. He'd walk along with bale after bale of hay on his shoulder without breaking sweat. Fedor couldn't have been more different, he was small, wiry and restless. Always ready with a smile, he had an open face, with dark good looks and blue eyes that made the girls melt. In fact, I think he never really ever thought about much else other than girls. 'What about those German girls, eh, Stefan? Weren't they hot? They were so pretty, I wished I could've stayed there you know? I really do.'

The endless slog of the farm work threw us together, I felt as if I'd known Mikola and Fedor all my life, it was like having two brothers.

It was a relief when the weekends came, we only worked on a Saturday morning and the rest of the time was our own. Sometimes, one of us would be sent down to the village to run errands for Mr Robinson. On one of those Saturday mornings, I'd taken a slow walk down from the farm, and I found myself standing outside the garage. A mechanic was crouched down next to a motorbike, applying a shine to the tailpipe and the mudguards. It was a beautiful machine. He straightened up and saw me looking. 'You like my motorbike? I've had it two years now. It's a Royal Enfield Bullet. A great bike, but I'm selling it 'cause they've just made a new, more powerful model. You want to buy it?'

Oh, I wanted it all right. He told me how much he was asking, and I can't recall the price I paid, but I know it amounted to nearly all the money I'd saved up over the last year. I agreed the price with him and to collect it the following Saturday. He directed me to the Post Office so I could get myself a licence. I had just enough money on me to pay for it, under the watchful eye of the Post Office counter clerk, so I completed the form, with his firm hand of assistance, paid my money and put it in my wallet, all ready for the following week.

That was a long seven days. The first chance I got on the following Saturday I slipped away from the farm and hurried down to the garage. I was greeted with a smile as I held out a bundle of notes. He filled up the tank with petrol, and then he showed me how to use the controls. After a few wobbles around the village square, I roared away leaving a cloud of smoke behind me. I rode back to the farm. The first half a mile I took it steady, but then I did what all young men do when they get on a motorbike; I revved the engine hard and felt the wind on my face and in my hair. I flew like an arrow through those country lanes. As I turned into the entrance of the main farmyard, everyone looked across. Mikola and Fedor stood up from their usual spot on the steps up to the hayloft where they liked to sit and smoke. They gazed in astonishment as I rode up to them and then stopped. 'Stefan, that is one hell of a machine you've got there. It's a beast.' Mikola grinned at me and took a pull on his cigarette. Pawel, Otto and Karel came rushing out from behind one of the barns and took it in turns to jump on the back and have a ride around the farm. Everyone whooped and cheered, and I revved the motorbike hard. Somehow, the Kozak fire inside us blazed, and we didn't care. It was a show of strength in a way, however small, just to show the world we existed. It was the most fun we'd all had for a while, there were six smiles spread wide across six faces. Until Mr Robinson came hurtling out of the main farmhouse, his face all red. It looked like he was about to explode.

'Hey! What do you think you're playing at? You can't ride around here like that! You'll scare the animals! I won't have this. This motorbike is not to be used here on the farm, is that understood?' Without waiting for any of us to answer him, he stormed back into the farmhouse. I turned the engine off, and there was a moment when nothing was said. I wheeled the motorbike into the barn and then went to the farmhouse. 'Mr Robinson, I'm sorry about the bike, I don't want any trouble.'

Mr Robinson stared at me for a second or two. He had a look about him that I wasn't sure of. 'Listen,' he said, 'you've come here, we've given you work and you've got somewhere to live and enough to eat, and we pay you a wage! You should respect that. But this business with the motorbike, it's not acceptable.'

'I bought it with my own money.' I replied.

Mr Robinson tapped his fingers on the kitchen table. 'I'm afraid I'll have to restrict your use of it to weekends only. Under no circumstances can you use it on farm land.'

It felt just like being back in the Soviet Union. All we'd done was fool around with a motorbike. I thought about what he said, and I knew that, if it were his own sons, he would have allowed it, but because of who we were, he'd taken a hard line.

Mikola, Fedor and I resolved to get away from the farm work as soon as we could. So, the following Saturday I took Fedor with me and we rode off to the nearest city, Worcester.

It was a grand place. There was a sense of majesty as we rode around. Some of the buildings were quite magnificent. We passed by some old school buildings that looked a hundred years old, with carvings of hideous faces in their brickwork – I wondered what those carvings could be. At times, we passed by the River Severn, and saw swans floating along, with streams of gold flickering on the top of the water. A fresh breeze swept over us.

We'd set off early, with good reason. The farm work would have to wait, we wanted to see where the real work was, if any. The plan was to sneak back before anyone noticed we'd gone. The streets were lit up by lamps mounted on tall pillars, we rode around with the Bullet's headlamp throwing a beam in front of us. It was a pre-dawn world we were riding through, and we saw many people. They walked with a silent grace, their steps full of purpose, with bags slung over their shoulders. Some rode on bicycles. I slowed right down, and we reached a junction into which streams of men were pouring. I turned into it and rode to the end. The road stopped right there, we could go no further. I turned the engine off. Fedor and I got off the motorbike and stood and watched as people walked into a large building in front of us. It was a big concrete box-like building, an ugly construction. There was a large chimney sticking up into the sky, and after all the people had gone into the building and a hooter had sounded, smoke began to billow out of that chimney.

'What do you think?' I turned to Fedor.

'Looks like some sort of factory. There weren't many girls going in there though, were there?'

'Fedor, I'm sure there are enough girls in there to keep you happy. Do you think we should try and get some work here?'

'Well, the farm work's okay, but we don't earn much there, and just lately Mr Robinson's been giving us a hard time.'

Before I could reply, we were interrupted by a man running towards us, 'Hey! You two! We need men like you. Here.' He thrust papers into our hands. 'We've got lots of orders, and we're getting a lot of business right now, so if you two fellows are interested, we can pay you good money.'

Of course, we were interested, so that's what we did. It took some sorting out, to get our papers stamped again, and to get authorisation. We had to seek out accommodation and move our belongings, but a couple of weeks later, the three of us, Mikola, Fedor and I, were all walking together towards that factory. It was called Metal Box.

Each of us found lodgings in the city, and at least we had our own room rather than sharing with others in a hostel, listening to each other snoring at night.

On our first day we walked onto the factory floor to be greeted by the noise of machines so loud we couldn't speak to each other. We were taken through to an area at the back which was quieter and our foreman, Roger, spoke to us, 'Right then, you three'll start off on the factory floor, where I can see you. We'll have you working on all the different parts of the production line to see where you fit in best, and so you know all about the run from start to finish. Then, once we've seen you through your first few weeks, we'll assign you to a Department suitable for you, and for the Company. And get this: I won't stand for any idling. You'll earn good money here, but you'll have to work for it. If I catch any of you lot fucking off outside for a crafty fag, you'll be out of here with my boot up your backside. Got that?'

The three of us nodded in unison. We got the message all too clear.

The first week flew by, and I have to say I enjoyed myself. It made a change from standing in a field with the rain soaking you to the skin. The machines fascinated me. Since I'd bought my motorbike, I'd enjoyed tinkering with it. One of our Polish friends on the farm, Otto, was a mechanic, and he'd shown me how to tune it up, change the oil and keep it in good condition. By contrast to the gentle roar of the motorbike engine, the machines in the factory were monsters. They scared me. They pounded away, making such a racket; I thought they might chew me up. A fellow worker, one of the older ones, Arthur, helped me out. He showed me what to do, I was like an apprentice to him. I followed Arthur around that factory floor and, as I did, it seemed like Roger's eyes were on me. Every time I turned around, he was there. It was very different to working on the farm, there were few opportunities to sneak off for a smoke or a daydream in a sunny glade or on a haystack, but the rewards were so much greater! At the end of our first week I opened my brown paper wage packet and found I'd earned three times the amount I was paid on the farm. Arthur smiled as he watched me open that envelope, 'Not a bad week's work eh? I think you'll do all right for yourself here you know, Steve.'

That's what they all called me at the factory. Steve. I liked the sound of it, and it gave me a new beginning, like I was someone brand new, without the load that I carried inside my heart.

The three of us prospered, it felt like we were moving up in the world a little. Now and again, we encountered some hostility from a few of the locals, some name calling and more whispered *bloody foreigners* comments floating into our ears. All we could do was hold ourselves up and look people in the eye. There was nothing for us to be ashamed of. We were working hard, and behaving ourselves, well perhaps apart from Fedor's roving eye. Whenever a pretty girl came anywhere near us, he'd be smiling away and trying to charm her with a bit of chat. Once or twice, in the local tavern, he'd get a stare from a fellow to let him know that the girl he was flirting with was taken.

Factory life was generally good. They worked us hard, but paid us well, so there was no cause for us to complain. Most of the locals were friendly enough, and I developed a good bond with Arthur, who was supervising me.

There were others at the factory from areas of Europe who had also been devastated by the war. The factory provided work for many of them as well as us Ukrainians. I worked alongside many Poles. My approach was to try and get on with all my workmates, whoever they were, but history between Poland and Ukraine is of two countries constantly at war with each other. Poland conquered a good portion of western Ukraine at various times through history, much blood had been shed, both that of Poles and Ukrainians.

The Poles always seemed to hold the view they were superior to us somehow. That always made us smile. Our cultural heritage was as rich as theirs, and the Ukrainian identity is strong, always has been, otherwise we'd have been swallowed up long ago by those of our neighbours who liked to wage war.

One day, a Pole, his name I can't recall, came up to me at the factory when none of the supervisors were around. He was a young fellow, 'Hey, you're a Ukrainian aren't you?'

I looked at him without flinching, our eyes locked onto each other, and I could see his brow was twisted and his lip rolled up. 'I am,' I replied.

'Well, I want you to explain something to me. When our glorious Polish infantry invaded Ukraine in 1918, why did your people conceal harrows on the ground to disable our horses and cripple them? That was barbaric! Everyone knows that horses are beautiful creatures and hard working. In all wars, it's always been an accepted fact that horses should be protected at all times. What your people did was shameful! Why did they do that?'

He looked at me hard once again, tilting his head to one side to emphasise the question. My eyes dropped downwards as his words seemed to linger in the air, but then the Kozak spirit rose inside me and I looked up again. 'I don't know,' I said to him, 'I wasn't there, so I can't say what happened.'

His lip rolled up again and his eyes narrowed, but before he could say anything else I spoke again, 'Why do you think they did that?! The Poles were riding onto our native Ukrainian soil! Our land! We'd do anything to defend it, because it belongs to us, no-one else! If you Poles bring horses onto our land, we'll do whatever we have to. If we cripple them, then that's tough. Don't think I'm a barbarian - I love horses. As you say, they are beautiful animals.'

The Pole stood there, with a couple of his friends. I stared right into his eyes, and I waited, to see what his response would be, but he said nothing, and he and his friends turned around and walked away. So that was that.

At the end of the working week, it was our custom to visit the local tavern, the Railway Inn, for a couple of pints of beer. It was usually overflowing with people, especially in the summer and, the three of us would sit at a table and talk to other men from the factory. Fedor would be looking at any pretty girl that happened to pass by.

It was Arthur who took me to the Railway Inn at the end of my first week; I was pleased about that, it made me feel accepted.

'So, Steve, are you Polish or Ukrainian?' he asked.

'Ukrainian.'

'Whereabouts are you from in Ukraine?'

'A town called Vinnitsya.'

Arthur shrugged his shoulders, 'Never heard of it.'

'It's not far from Kiev. Ukraine is a very beautiful country, Arthur, you should see it.'

'I have seen it, Steve. I was there at the end of the War. You're right, it is a lovely place. I was down in the Crimea. We were with the Russians just after they'd seen the Nazis off. Some terrible things happened, Steve, really terrible.' His face turned white as he remembered and he stumbled over his next words. 'Our Commanding Officer was under orders to help them Russians out. We did whatever we were asked to do, that's how it is when you're in the Army. There was one time when a group of Ukrainian sailors at one of the ports hoisted up the Ukrainian flag. You know, the blue and yellow one. What they did was take down the Russian flag and replaced it with theirs. Now, of course, that state of affairs didn't last long. The Russians arrested them. I think there was about twelve of them altogether. They rigged up a court martial right there and then and found them all guilty of treason. Sentenced them to death on the spot, just like that. They asked our Commanding Officer to provide a firing squad, and he agreed. We couldn't believe it when he gave us the order. I never could understand why he agreed to it. I expect they probably paid him. Orders are orders, so that's what we had to do.'

He looked at me with very sad eyes as he told this story, and it made me angry. Not because of Arthur, but because, once again, as ever, any show of patriotism from Ukrainians was brutally crushed.

Arthur was a good fellow, but it was strange working with someone who'd shot and killed fellow Ukrainians in cold blood, even though it was under military orders. It was enough to test my faith in humanity.

Our lives were quite settled in England and the years passed quickly. It wasn't so long before we reached 1952 and, by then, I was 25 years old. I grew into the habit of keeping up with what was happening in the world by reading an English newspaper most days, or trying to anyway. I always scoured the news for anything about our homeland, looking for any cracks to appear in the Soviet Union. Nothing much was reported. The Soviets had established a communist state and their curtain of iron repelled anyone who wanted to get in and denied anyone who wished to leave. I searched inside myself, my heart was torn, and my head was a mess of jumbled thoughts as I considered whether I should try to write home. I sat down with a pen and paper many times, but what could I say? I knew the authorities would intercept any letters. Eventually, I summoned up enough Kozak courage to stop my hand from shaking, enough to scribble a few sentences. Just to let my Mother know, if she was still around, that I was alive and thinking of them. I hoped the letter would get through. Many times I wrote, but nothing ever came back.

In March of the following year, 1953, I unfolded the newspaper one evening and something right there on the page jumped out at me. It was a piece of news I'd hoped to hear many times over the years. Stalin was dead. A smile spread itself across my face, and jolted me out of my early evening doziness. I jumped up out of my chair, folded the newspaper under my arm, and ran all the way to Mikola's house,

'Look! Look at this!' I passed the newspaper to him, still jumping up and down like a madman.

'Stefan, sit down before you injure yourself,' he gestured towards an armchair, so I sat in it, but I couldn't stop fidgeting. I was tapping my fingers on the arms of the chair, and my feet wouldn't stop dancing. Mikola scanned the page of the newspaper, his eyes widened and he let out a low whistle. 'You know what, Stefan, this calls for a little celebration.' He got up, walked into his kitchen and returned with a bottle.

'A good glass of this *Scotska horilka** should do it.'

He poured two generous glasses and we clinked them together. We drank. One of our worst enemies was gone, without doubt making the world a better place.

What followed over the next two or three years was a disappointment. Khruschev became the Soviet leader, but apart from one or two minor concessions or blunders, things stayed the same. Any letters I wrote still didn't get through.

Well, the years just seemed to slip by like water down a drainpipe. 1957 arrived, and by then, the Soviets were sending rockets into space, in competition with the Americans. What a joke. The Soviets exploring space while their citizens live their lives as virtual prisoners. I was so angry, but all I could do was swallow it down, yet again, just like we'd always done.

One day I was round at Mikola's house, when Fedor called in. He didn't seem his usual self, he shuffled in, with his head bowed slightly and with the hint of smile on him.

'Hello Fedor, are you all right?' said Mikola.

'I . . . I've got some news for you,' replied Fedor.

Both Mikola and I looked expectantly at him, waiting for him to tell us more. There was a pause, like a leaf floating down from a tree in a cool summer breeze.

He finally spat it out, 'I'm getting married!' The two of us jumped up, shook his hand and slapped him on his shoulders. Mikola poured large measures of *Scotska horilka* and we toasted the man.

'Which one is she?' I asked him.

Fedor chuckled at that. 'It's Araciella.'

'The Italian? Well, my brother, she's a beauty,' said Mikola, 'for sure, any babies that God bestows upon the two of you will be truly divine.'

A few weeks later, in the first week of December, we attended Fedor and Araciella's marriage ceremony. It was a warm evening for the time of year with a strong winter sun bursting through the trees. Mikola and I stood with Fedor at the church as we waited for Araciella to arrive. After a few agonising minutes during which several cigarettes were smoked, and anxious glances were cast up and down the road, a car pulled up. Fedor rushed into the church with Mikola, who was his best man.

Araciella stepped out of the car. She glided up the steps and into the church, like a fairy tale princess. Her olive skin was like gold in a sea of pure white ruffles and curves. She looked a dream. The ceremony seemed to fly by, and I stood there thinking to myself, *maybe I need to start looking for a wife*. The two of them took a slow walk down the aisle, looking so happy. People reached across to shake Fedor's hand or plant a kiss on Araciella's cheek. There was a good sized congregation in attendance, and a small reception was planned for the friends of the bride and groom. Fedor and Araciella stood outside the church basking in the glow of their union in the eyes of God. Mikola, I, and several others departed to a nearby friend's house where the reception was to take place. We'd already decorated a room with candles and flowers, and just needed to set out the plates of food. We'd prepared a wonderful selection of cold meats, boiled eggs, salads and fine breads, and of course a fancy, plaited *korovai**.

We heard a car pull up and waited, just for a minute or two. Fedor and Araciella burst into the room and drank the traditional glass of *horilka* and threw salt over their shoulders, while the rest of us looked on and clapped. A traditional Ukrainian wedding song crackled in the background. They walked further into the room and I found myself looking at Araciella. She had curves in all the right places, and her wedding dress fitted her snugly showing off her figure. I wondered to myself how soon it would be before she and Fedor had children. As they walked into the room together, Fedor wrapped an arm around her waist until it rested on one side of her stomach, and he softly patted her right there. I smiled at him, and he grinned right back, as if he knew what I'd been thinking. For sure, Fedor was well and truly on the road to starting his own family.

Chapter 13

Ukrainian proverb: Love will find a way. Indifference will find an excuse

'Well now, Stefan,' said Mikola as he rolled himself a cigarette, 'It was a good wedding, no?'

'Yes, it was a fine one. I think we did well for Fedor there,' I replied, as I too rolled one up.

'So, do you think it's time then?'

There was mischief in those eyes, Mikola was a fine fellow, a big strong man, and with a mind sharp as a *britva**. He knew what was going on in my head all right.

'I have been thinking . . . it doesn't look like we'll be getting back home anytime soon to our families, does it?'

It was the spring of 1958 and there was no sign of any thaw in the east. The Soviet Union had pulled its iron curtain around its borders and there was no way through. We'd read it in the newspapers and heard it on the radio.

'I can't argue with you. I've written so many letters back home now without any reply, I've lost count. If I write any more, I reckon I'll go mad.'

'I know. It's a curse. Those Soviet sons of bitches are vicious. They don't care about anyone.'

We lit our hand-rolled cigarettes. The Soviet Union had joined the space race, with their launch of Sputnik. They'd also sent a dog into space. What good was that? While we, as displaced persons, were too afraid to go back to our homes, they played their stupid games with rockets. We cursed them more than once.

'So, what are your thoughts? You talk about family.' Mikola took a pull on his cigarette, blew a cloud of smoke out, and kept his eyes fixed on me, those baby blue eyes that looked so innocent, that mesmerised me.

'I . . . I think it's time I got myself a wife. Look at me. I'm not getting any younger. I'll be thirty this year. Back home, a man my age would've married and be father to a houseful of children by now.'

'You're right. More and more of us Ukrainians are settling down now. You hear about it all the time. And of course, there's our good friend Fedor.'

I pondered this. Now, I wished Fedor all the best with Araciella, but I knew what I wanted. I always remembered what Oleksa said to me back in the Displaced Persons Camp in Regensburg: *we must fight to keep our traditions alive.*

That thought was never too far away from me, and when Fedor got married to Araciella, I pushed it to the back of my mind; I wanted him to be happy, and to have a long and prosperous life. But I wanted more. To uphold our traditions I knew I'd need someone like me, someone from back home.

'I'd like a Ukrainian girl for a wife. Where can I find one, eh?'

Mikola stubbed out his cigarette and began to roll another one. He raised his eyebrows and fixed his steady gaze on me. 'They're in short supply. There's not many around here. Look at Fedor, he couldn't get one could he? But if that's what you really want, then we must find a way.' He lit up his second cigarette. 'Listen, maybe we need to get around a bit more, to other towns. Look at this!' He thrust a newspaper at me. It was the latest copy of *Ukrayinska Dumka**. I flipped through it, and there were stories and information about Ukrainian communities in towns and cities all over Britain,

'You see, Stefan, there are places we can go, in search of a bride for you.'

So, that's what we did. On a Saturday we'd put on our best suits and polish up our shoes. Our hair would be slicked back and arranged in a neat pile on top of our heads, we scraped our faces smooth as china bowls, and slapped on a dab or two of aftershave. The Royal Enfield Bullet was our chariot – Mikola hopped on the back and clung on to me like a leech and we tore up the highways of England. We were on a mission. The bike took us to Kidderminster, Wolverhampton, Birmingham, Gloucester, Coventry, Manchester, Bradford and Nottingham. We met so many people and made so many friends. The community was growing – it was a good time. There were one or two occasions when I saw a lovely young girl, and she'd smile at me, but then I'd find out she was taken. There were one or two spinsters hanging around, but they were too old for me, I was a man in search of a wife to start a family with, but romance didn't happen for me. Mikola however, was a good ten years older than me, and so he struck up a friendship with one of the spinsters, Olga, and they corresponded with each other for years.

Once or twice over that summer, I was invited round to Fedor's house, with Mikola. Araciella had her baby and it was bawling its head off while we were there, but strangely I didn't find it annoying, it just made my heart ache even more.

Then, in the New Year, towards the end of January, on a cold, dark evening, I was sitting next to a fire in the back room of my home, warming myself. The cold had crept right into me; it felt as if my bones had frozen. I was sipping a mug of hot sweet tea and smoking a cigarette. The radio was on, but I wasn't really listening to it. There was a banging at the back door, and I smiled to myself as I stood up to answer it. It was Mikola, I recognised the knock. He came in and I brewed up a cup of tea for him. He sat and drank his tea back, and lit a cigarette,

'I've got something for you.' He pulled the latest copy of *Ukrayinska Dumka* out of his coat pocket and unfolded it, turning to one of the middle pages. He handed it to me. It was the news section that caught my eye. A wedding had taken place in London – the wedding of a Ukrainian man to a girl who had travelled from Poland,

'Mikola,' I said, lifting my head up from the newspaper, 'I'm looking for a Ukrainian bride, not a Polish one.'

'Stefan, Stefan! You know your trouble don't you – you always jump to conclusions too quickly. Read it again, more carefully this time.'

I lowered my head once again and this time the words jumped right out at me: Ukrainian man from London marries his bride. Recently arrived in England from Poland, Lubya is a girl who hails from the West of Ukraine and is delighted to have found a Ukrainian husband.

I passed the newspaper back to Mikola,

'So,' I replied, 'maybe there is a way . . .'

'See this fellow in the photograph? I know him. He's from the same town as me, Brody. I've known him all my life.' He thrust the paper back at me. There were two photographs, one of the happy couple and another of the bride next to the man who had been instrumental in arranging for their meeting and their subsequent marriage.

'He's called Sotnik. He was one of the fellows on the local Council, a learned fellow indeed.'

'Yes.' I lifted my head up from the newspaper. 'Perhaps I should write to the newspaper, to see if I can get more information.'

'No. In situations like this you need to seize your chance! Life is short, letters can pass back and forth and nothing changes. We need to get down there, to see the men who work on the *Dumka*. Maybe they can help us.'

'You're right.'

The following Saturday, we wrapped ourselves up with heavy coats, scarves, hats, gloves, thick socks and big boots, and we climbed onto the Bullet and roared onto the nearest road that headed south. London was our destination, to Holland Park where the Association of Ukrainians in Great Britain was based. It was a dark, cold morning and our clothes weren't thick enough to keep the chill from penetrating through to our bodies. Still, we kept on without stopping. All the way to the outskirts of London, by which time the sun was rising up, throwing its golden rays over the horizon. Even so, the cold gripped us tight as we blundered our way across the city, stopping to ask directions on frequent occasions.

Eventually, we found Holland Park and were relieved to be able to get off the bike and stamp some heat into ourselves. A nearby café caught our eye and we wandered across for a hot cup of tea and a sausage roll.

It was ten o'clock and we wandered through the streets of Holland Park, looking for the blue and the yellow, and those distinctive letters we knew so well. It took just about 20 minutes of walking through those tall, white-painted houses and there it was. We walked up a set of eight stone steps to a large, shiny black front door with a brass knocker. A brass plate on the wall had the *tryzub** engraved into it. That made me smile – the national emblem! That trident shape symbolic of Ukrainian freedom – the freedom we all hungered for.

We rapped on that door, and it was opened by a smiling young man who was most welcoming. An older man then greeted us in the hallway, and handshakes were exchanged. 'I'm Boris, one of the staff here. What can I do for you fellows?'

Mikola pulled the newspaper out of his jacket and explained that we trying to get in touch with someone. Boris looked us up and down – we must have looked like a pair of wild ones, with our wind-beaten faces and our crumpled suits, and then he showed us into a sitting area where we sat down and he nodded to the young man who had followed us. He reappeared shortly afterwards with a tray of tea and biscuits.

'You see, I know the fellow in this photograph.' Mikola thrust the newspaper towards Boris, pointing at the photograph. 'His name's Sotnik. I can't remember his first name – I don't think anyone ever used it. He's from the same town as me in Ukraine, Brody. I knew him quite well, everybody knew him. Now, it looks as if he's ended up in Poland. Now, Boris,' said Mikola pausing to take a mouthful of hot tea, 'you know as well as I do that there aren't many Ukrainian women here in Britain. You see, Stefan here wants to get married, settle down and start a family, but he wants to preserve our way of life: he's looking for a Ukrainian bride.'

Boris smiled at the two of us as he held a cup of steamy tea to his lips,

'My friends, of course we here at the Association will do everything we can to help you. But we'll need all your details and to see your papers.'

Mikola and I produced our registration documents and our health papers with our addresses on them. Boris looked at them closely.

'Okay, young men, I'd like to help you. It is our role here at the Association to promote and preserve the Ukrainian heritage, our way of life and our customs. Let me get you this man's address. He really is quite a fellow. We get letters from him every week, and he's already assisted Ukrainian couples to get together many times. You see, after the war ended, UPA stayed active in the West of Ukraine, in and around the Carpathian Mountains. They were fighting for freedom, so any non-Ukrainians that entered their territory were attacked. There were many ambushes and many deaths. In the end the Poles went in with their army. There were people who lived in villages near those mountains who were good people. The men from UPA could walk into those villages whenever it was safe to do so, and the villagers would feed them – or sometimes food was taken out to them. Anyhow, after a year or two of ambushes and attacks, the Poles poured into those villages and told everyone they had two hours to pack up and leave. Some of those people left behind their homes and many acres of farmland. Then they were shipped right across to the West of Poland – to the Recovered Lands. That's what happened to Sotnik. He ended up near the town of Wolow, in a small village called Uskorz Wielki. He does what he can to promote the Ukrainian language, mainly through songs. He plays the mandolin, you see. The situation in the Recovered Lands is the reverse to that of our people here in Britain. Here, we have a shortage of women. Over there is a shortage of men.'

He marched off out of the room and came back a few minutes later with an envelope.

'Here is Sotnik's address. Letters to and from him all seem to be getting through, unlike to our homes in Ukraine. Damn those Soviet sons of bitches!'

Neither Mikola nor I could disagree. Firm handshakes were exchanged as we departed and he urged us to visit again. 'Enjoy your visit to London! If you should pass this way again then please call in, we'll be very happy to see you both!'

Outside, on the pavement, I carefully slipped the envelope into my jacket pocket.

'Well, Stefan, it looks like we got what we came for,' said Mikola, 'Now, let's get over to Kilburn as we planned. We've got a great night ahead of us and now we can really celebrate!'

Mikola's nephew lived in Kilburn, a fellow called Stefan Derevyanka. He'd served in the Polish Army and ended up in Italy at the end of the war. Then, the same as the rest of us, he came to Britain as a refugee. Not long afterwards he'd met and married Julie, an Irish nurse. How Mikola came to be in touch with him I don't know, but, after we'd jumped on the Bullet and shot across the City, we found their flat, and walked up to the third floor, knocked on their front door, and were greeted with a flurry of smiles, handshakes, slaps on the shoulder, a kiss on the cheek from Julie and the next thing we knew we were sitting in their living room with a glass of whisky in our hand. It was still only five minutes to midday.

I'd never met Derevyanka before, but within half an hour I felt as if I'd known him all my life. He worked at the Ford car factory in Dagenham, and at the weekend he made the most of every minute.

Julie cooked us all a lovely dinner of potatoes and stew, and then we had a walk into Kilburn. The four of us went to a pub, one of Derevyanka's regular haunts. He came back from the bar with three pints of a beer that was completely black with what looked like several spoonfuls of cream on top,

'Hey fellows, have you tried this? It's called Guinness, all the Irish around here drink it, and it goes down nicely after a lovely lunch.'

I took a cautious sip of the dark brew. It was so bitter, but also like velvet, it slid down inside you like magic. Mikola dished out cigarettes and we chatted away. Derevyanka was a big talker. So was Julie. Derevyanka told us all about life in London, working at the car plant. Julie worked as a nurse in one of the hospitals. As usual, Mikola had a few stories to tell, it was a great atmosphere, but that envelope in my pocket was on my mind. Several times I surreptitiously patted my jacket just to feel the crunch of it – just to make sure it was still there. I don't mind admitting it, I was lonely. Even though I was right in the middle of a busy pub at lunch time, my loneliness ate into me. Strange how, even in company, a man can feel adrift somehow. As I sat there listening to the stories pouring forth, I thought of Mother and Father. They'd married and raised us boys in that house back in Vinnitsya. I knew that was what I wanted. To try and put those pieces back in place. To make it all right, if that was possible. Whilst around me, the drinks flowed and merriment and laughter rang around my ears, I was contemplating on life and the future.

It was a raucous evening at the flat in Kilburn. Derevyanka loved to play cards, and, in the evening, several fellows came round for a game. The drinks flowed, Julie was a great hostess – she brought out trays of sandwiches and snacks. The *Scotska* and the *horilka* flowed like water, and there was always a glass of beer to hand. It was a wild night.

The next morning I woke up with a throbbing in my head, but with a resolution in my heart that I would use the information given to me by the folks in London to build a future.

The next day, back in Worcester, I sat down and wrote a letter. The words flowed out of me. It was the story of my life, all about where I was from. The schools I went to, my friends and my family, the Ukrainian poetry I loved. All in all, I wrote six pages, to this fellow Sotnik, and I slipped in a photograph of myself. I had to wait until the following Monday before posting it.

A month or so later, I came home from work to find an airmail envelope on the doormat. I ripped it open in the space of a second, and I scanned my eyes across it. Then, I sat down, took my coat and my boots off, and read through it more slowly. It was encouraging. Sotnik asked me to provide a reference from someone who could verify who I was, and then he said he hoped he could help me. Of course, I asked Mikola, who was only too happy to oblige and I entered into a correspondence with Sotnik.

Within a few weeks of letters flying across the sea and over the land, Sotnik wrote a letter to me that was to change my life:

Dear Stefan,

I have some good news. There is a family here that have five daughters – the Poruczniks. One of them has said she'd like to get to know a Ukrainian man, maybe with a view to marriage. Her name is Maria. She's aged 20, and is a lovely girl. I've spoken with her parents, and they are of the opinion that she is ready for a courtship. But first of all, her parents have asked for you to write to her and get to know her.

Yours,

Sotnik

He provided the address, and that was all I needed. With a pad of paper in front of me and a pen in my hand, I sat down the very next evening to write to Maria. It was more difficult than I expected. Several attempts were required. I'd never written to a girl before – I wanted to make a good impression. Eventually, I managed to put together a couple of pages about myself, and enclosed a photograph.

Over the next few months, we exchanged many letters, and one or two photographs. In the evenings, I'd read through her letters and look at her photograph. She was a beautiful young woman, with dark hair and sparkling eyes. After we'd exchanged numerous letters, too many to count, I nervously, with my hand shaking, wrote a letter to her father asking whether he'd consider allowing Maria to meet me, with a view to a possible marriage. A week went by, and then another. I smoked too much, and couldn't stop drumming my fingers – keeping busy helped, so I took whatever overtime was available at the factory.

The next time I came home and saw an airmail envelope on the doormat, I felt a surge run through me – an electric spark; a flame rising. I grabbed the envelope and tore it open. I paced up and down as I read:

Dear Stefan,

Thank you for your letter. I am very pleased that you and Maria have continued to write to each other over this last year. She has grown very fond of you. I am a man of few words, so I'd like to give you permission to meet with Maria, and if all goes well, you have my consent to get married. May God bless you.

Yours,

Mikhaylo Porucznik

And so, she came. Arrangements were made, a flight was booked

– a local Ukrainian couple, Mr and Mrs Lipoviy, kindly agreed for Maria to stay with them while we courted. I booked a week's holiday from work.

She arrived on a Saturday morning, on the 1st of October, 1959. As I waited on the platform for the train to arrive, I shoved a finger into my freshly starched shirt collar to ease it, and kept straightening my tie. I was dressed in my best suit and my hair was swept back into a mop on top of my head, I resisted the urge to run my fingers through it. I paced up and down, those brightly polished shoes clicking on the platform over and over again, like a drum beating. The train came in on time, and my heart thudded like never before, I struggled to hold myself in. The train stopped with a hiss and smoke billowed into the station. A large suitcase appeared from one of the carriage doors, its owner struggling to manoeuvre it, so I rushed across to that door and helped with the suitcase, it was so big it would hardly fit through. Eventually, I managed to prise it free and heaved it onto the platform, and then I looked up.

'Maria?' I offered my hand and, after she'd stepped down from the train, she took hold of it. It was so warm and soft I didn't want to let go of it. Momentarily, I was lost for something to say as I gazed at her. She was so fine. More beautiful than any photograph could ever do justice to. With dark hair, down to her shoulders, incredible green eyes, and a face like porcelain. She hypnotised me.

'Hello, Stefan.' Her voice sang into my ears and pulled me out of my dumbstruck state.

'Hello, Maria,' I replied, trying to speak with some authority, whilst all the time, inside I was melting. 'Welcome to Worcester. Let me take your things.'

I picked up the suitcase, not the easiest of tasks because of its size and weight, and ushered Maria out to a taxi. The taxi took us back to Mr and Mrs Lipoviy's house, and I found myself jabbering away a little foolishly along the way, while Maria sat and listened, smiling serenely. Mrs Lipoviy served up a beautiful lunch, and, during the course of the meal, I managed to regain my composure.

Over the course of the following week, the two of us walked, arm in arm, through the town. Autumn clouds hovered above, threatening to throw rain down on us, but it stayed dry. We stopped in cafés, we walked in the park, with leaves swirling round our feet. Somehow, it all felt so right as we talked about everything. In the café, with a cup of strong tea in front of each of us, we contemplated our lives.

'We are scattered, Maria,' I said. 'Like seed blown out of an open hand by a hurricane, we Ukrainians fall to the ground wherever the wind blows us. And so, we have no choice but to root ourselves into the land where we fall. A piece of Ukraine on foreign soil, with the Kozak blood and fire, that's what we bring. We've got strength. Not just physical strength, but the force to get things done. If there's a problem we fix it. Ask anyone at the factory – they'll tell you.'

Maria listened and nodded, and then replied. 'The world can't begin to recognise the terrors that have come down on us. My family, as you know, was evicted by gunpoint from our home in Lemkovyna. The Poles wanted us out, to break UPA. We fed the insurgents whenever we could. And why not? They were good Ukrainian boys who just wanted to free their own land. There is no better reason to fight.'

'Our battle is a long one. All we can do is stay true to who we are, and that's what we'll do. I need a wife to join me. To live beside me, and to stand firm in the faces of those who would seek to deny us our heritage.' I dropped down onto one knee and I took Maria's hand.

'Will you marry me?'

Maria looked down on me with her wide, open face and her sparkling green eyes. 'Yes. Yes! Of course I will, Stefan. We'll make a life together. Ukraine is in our hearts – we can never let it go.'

And so it was. We married. It took a few weeks to make all the arrangements, but on a crisp, sunny autumn Saturday, the 15th November 1959, we took our vows at the local Catholic Church in Worcester. A Ukrainian priest from Wolverhampton, Myzichka, agreed to preside over the ceremony in front of a congregation of 20.

On the morning of the wedding, I'd got my *dryshba**, a fellow called Schultz, a German who shared the same lodgings as me in the St John's district of Worcester, to help me get ready. In true Ukrainian tradition, Mikola was a second *dryshba*, and Fedor a third. I chose Schultz because he was reliable, I didn't want anything to go wrong on the day, Mikola was a good friend, but a terrible time-keeper. The other reason I chose Schultz was, because he worked in a tailors, he had a selection of very fine suits. We were about the same size, so I borrowed one from him for the wedding. It was more important to make sure Maria had a wedding dress she was happy with, so that's what I spent my money on. Anyhow, the suit was very smart.

On the morning of the wedding I got up and began my preparations, with Schultz in attendance to make sure nothing was wrong with the way I looked. He used a special clothes brush to make sure there were no specks or strands of cotton on me, and then he neatly folded a handkerchief and placed it carefully in my top pocket, using the back of his hand to flatten it into place. He scolded me for placing my wallet in the jacket side pocket, and insisted I place it in the breast pocket inside the jacket. He reckoned it would ruin the look. I looked at myself in a mirror – I felt like a prince! Finally, after several inspections and minor adjustments, Schultz stopped fussing. I had a small pile of belongings on the side board in my room, where I was getting ready. There was a pack of cigarettes, my keys and a pocket knife. I knew Schultz would never let me take any of these in case they ruined the look of my suit, but I wondered whether I should take a pack of cigarettes with me. I decided against it, after all it was my wedding day; my friends would be there to give me one if I needed it. Then, my eyes fell upon the wooden bracelet. It was still with me, after all this time. That piece of Ukraine, those small beads of oak were still the closest I'd been to my own country for a long time. While Schultz was distracted, I slipped them into my jacket side pocket. I hoped they'd bring me luck, and at least, if we could not be in Ukraine, then part of it would be with us.

Schultz got me to the church in plenty of time, the service was due to commence at two o'clock. We smoked a few cigarettes outside while we waited for the rest of the congregation to arrive.

The autumn sunshine was with us. The guests began to arrive and with the appointed hour approaching, Schultz ushered me into the church where I took my seat at the front. A few minutes later Mikola and Fedor arrived and joined us on the front row, stopping in front of me to shake my hand and give me blessings from God. There was a cool serenity in the air that was reflected in my mood. I was in no doubt about Maria; she was the girl for me, the one I wanted to hold in my arms forever. My thoughts were invaded by the organ as it exploded into majestic harmony, and filled every corner and crack of the church with a sound like heaven. She was on her way to me!

The ceremony passed by in something of a blur. I just remember my lovely Maria next to me in her billowing wedding dress, looking like an angel. The priest took us through the vows and we both said 'I will'. I kissed her lovely lips and finally she was mine, and I was hers.

The wedding party strolled out of that church into that bright autumnal sunshine, we all blinked and then held ourselves up straight and true, with big smiles, for a few photographs. Then, it was on to a small reception at the house of Mr and Mrs Lipoviy. They had a large dining room and it was there that Maria and I went to celebrate our union in the eyes of God, with all our friends. A meal consisting of soup, roast chicken with potatoes and vegetables, and finally a sponge pudding, was served to us by the wives of some of my friends. It was a grand feast. I was proud, and never happier.

Then we pulled back the chairs and pushed the table to one side. Bottles of *horilka* appeared and glasses were pushed into the hands of the men for toasting. Maria and I cut our wedding cake and our union was sealed. We kissed and then I took her in my arms for a slow waltz as a man called Ivan stepped forward with an accordion. He played many of the old Ukrainian tunes, beginning first with some of those slow waltzes and then came the *hopak** and the *kolomyjka**. The *horilka* flowed, the boys loosened their ties and things got wild, with much stamping and yelping. We linked arms and span around in a circle until the world was a haze around us. In those moments, it felt as if the world was ours.

Of course, as was always the case, the night ended with songs and plenty of them. The men all sang like Kozaks, the women like nightingales. We were a joyous choir, a scene snatched right from the history of Ukraine. That's how it always was in the old days. The spirit of those times was with us.

Midnight came and went, and, finally, the last of our guests tumbled out of the front door and said their goodbyes, with handshakes for me and kisses for my lovely bride, Maria. Now, she was all mine. We'd arranged to rent a room at the house of Mr and Mrs Lipoviy, with our rental period beginning straight after the reception. They had five spare rooms which they rented out. It was a grand old house, much like a palace, and it would certainly be a suitable place for us to begin our married life.

We climbed the stairs together slowly; we had the rest of our lives to spend together so there was no need to rush. Besides that, it had been a long day. At the top of the stairs we turned and walked along the landing to our room. The door creaked open as I pushed it, and we walked into a delicate perfume, a wonderful sight was there for us to behold. The room had been filled with bunches of flowers.

'Oh, Stefan, this is beautiful!' said Maria, collapsing onto the bed. It was like a fairytale. I kicked off my shoes, and then walked over to the window and drew the curtains. I turned and smiled at Maria,

'I'll just go to the bathroom, while you get undressed if you like,' I said.

'Thank you, Stefan, but wait.' She jumped up. 'Just take off your jacket and make yourself a little more comfortable first.'

She came over to me and helped me with my jacket. I was about to throw it over a nearby chair, but then remembered how fussy Schultz was, so I took the wallet out of the breast pocket and placed it on the chest of drawers. Then I fished out the wooden bracelet and smiled to myself. I held it up and looked at it briefly, before placing it next to the wallet. Next to me, Maria gasped. She reached across and picked it up, all the time her eyes growing wider and wider. I saw her eyes as I'd never seen them before. Or maybe they looked more familiar than ever. I felt myself spinning back to another time and place, those eyes had looked into my own some years before, I was sure of that.

They were truly Ukrainian eyes.

Chapter 14

Ukrainian proverb: The malicious cow disturbs the whole herd

Four years went by. The summer of 1963 had come and gone and the cool breezes of autumn blew through our house. It was our first house together – our own little palace, modest though it was. I'd saved and scraped together pennies and pounds; done as much overtime as I could, and I'd sold the Bullet. It tore a piece of me away when I watched it zoom away down the road, but it had to be done, for the family.

Maria and I hadn't wasted any time; we were proud parents of two bouncing, noisy children. Our first baby was Anna Helena, born in the early autumn of 1960, named after two of Maria's younger sisters. Anna had a lovely mop of dark hair and a pair of piercing green eyes, much like Maria's.

Andriy Volodimir arrived in the late autumn of 1962. I wanted to call him Volodimir, after my long-lost brother. Maria persuaded me against it; she thought our baby boy should have a name that would fit in better in England – Andriy, or Andrew in its English form. In the end I agreed, but Volodimir was not forgotten.

Our house in Vincent Road, Worcester, was a two-bedroom terrace, with a kitchen, an outside toilet and two living rooms. Almost as soon as we knew Maria was expecting our first baby, I was jolted out of my evening with the newspaper by my wife telling me she wouldn't be prepared to live at Mr and Mrs Lipoviy's house once we had a child. She insisted, and kept insisting, that we should get our own home, away from the interferences and the pettiness of living with a landlady. Mrs Lipoviy was very nice, but she was also very nosey. Maria and I needed our own space. I began looking for somewhere, and Vincent Road was where we ended up. I used up all my savings to buy that house, every penny. It was a good house, a real family home. With the aid of a grant from the Council, we built a bathroom on the ground floor, and a third bedroom above it. Bit by bit, we decorated and furnished. We got hold of second-hand beds and wardrobes for the bedrooms from a shop down the road, and a table and chairs for the kitchen. We purchased a couple of old sofas that were past their best, but they were comfortable enough. One or two cabinets got a home in our house, we did the best we could without much money. I even managed, at one point, to get hold of a television. A fellow on our street was moving and wanted to get rid of it. It was an early model and it crackled and flickered a little bit, so I didn't have to pay him much for it.

We sat and watched the news in moving pictures, which was better for us, because sometimes we couldn't always understand what they were saying on the radio. There was so much going on in the world, and there was one man who stood out above all the others, John F Kennedy, the President of the USA. When the Soviets tried to position missiles in Cuba he stopped them. Under his leadership, the USA sent aid out to many parts of the world; he appeared on the television so many times and spoke of working for world peace. Meanwhile the Soviet communists hid behind their curtain of iron. That curtain was wrapped around them, turning them into a giant all-conquering machine, waiting to take over more and more of the world, just as they'd done with our beloved Ukraine. None of us knew what was happening inside that machine, but, from past experience, we had some idea.

Kennedy though, he was a peacemaker, a man who could really change things. That's how we saw him. Maybe there was a chance, somehow, that he could do something to get us our Ukraine back. At that time it seemed unlikely, but inside we held onto a small breath of hope.

I was just grateful to be living in a democratic country where you didn't have to look over your shoulder all the time. A place where you could practise whatever religion you chose, without any trouble from anyone. Okay, now and again, you'd get someone whispering about *bloody foreigners*, but it wasn't so often. I was accepted at my workplace, and on the street where I lived. My wife and my family were also accepted. I felt much safer than living under Soviet rule. The British love to complain about everything, but don't we all? Under the Soviets we weren't allowed to do that, they crushed our souls, tried to suck us into their machine. Of course, we stood firm always, with our Kozak blood keeping us strong, pushing the fear down. Whatever they'd done to us over the years, they couldn't break us. They wanted us to snap like a dead twig held up in a strong wind, but we'd always managed to bend towards the eye of the hurricane. We fought a battle we knew we could never win, but we never gave up.

It wasn't long before an event occurred that was to shred our hopes once again. It was a week before Andriy's first birthday, November 1963, and the world seemed to go frantic. The programmes on the television were interrupted by bulletins presented by newsreaders with frowning faces. The President had been shot! We could hardly take our eyes off the television all night, waiting for more news. In between waiting for further announcements, I switched on the radio in the kitchen and tuned into a BBC station. I listened carefully as the hysterical outpourings of eyewitnesses were broadcast, and heard that Kennedy had been taken to hospital. We waited and we hoped, but deep inside I had a bad feeling. I smoked too many cigarettes and paced up and down the kitchen until finally, 'Stefan! Quick, come here!' called Maria.

The face on the television screen was solemn. The presenter spewed out his words as if he didn't want to believe them, '*It has been confirmed from Parkland Hospital in Dallas, Texas that President Kennedy is dead . . .*'

I couldn't listen any more. I just walked back into the kitchen and lit another cigarette. Maria came through to me. 'Stefan,' she put her arms around me, 'Come on, it's late. I can see you're upset, but you've got work tomorrow. Come on now. We have to carry on. Everything will work out for the best.'

With her arms around me, I felt some of the tension drain away from me. On our way up to bed we looked in on Anna, and on Andriy. They were both soundly asleep, thankfully oblivious to the political turmoil that was engulfing the planet.

The next evening, after work, I called round to see Mikola. He brewed up some tea, and we sat at the table smoking cigarettes. 'So, what do you think about Kennedy's assassination then, eh?' said Mikola.

'You know as well I who did it. The Soviets! Damn those bastards all to Hell! Will they never stop, with their communist shit! They just keep taking whatever they can, whenever they can. They don't care about anyone, not even their own people!'

'I can't argue with you. The Soviets are vicious dogs, if they think someone is a threat to them, they just wipe him out.'

Mikola stood up, reached into a cupboard and slammed a bottle of *Scotska horilka* and two glasses down onto the table. Generous measures were poured and we drank to John F Kennedy, and we cursed the Soviets. I wished they would all climb into their Sputniks, shoot off into space and never come back.

The children were growing up; Maria and I worked hard to keep our home going, and to make a life for our family. The Metal Box Company was good enough to offer Maria a job, and she took it. We earned enough money to pay the bills, and furnish our home. The children had enough to eat and were clothed well. For the first time in my life I felt free from fear. Okay, one or two of the English looked down on us; they thought we shouldn't be there, but what choice did we have? Of course, I would rather have returned to my home, to the places and the people I knew, but the fear held me back. To return was to walk into a cauldron of suspicion. The Soviets were madmen, their communist doctrines were woven into their hearts. Anyone who should disagree was eradicated.

1966 arrived. Andriy was three and Anna was five, and things were a little easier for us. We were managing well, and the future looked bright. England was beginning to prosper once again, and the World Cup was being held there. It was an opportunity for England to show the world what it could do, both in playing the game of football, and in organising the tournament. On our crackly old television, we watched many of the games. Mikola was a frequent visitor at that time. He loved football. The two of us watched, enthralled, as England, with Bobby Charlton, made progress through to the semi-finals, where they were drawn to play Portugal.

In the other semi-final, which was played the day before the Final itself, it was West Germany against the Soviet Union. The game was of interest to us, because of course we wanted the Soviets to lose, preferably to be humiliated, but then again, as we watched them play and looked at the players, we realised that many of the team were Ukrainian. The names were from our home country, we could see that.

'Damn those Soviet thieves!' said Mikola. 'Not only do they steal our land and everything on it, they steal our footballers!'

There was Porkuyan and Sabo in the first eleven and on the substitute's bench was Serebryanikov. All three of them were Ukrainian sportsmen who were being denied the chance to wear the blue and the yellow of Ukraine. Not only did they take our young men, but also one or two from Georgia and Azerbaijan. It filled me with disgust to see that Soviet hammer and sickle emblem worn by Ukrainians on the sports field, but I guess those boys just wanted to play their football – and knowing the Soviets, they were probably never given a realistic choice. The frozen wastes of Siberia were always an option for any that refused to play.

Anyhow, we watched, with a strange mix of emotions inside. Part of us wanted our boys to do well, but for the Soviets to be thrashed. The West Germans were a solid team and for a while it was a close game, but once they'd taken a two goal lead it was virtually over. It was nice to see our boy, Porkuyan, score a late consolation but if only he'd been wearing the blue and the yellow, then I would have jumped through the ceiling.

A few days later, Wembley Stadium in London was full of cheering supporters. The whole of England stopped. Every ounce of every man, woman and child was willing England to beat the West Germans and be crowned world champions. Mikola and I were cheering them on too. After all, we had a lot to be grateful for. The English had given us a home and the freedom to be who we were. Okay, we were restricted in the kind of work we could do, but we had homes and we had enough to eat. The houses in which we lived had heating and running water. We couldn't complain.

The Germans took an early lead, but England came back strongly and were ahead by two goals to one, with just a couple of minutes to go. A nation stood still, not daring to even breathe. Then, from nowhere, a calamity! An equaliser from the Germans sent the game into extra-time. That created a hush in all of us. I could feel it all around, and I knew it was hanging right over everyone, up and down the whole country.

In extra-time, England scored to make it three to two, but there was a controversy. The shot, by England striker Geoff Hurst, had smashed onto the underside of the crossbar and bounced down. The Germans disputed whether it had crossed the line. In the end it was a Russian linesman who confirmed that the goal should stand. Mikola and I smiled at each other as we watched the linesman talking to the referee. 'That bloody Soviet fool,' said Mikola, 'he looks half asleep. Does he know what the hell he's doing?'

It didn't matter in the end, because Hurst scored again, and England won the game! Euphoria swept over England, and we all got caught up in its wave! The celebrations went on for days with people coming out onto the street cheering and singing. It was open house along our road for at least a week. I could walk into a neighbour's front door at anytime, and a glass of beer would be in my hand in the space of a few seconds. It was pure joy.

The years following this saw the Ukrainian community in Britain develop and grow. Someone, at some time, I guess it must have been the Association of Ukrainians in Great Britain, bought a huge ex-army site in Weston-on-Trent, Derbyshire, which began to be used for regular rallies by Ukrainians from all over the country. It was a great place and was given the name *Tarasivka*. There was a hall, large enough to stage concerts. There were groups of barracks and two large fields, suitable for camping. There was a football pitch, volleyball pitch and even a small swimming pool. And, if you walked down the road, past the nearby woods, there were further facilities – a hostelry with a bar and numerous dwellings that served as retirement homes.

Several times a year, but more so in the summer, hundreds of Ukrainians would travel there, some by car, but also many by coach from the bigger Ukrainian communities such as Manchester, Bradford, Wolverhampton, Leeds or Coventry.

Tarasivka was an oasis. It was as if God had planted a small piece of Ukraine right in the middle of England. We could socialise and eat picnics together, and meet up with old friends. In the afternoons, the young boys and girls would stage a concert, with traditional music, singing and dance. It was a wonderful sight to see the youngsters keeping up those traditions. A chapel was built for church services. At the back of the hall, on a small part of the field, a bazaar would be set up, and we could go and buy embroidered tablecloths, books, greetings cards or recordings of Ukrainian music, all sorts of things. In the evenings they would hold a *zabava**. A band would play, usually consisting of mandolins, accordions, a drummer and maybe a guitarist. Maria and I would have a dance in the early stages of the evening, and then let the youngsters cut loose. We'd sit back and watch the boys and girls getting to know each other.

Once Anna reached ten and Andriy was eight, they spent many weeks of many summers at *Tarasivka*, at the yearly camp that was held there. Not only did they immerse themselves in Ukrainian culture, it helped them to become more independent. The Soviets may have taken Ukraine from us, but they couldn't steal it from inside us. Anna and Andriy grew up some more and started senior school, and I don't know where those years went. They trickled by like rainwater on a window pane.

Every day I thought about my family back home. It tormented me to think about Mother, and what would have become of her. I hoped and prayed she hadn't been harmed. I was never able to free myself of the regret that we'd left her on her own. And what of my big brother, Volodimir? I imagined him shivering in some ramshackle hut in the depths of freezing Siberia. I had no doubt that's where he would have ended up. After all that had happened to me and my family, I still wanted to go home, to walk again on Ukrainian soil. To gaze across the steppes in the steamy heat of summer and drink in that blue, blue sky. I wanted to, once again, breathe that mountain air.

Mikola was a good friend to our family, and a frequent visitor to our house. I remember one evening, it was in 1974, he came round and we were playing cards and having a smoke and just talking in general when, there was a dull hiss, and all the lights went out. 'Hell and fire, looks like a fuse has blown!' said Mikola.

'Don't worry, I'll go and see.'

I fumbled my across the room, using the furniture to guide me, and pulled the curtains open to let in some of the light from the moon and stars. A gentle shaft of light from the sky above shot into my face and I was about to feel my way to the kitchen to the fuse box, when I spotted something. There were no lights on in any of the neighbouring houses. 'Mikola, I don't think this is just a fuse, all the lights round here are out.' I grabbed a torch from a kitchen cupboard and checked all the lights and power sockets. They were all dead.

'You know what?' I reported back. 'Everything they've been saying on the news is true. The miners' strike has caused this power failure. This is what they've been threatening. I've bought some candles just in case.'

I lit one of the candles, and was thankful that Maria and the children had gone to bed. Mikola and I smoked a few more cigarettes in the dim light, 'I'll tell you what this reminds me of,' said Mikola, 'it's just like living under the Soviets. Nothing ever worked properly there under the communists. There are forces at work in England that would seek to drag it into a communist state. I wouldn't be surprised to find there are Soviets here in England, trying to spread their propaganda and their doctrines. We know what that means eh, Stefan? It means poverty and persecution. I hope the Government stays strong.'

The power cuts didn't last too long, much to the disappointment of Anna and Andriy. They enjoyed living by candlelight, it was magic to them, but for the rest of us, it was a relief to get back to normal.

Apart from the miners' strike, and other minor industrial unrest that occurred at times through the seventies, the other dilemma we faced was the nuclear weapons race. The Yanks and the Soviets were locked in a battle neither could win. The rest of the world looked on, and swallowed their fear down, and pretended that everything would be okay. It just needed one madman to push a button and we'd all be fried, and the earth around us would be injected with radioactive poison. We lived day to day. All we could do was keep working and pay our way, just like all ordinary people do.

It was often hard, existing as a foreigner in a country not your own. Wherever you went, amongst the native population, it was as an outsider. We looked different and we couldn't speak English so well. Sometimes, I'd walk into a shop and, as soon as I opened my mouth and spoke, the atmosphere changed. People hushed their voices and glanced sideways at me. I guess it was only natural really, so at the end of a working day I looked forward to coming home and relaxing, in a Ukrainian household, with my lovely wife and children. As they grew older, Anna and Andriy often preferred to spend time alone in their bedrooms. Anna would be reading a book or sewing, and Andriy was learning to play the guitar, so it was better for all of us that he stayed in his room, but one thing was guaranteed to get us all running into the living room, and that was when we saw anything to do with Ukraine on the television. There was a talent show called Opportunity Knocks hosted by a fellow called Hughie Green. One of us would be watching the show, and then a cry would go up, 'Ukrainians on television. Quick!' The children would scramble down to the living room from all parts of the house, and we'd gather together to watch. It would always be a troupe of Ukrainian dancers, boys and girls from somewhere in Britain who had been taught the traditional Kozak dances, the boys wearing the embroidered shirts and the *sharivari*, and the girls with lots of coloured ribbons in their hair, and also with embroidered clothing. I can't describe the joy I felt to watch them. For five minutes, probably less, it felt to all of us that Ukraine was still alive.

There was also a film, *Taras Bulba*, an American production of the novel by Gogol about Ukrainian Kozaks. It starred Yul Brynner and Tony Curtis. Whenever it was on the television, we'd all gather together to watch it. We loved it. It was a part of our history when we had warriors who were prepared to fight our enemies, and it was something we needed to hold onto.

Our good friend Mikola passed away in April 1977, and as we stood in prayer at his funeral I wondered whether we'd all be under the ground before Ukraine might be free.

My 50th birthday came and went in the following year, and by then I'd pretty much given up hope of ever getting back home. England had been my home for nearly 30 years – much longer than the years I'd spent growing up in Ukraine. It was a strange situation to be in. I hadn't chosen to leave Ukraine, but England was where I'd landed and I'd done my best to be a part of what was around me. All we Ukrainians did. We knew how to work hard, we earned every penny that was paid to us, and we were grateful, but it couldn't change the Kozak inside us. Our eyes were eastern, that's where we belonged. That's where we should have been.

As we continued to look upon the world we began to see changes. In Poland, a fellow called Lech Walesa led a protest and a revolution against communism. Years later, following many battles, all carried out in peaceful protest, he succeeded in removing Poland from communist rule and in achieving independence for his country.

For Ukrainians the world over, hope began to build. Walesa had inspired us. If he could do it, then why not us Ukrainians? To break the communist chain that was locked around us, we needed to do something. Of course, it was easier for Walesa, because Poland was not actually part of the Soviet Union, but it showed the world that ordinary people didn't want communism.

Anna and Andriy grew up some more and, in 1982, Anna got married to a fellow, also called Stefan, from Coventry. A traditional wedding was held in Stefan's city and a reception at the local Ukrainian club. It wasn't long before they produced our first grandson, Marko. The years were passing quickly.

In 1984, the mineworkers were at it again. Most evenings, we would watch the news on television to see what was happening, and I shook my head when I heard the mineworkers' leader talking. The militants had the language of the communist, and I had no doubt the Soviets were infiltrating. For England to go through a revolution similar to the Russian one was unthinkable, but strange things have happened in the world. The forces of communism are like a creeping rash, they get everywhere and they aren't easy to get rid of. Any opportunity to spread their doctrine would draw the communists like flies to an open sore. They would use any methods they could to feed the masses lies and propaganda. For a whole year the mineworkers battled, but Margaret Thatcher, the Prime Minister, beat them in the end. There were some bloody clashes with the police. The images on our television screens were graphic. The police were armed with truncheons and they weren't afraid to use them. It was a war. Mrs Thatcher held on and used the brute force of authority to smash the miners back. They weakened, until their campaign faltered and died off. Many saw this as a heavy defeat for the working man, others as a victory for democracy. I was just glad the communists had faded into the background.

Then, in April 1986, something happened that was to carve a scar as big as a Kozak sword slash right across all Ukrainian hearts. It was the 26th of April to be exact. Easter had come and gone and summer was on its way. It was a time of year when there was always much to rejoice over. The flowers were beginning to jump up towards the sky in search of rays from a golden spring sun. People all around were coming out of their houses to tend their front gardens. To mow their lawns, and plant flowers to add colour into their own, and everyone's lives. We didn't have much garden at our house, but I tried to make the most of what was there. I grew vegetables in our back garden. They tasted so good, so much better that the ones from the shops. I could grow just about anything; people around us said I had 'green fingers'. When people said things like that to me, it made me smile, but it also made me a little sad. It reminded me of my brother, Volodimir. Any green fingers I had came from him. On our land back home, we often worked side by side, and Volodimir had the knack, he had that bond with the land beneath him. Plants would push their way out of the soil up to him, to feel his caress. Under him, our garden grew, and I learned from him. We had plump, luscious tomatoes, cucumbers and rows of full of potatoes, carrots and onions.

On this particular day, I came in from the garden as the sun was setting, tired but contented. I pulled off my shoes and then Maria made me a cup of tea. I went through to the living room and turned on the television, and as I waited for the picture to appear, I took a few sips of tea. The early evening news broadcast was the one I liked to watch, to see what was happening in the world. The music at the beginning, with its dramatic stabbed notes, was just fading out and, as always, the newsreader's face looked out at me. I took a sip from my cup and listened to him as he read the opening news story. The words *nuclear disaster* and *Ukraine* made me start. I dumped my cup on a side table and leaned closer. My heart beat so hard inside I thought it might burst, as I looked and listened in horror to a news story from Ukraine about a place in the north called Chornobyl. It was the site of a nuclear power station, and an accident had occurred. There was a film taken from a helicopter showing a pillar of smoke erupting from the tower. The newsreader confirmed this was releasing a gigantic cloud of radioactive dust into the atmosphere. I felt sick, right from my stomach into every bit of me. I wanted to stand up and kick the screen in, to stop the broadcast and break the television so I couldn't look at it. Instead, I froze. I sat there, ready to explode, but motionless, like a statue, listening to the detail, and burning inside with hate for the Soviets. Damn them all to Hell! I watched as more pictures came in from Ukraine of fire-fighters trying to douse the radioactive inferno with jets of water. It wasn't making much difference. The newsreader finished the broadcast by saying there had been some deaths, about 50 or so, and then the report finished. I was left with my head spinning and my heart slashed open.

Over the next few days, I listened to every news broadcast there was. I watched, in horror, as they continued to battle the radioactive fire. For 12 days, those fire-fighters worked tirelessly, with determination, with little consideration for their own welfare. They were heroes. The recovery operation was frantic and disorganised. The pictures on the television showed lead and sand being dropped into the tower from a helicopter to douse the flames. The day after, they found the temperature was rising once again, releasing further radioactive dust from the reactor. That was so typical of the Soviets! They had no idea how to stop the fire. They caused so much damage to our beloved Ukraine, they can never be forgiven. To poison our land in this way, to cause ill health with cancers and deformities in children, that could only be the act of evil madmen.

One day, I hoped a radioactive rain would fall onto their land, soaking into the water below, infiltrating everything around them. Let them taste it. Let them feel it. Let them sit and wonder where the next mouthful of decent food would come from, but not the ordinary people or the children. Just the leaders, those communist elite, those bloodthirsty villains sitting in the Kremlin scheming and plotting. How I wished I could burn that monstrous den of devils down. That's what they deserved. They'd been only too eager to inflict years of pain and suffering on our Ukrainian nation.

I followed the situation at Chornobyl over a period of a few weeks. Much was written in the *Ukrayinska Dumka* on the subject, but words count for nothing, not when people are dying or placed in danger.

The nearby town of Pripyat, a town built for the purpose of housing the workers of the Chornobyl Power Station, had become a ghost town. All the dwellings had been abandoned, and worst of all, a newly built fun fair sat rotting. It never got used by the local children. The townspeople had worked hard to create prosperity in the region, to give their children a good life. As all parents do, they wanted their children to grow up free of fear and with every day full of smiles and laughter. It was taken away from them in the space of a few hours, when a radioactive cloud was allowed to cover the land like a toxic blanket. The people were left with no choice. Because of the Soviets, all the people of Pripyat were forced to leave their homes.

Chapter 15

Ukrainian proverb: When the flag is unfurled, all reason is in the trumpet

I looked at the face on the television screen and thought to myself, you're no different to any of the others. You're a liar, feeding the world propaganda. What was all that rubbish about perestroika and glasnost? Just another Soviet fairy story to fool the world into thinking that things could be different. How could the Soviets justify creating a state where everyone was supposed to be equal when, if you said anything they disagreed with, you were persecuted?

I was watching the evening news round at Fedor's house, who slowly shook his head and said, 'They're a treacherous breed, and I don't like the look of this Muscovite any more than the others.' He was talking about Gorbachev. The Soviet leader sounded like he might be different to the others, but under him, as ever, Ukraine got mutilated. Following the nuclear disaster at Chornobyl, many people were displaced and plunged into uncertainty and poverty. His apologies jarred in our ears. How could we believe a word he said?

'You know as well as I, there is no truth in the world and there never will be.' I replied.

All over the world there was turmoil. The Soviets were fighting a war in Afghanistan; they'd rolled their tanks across the border back in 1979. It was part of their mission to spread communism. It was crazy! Why try and push ideas onto a people who don't want them? The Soviets were aggressive and brutal, always looking to gain territory from their neighbours, always looking to poke their noses into other people's business. That's what they'd always done.

But, a surprise arrived in 1987 that made me raise my eyebrows. The USA and the Soviets agreed to reduce their stockpiles of nuclear weapons, and the world breathed a little easier. Maybe things were changing.

Meanwhile, I became a granddad three times over! Anna gave birth to another two boys, Mikhaylo and Simon. It was a great time for me, and Maria, to see those young boys grow up, learning the Ukrainian language, and the customs from back home, but at the same time, I was starting to feel my age. I was 60 years old, and my body was creaking. I had so many aches all over my body, but that's what happens as a person ages. I wondered many times whether I'd ever get back home and walk again on Ukrainian soil. That Iron Curtain was drawn right across those eastern territories, including my beloved Ukraine, and it seemed like it would stay right there forever.

But, one evening, I was watching the late news on a warm evening in June. Ronald Reagan was the president of the USA at that time and he was visiting East Berlin. I watched, wondering what the purpose of his visit might be. I had no doubt it would be to further the prosperity of the USA and to forge stronger links with the Soviets. It made my stomach turn to see Reagan shaking hands with Gorbachev. It was like watching two bullies slap each other on the back and sanction each other's aggression towards other, smaller nations. Then Reagan made his speech, and I leaned forward to listen closer. I didn't expect the ex-screen cowboy to say very much,

'We welcome change and openness; for we believe that freedom and security go together, that the advance of human liberty can only strengthen the cause of world peace. There is one sign the Soviets can make that would be unmistakable, that would advance dramatically the cause of freedom and peace. General Secretary Gorbachev, if you seek peace, if you seek prosperity for the Soviet Union and Eastern Europe, if you seek liberalization, come here to this gate. Mr. Gorbachev, open this gate. Mr. Gorbachev, tear down this wall!'

They were strong, powerful words. The speech echoed around the Ukrainian communities and through the Ukrainian press. It felt like something was in the air . . .

Andriy moved away to Nottingham to study at the University there, and, afterwards, settled down there with Mandy, his girlfriend. Maria and I were on our own, although our children kept in touch and visited often.

As ever, the world just kept moving on. After many years of service to the Metal Box Company, I was made redundant – replaced by mechanisation. Well, it was the modern way. Things weren't so bad though, our mortgage was paid off and I got a generous redundancy package, so I took early retirement.

We reached 1989, the years sliding past like a rich man making money. The Soviets pulled out of Afghanistan, having failed to win that war, and then, just a few months later, we witnessed scenes on television that were simply astonishing. Hundreds of people, or maybe even thousands, swarmed around the Berlin Wall. Some youngsters danced on the top of the wall; others tore away at the bricks. It got more and more frantic and the joyful noise of freedom smashing down a wall of oppression poured out of the television until a section of that wall fell away, the dancers on the top leaping to safety. It wasn't long before it all crumbled into bricks.

'Nobody wants the communists any more do they, Stefan?' said Maria, as we watched it together.

'Maybe now is the time for a new dawn,' I replied. 'Maybe we're seeing the start of a cure for the communist disease.'

Brick by brick, that wall in Berlin got dismantled, and people from both sides embraced each other as Germany took its first steps towards reunification.

Communism took a massive body blow that day, and it never recovered. Slowly, the belief that Ukraine could be free began to spread inside us like the glow from a glass of *horilka*.

A fellow came to prominence in leading Ukraine towards independence. His name was Leonid Kravchuk. In Ukraine, there were numerous strikes and demonstrations by ordinary people who wanted democracy and freedom. I braced myself as I looked at the images on the television screen of people up and down the length and breadth of Ukraine who were massed together, singing in protest, and for democracy and freedom. I sat waiting for the riot police to go charging in, with batons and water cannons. I expected to see images of people being cuffed and beaten to the ground by the uniformed thugs of the administration, but it didn't happen.

Kravchuk was the architect. He guided Ukraine away from communist rule towards independence, and for that I thank him from the bottom of my shoes and from the deepest reaches of my heart.

On December 1st, 1991, Ukraine held a referendum and a presidential election. The result was in no doubt. A huge majority resulted in a free Ukraine with Kravchuk as its first president. I could hardly believe it. Maria and I hugged each other as the results were announced. Ukraine was free of its Soviet yoke!

All over England, and the rest of the world, the Ukrainian diaspora could celebrate and really feel free. For the first time, we could say we were a truly independent nation. Ukraine was a part of Europe and had its own place in the world. I gave thanks to God.

And so, the question remained whether I should try and make contact with my family again. So many times I'd tried. Over the years I'd written dozens of letters, all of them ripped open by Soviet officials and probably destroyed. Of course, I knew I had to try!

I sat down with a pen and a pad of writing paper. Almost 50 years had gone by since I had last walked on Ukrainian soil and I pondered who I should write to. My heart and my head ached so much as I forced myself to face the fact that Mother was surely no longer alive. She would have been more than 90 years old. With all the hardships she'd gone through, I doubted whether she would still be here. I prayed that, wherever she was, she'd forgive me for leaving her; I'd missed her so much over the years, my beautiful, wonderful Mother! I still remember her arms around me, that warm embrace, that aroma of a mother's bosom, that aura of life she had around her. She breathed so much of that into us. I smiled whenever I saw her – I still do see her in my dreams and she's there in my heart. She lives inside me.

And what of my big brother, Volodimir? Where had he ended up? Was he like me, one of the displaced? Or had he made it back home somehow? Slowly, with the pen crawling across the page, I wrote the letter – I decided I'd write to Volodimir, all the while praying he was still alive. Even if his heartbeat wasn't near to mine, it would still beat in time together with mine for all eternity, that's how close we were.

It wasn't a long letter, I just told my story in a few words and asked for someone or somebody to write back. It was January 1992 and we'd just celebrated our Christmas. It just so happened that my old friend Fedor had received a visitor from Ukraine around that time. His guest was the first wave of adventurers from beyond that border. Many young Ukrainians took the opportunity to see a bit of the world once they were free of the shackles of communism. They were pouring out of Ukraine day after day. Fedor's nephew had come to see him, a young man called Theo, who hailed from the same town as Fedor, Rivne. Fedor invited me round one evening to meet him so I drove over there one Friday night. Fedor, and his wife Araciella, laid on a spread, with a selection of sandwiches, cold meats and pickles and plenty of cakes and pastries. It was a fine spread indeed. One or two of Fedor's other friends were there and the atmosphere was of a quiet joyousness, of a celebration that Ukraine was no longer a slave nation.

'So Theo, how is life in Ukraine right now?' I asked.

'It's hard. But it's also exciting. Everything's changing. Some things are getting better, other things are getting worse. We're finding our way; it's an adventure every day. Sometimes you wonder where the next piece of bread will come from, but something always turns up. There's always some deal or something you can do for someone, and then you can earn some cash. That's what it's all about, no?'

'Listen to me,' I said, 'it's hard work here in England, but at least you can try to make things better for yourself. That's what all of us Ukrainians have done. Now, it's time for your generation to show the world what you can do, eh?'

Theo looked at me and nodded with a smile across his face. I sensed there was a new beginning for Ukrainians across the world, and that Theo could be part of that. I wished him the best in his future endeavours, but there was one favour I needed to ask him. 'I have a letter, to my family in Vinnitsya. Would you be able to post it to them when you get back home?'

'Of course I can, Stefan, as soon as I get to the nearest post box I'll drop it in.'

The party carried on at Fedor's, and I stayed for a little while longer, and then said my goodbyes. When I got home, I went upstairs, got undressed and went to bed. Sleep was slow coming; I drifted in and out of slumber, with dreamy thoughts of home invading my head.

The following weeks passed by like slow motion. I checked the mail every day, but nothing came, until one day in the first, crisp dawns of February.

It was a Saturday and Anna, Stefan and their three boys were visiting us. As usual, I'd gone out to the town to buy some milk, a few groceries, and a newspaper. I got back to see Anna sitting at the kitchen table with an airmail envelope on the table in front of her.

'Hello, Dad,' she said as I stood looking at the letter, 'it's addressed to you. It's from Ukraine.' I dumped the shopping bag down on a chair. The letter was there looking at me, daring me to pick it up and open it. My hand trembled as I reached for it and held it up. Sure enough, the postmark was from Ukraine, and the stamp appeared to be Ukrainian. I put it back down on the table, and started to unpack my shopping.

'Aren't you going to open it?' asked Anna.

'I'm just going to unpack this shopping,' I replied, and busied myself with loading up the fridge and the cupboards with the items I'd bought. Once I'd done that I walked across the kitchen and picked up the kettle, and filled it up with cold water from the tap.

'Well,' Anna was watching me as I moved around the kitchen, 'aren't you going to open it?'

I didn't answer her, not because I didn't want to, or because I was being rude to her. There were no words I could say right then. My mind was a swirling jigsaw of broken thoughts. The kettle boiled. Anna sat quietly as I made myself a cup of coffee. The letter was screaming at me as I sat down at the table, screaming for me to pick it up and rip it open. The steam from my cup of coffee drifted up towards the ceiling and deposited drops of moisture on my forehead, which, together with the strong coffee aroma, got my pulse racing. I rubbed my hands through my hair and then I scooped up the envelope and began to open it, taking care not to damage it. Inside were two small sheets of paper. I unfolded them, and Maria came and sat at the table as I began to read. The tears flowed down my cheeks almost as soon as I read the first few words from my nephew, also called Stefan, like me! He was the son of my brother, Volodimir. I praised the Lord that Volodimir had survived and produced a family.

    I then found out that Mother passed away in 1980, she lived until she was 90 and passed away peacefully in her sleep. I put the letter down and clasped my hands together in thanks to the Lord that she'd lived so long. I picked the letter up again to discover that Volodimir passed away the following year, 1981. He'd been watching television with his family one evening and excused himself to go outside and tidy the yard. After he'd been gone a while, they went to see where he was and found he'd collapsed from a heart attack and died. As I took in those words, I steeled myself like a Kozak. I sat there, my shoulders shaking, I couldn't hold myself back, and the tears streamed down my face. Anna and Maria put their arms around me as I sobbed. It's hard to describe how I felt. It was as if I'd lived in one world and then been whisked away to another. My memories came flooding back stronger than ever. In my head I was back there with Mother, in the kitchen, with the fire burning in the oven, the heat melting into me, keeping me warm. Right then, I knew for certain I'd never see her again, and, although I'd expected that to be the case, seeing it written down carved a deep wound inside me. As for Volodimir, the knowledge that he died so young, only 55, it ached inside me. Alive or dead, he was still my brother, and I knew he was looking over me – somehow I felt closer than ever to him; maybe because I knew he was up in Heaven with the angels.

    I read that letter from start to finish. It took me about half an hour to get through it, even though it was only two sheets of paper. Every word and every sentence tore through me. I smoked cigarettes as I read. Then I read it through again.

    Sometimes, freedom wasn't so easy, not when your family had

lived through times like we had. Of all my family, I was the luckiest, and the only one still alive. My journey had been hard and long, but after reading through that letter several times, I knew there was one more journey I would need to make.

Many more letters flew back and forth from England to Ukraine as I wrote to the children of Volodimir: Tanya, Mikola and Stefan. Photographs were also exchanged and there were many old portraits of a big extended family standing next to my beloved Mother and brother. Preparations needed to be made. An application form for a passport was completed and sent off to the authorities, and I arranged a visit to my doctor for a health check and for the vaccinations needed.

Meanwhile, Anna and Stefan booked flights to Ukraine to visit in July of that very year, because they already held passports. Andriy was unable to go because he'd recently become a father himself – another grandson for me, Joe. I was starting to feel old!

Maria and I looked after three of our grandsons while Anna and Stefan made their trip back to Vinnitsya, back to our old family home. They came back wide-eyed and full of stories of their trip, and their meeting with my niece and nephews.

'Dad, it was wonderful,' said Anna, 'they met us at the airport. Tanya was there, with her husband Volodko, and also Stefan and Mikola. They greeted us in the traditional way with bread and salt. I cried. I couldn't help myself. To be in Ukraine was an incredible feeling and they really welcomed us. From them on, it was like one big party. They took us everywhere during the day, all over Ukraine, and in the evenings there was food and drink, and we had music, we danced. Stefan played some tunes to them on an accordion. We had the time of our lives!'

As I listened to her a glow spread inside me, it filled every inch of me. I felt so warm and so happy I could have exploded with joy.

So, we sat and we planned for the following year. It required so much organising it gave me a headache at times. Andriy's wife was expecting yet another child so he wouldn't be able to come, a busy boy that son of mine. The trip would include Maria and I, Anna and Stefan, and their three boys, Marko, Mihasz and Simon. And so, it was all organised, once again, for the month of July 1993. I would be going home!

The letters to and from my nieces and nephews continued, and the occasional phone call. The summer faded away, the leaves fell from the trees and the winds blew cooler. My wait to go home had been a long one, so another year wouldn't make much difference. Besides, I'd never been on an aeroplane before and, although Anna reassured me that there was nothing to fear, I was beginning to get anxious.

I had other things to worry about too. How would things be back at home and how would I react? Once again I thought about our house back in Vinnitsya as I'd done a million times before. With that set of three wooden steps leading up to the side door, that Father painted every so often to keep them clean and in good condition. I wondered if they would still be there and what colour they might be. He always painted them a strong red colour – like over-ripe tomatoes.

Once I'd gone up those steps I'd be standing at that door, with its four wooden panels and cast iron handle. Father used a heavy stain on that door, it was a golden shade of brown with a sharp aroma wafting from its surface, and it always made my nose twitch. That shade of golden brown always made me feel like I was entering a palace. On entering the house, a blast of warm air from the stove always engulfed me, and usually it was accompanied by the smell of cooking or baking, my favourite was when Mother made biscuits. My mouth watered just thinking about them. If there were biscuits Mother usually gave me one, and I'd sit at the table eating it, while looking up at that icon of Jesus and his Apostles at the Last Supper. The gold painted frame that held the icon was so beautifully and ornately carved, it was a wonder to me. That's what I wanted: to see that icon and several others of religious scenes around the house, all with similar frames.

Things would be different though, that could only be expected. There would be different furniture and carpets, and I expected the walls to be a different colour. My mind raced through the possibilities, day after day. So much so, that I did my best to keep myself busy.

Some years back, I'd constructed a canopy at the back of our house, a roof over the back yard, which we sat under in the summer. Over the last few years, I'd wondered whether I could convert this canopy into a conservatory. A collection of wooden panels, battens and some old windows and doors were stacked at the back of my garage for this very purpose. With so much going on in my head and in my heart, there would never be a better time to start this project. Throughout the rest of that year, right up until Christmas, I was a hurricane in that back yard, sawing planks of wood, hammering panels together and drilling and screwing down wooden frames. It was good for me to keep busy in this way. It took my mind off things a little. The weather was kind to me, and by mid-December I'd constructed the shell of what would become a conservatory for Maria and me.

Before the first frosts crept in, I managed to weather-proof the outside of the shell with paint and bitumen, and Maria and I celebrated British Christmas by having our dinner out there. A Calor gas heater provided some warmth, and I decked the inside of the room with fairy lights and candles. It was like being in our own little palace.

In the New Year of course, we celebrated our own Ukrainian Christmas, which follows the Julian calendar, and is in the first week of January. We had a full house this time, with both Anna and Andriy, their spouses and all our grandchildren. It was great for us all to be together for a first Christmas at a time when Ukraine was finally free and no longer a slave nation to the Soviets. We thanked the Lord and we partook of our Christmas Eve meal more proud than ever of who we were.

My papers arrived shortly afterwards, and were all in order, we had our tickets, and the time was coming ever closer. Maria had been on aeroplanes quite a few times to visit her family in Poland, but air travel was something I'd never experienced. I'd travelled by road, by rail and over the sea, but the idea of taking to the sky turned my knuckles white and my hair, even though it was already grey, somersaulted into white almost overnight. At night, when I looked up at the sky, I'd often see shooting stars or aeroplanes flashing their lights, but I couldn't bear to stand there too long. My ears would start ringing and I'd rush to get indoors, with images of rockets firing through my head, just like when I was wandering through Europe in wartime, with explosions shuddering right through me, with enough power to take my head off and tear me to pieces. Sometimes, those rockets flew back and forth all day, exploding all around us. We huddled together in a ditch somewhere and prayed, hoping that our prayers would reach beyond the orange sulphurous fire clouds that hovered over us. That's how I remembered it. Those memories brought a sickness up into my stomach – a fear that threatened to turn me upside down. I sat down in an armchair and took a few breaths. Then I went into the conservatory and smoked a few cigarettes. Memories of the war were inside me waiting to come out and turn me into a wreck.

Finally, that Saturday in July came around. We took our two cars down to Heathrow airport in London. It was a steady drive, and I enjoyed it on the motorway. The M1 is a big, wide road and we started off nice and early at around seven, so there wasn't much traffic. As we got closer and followed signs to Heathrow Airport, we saw one or two planes coming in to land. A stirring in my guts brought a sick feeling up into my chest and I breathed a little harder. The idea of going up into the clouds in one of those things caused a tremble inside me. I tried not to let it show, just like I'd done so many times through my life. It was the Kozak way. Show no fear. That's what we did, and that's what got us through so many terrible times. Stefan, our son-in-law, negotiated his way through the site, with its many signs and lights, and roundabouts and roads leading to who knows where. I followed him, sticking close. We left our cars in the parking lot and got ourselves a trolley to put our luggage on. Once we were inside the main building I was a little more at ease because I couldn't see the planes and we were occupied with checking in and going through customs, so I was kept busy and that was good. Too much thinking wasn't good for me.

Inside, I was in a twisted up state. Part of me was excited about going back home to the land where I was born, and where I grew up, until the Nazis drove us out. Another part of me knew that the situation was broken beyond repair, I'd have to deal with how I would feel when I arrived back at the house I'd grown up in.

After a long wait and several announcements over the loudspeakers, we got on the plane, the seven of us, and we took our seats. Maria and I sat together in a row of three seats, with another passenger, while Anna, Stefan and their three boys were all together in the row behind us. It filled up quickly, and almost all the seats were taken.

After a safety briefing from the cabin crew, the plane began to move. I'd brought a newspaper onto the plane and, as the plane took off, I opened it up and held it right in front of me.

As the plane increased its speed and threw itself higher into the clouds, I sat motionless, with that newspaper in front of me. At one point I heard Anna call across to me, 'Dad, look out of the window. You can see the clouds.'

I wanted to turn my head and reply to her, but I couldn't. I was in a hole, a hole that was so deep there was no bottom to it. I stifled the fear building inside me and adopted the mask of the Kozak. I looked at the pictures in the newspaper, my mind was too frazzled to read any words. There was an article about Leonardo Da Vinci, and it brought to mind a painting in that old house I grew up in. The painting that leapt into my head was the one above the kitchen table, the one with Jesus and his Disciples sat at a long table, partaking of the last supper. It was that painting I'd looked at every morning and every evening as a boy. I wanted to be sitting at that table, eating a slice of bread and butter and looking up at Jesus and his followers, framed in gold, and with beautiful carvings adorning the image. That's where I wanted to be.

There were other paintings at my old home I wanted to see again. In the living room was one of the Holy Trinity, the Father, the Son and the Holy Ghost, also mounted in a golden frame, exquisitely carved. We'd also had one of the Virgin Mary with baby Jesus, and one of the Three Wise Men following a star, both of them in our living room also. I'd grown up with these paintings, and I wanted to see them again so badly, because I knew Father always held onto them in spite of everything. They represented a line that could not, or should not, be crossed. They represented faith.

My in-flight meal was dumped in front of me on the little fold-down table. It was a chicken dinner with roast potatoes, vegetables and gravy. But my appetite was poor; I managed just a few mouthfuls.

Four hours into our journey we were instructed to put on our safety belts and the pilot began to take the plane down. Even though I knew we were above Ukraine, I still couldn't bring myself to look out of the window. The engines switched from a steady, deep drone to a higher pitch that stretched my nerves to breaking point. I closed my eyes and waited, trying to breathe as normal, until there was a jolt and the plane landed on the runway. Finally, I persuaded myself to take a glance out of the window. I could see many metres of runway stretching all around us. Sunlight was streaming all around and daylight crept into the cabin as the door was opened. We all walked out onto a platform and then down a set of steel stairs.

As I stepped down onto the tarmac, I realised I was standing on Ukrainian soil for the first time in 50 years. I just stood there, and Kozak tears flowed from me. I couldn't stop myself. Maria put her arms around me and whispered to me,

'Stefan, you're back.' Anna and Stefan also put their arms around me and I was able to then stem my tears and feel joyous. My heart was full of sunshine as I stood beneath that Ukrainian sky. It was like magic, as if I'd been transported back in time, to the place where I was born.

Once inside the airport terminal, we collected our luggage and made our way through customs and into the Arrivals lounge. The building was a dismal sight, paint was flaking away from the doors and the sills of the windows were coated with a thick skin of dust. Inside, the linoleum flooring was peeling at the edges and was cracked in places. These deficiencies represented the legacy of Soviet neglect, and now we were seeing them with our own eyes. The officials checked our passports with typical cold-eyed efficiency, and then we all took our cases and bags down a final gangway into an open area with free-standing barriers dividing those arriving at the airport from those who had gathered to meet them.

'Stefan! Maria! Over here!' I saw a man waving at us, he had a big smile on his face and he walked towards us. As he came closer, I recognised him. It was Stefan, my nephew. I walked towards him and dropped my suitcase as we hugged each other. This was my brother's son! Maria, and Anna and her family all joined in with a group huddle and my other nephew, Mikola, and my niece Tanya and her husband, Volodko, joined us all in a rapturous embrace. Kisses were planted on cheeks, hands were shaken, and then Tanya spoke, 'Stefan, Maria and all your children and grandchildren, we welcome you to Ukraine.'

Her husband, Volodko, stepped forward with a platter, upon which was a loaf of bread and a dish of salt, the traditional Ukrainian welcome.

I must admit I was in something of a daze as we walked out of that building and I looked around me. It was one thirty and the sun was blazing above us, the sky was a misty blue, and beneath me was my beloved Ukrainian soil. The air I breathed was from a wind blowing across from those wonderful, magnificent Carpathian Mountains. It filled my nostrils, and my ears and all of my senses were tingling. I have to admit, it was strange, like stepping into a dream. We left the airport and we climbed into a minibus hired by my nephew and my journey back to Vinnitsya began.

The roads were bumpy and full of holes and cracks, a reminder once again of the extent of Soviet neglect. The constant bumping over holes in the road and the excessive engine hum made conversation impossible so I sat and took in the scenery.

We passed by many areas with settlements. There were blocks of high rise flats dotted around the landscape, one or two run-down shopping centres, and many sprawling estates, with houses of different sizes. One thing that was common to all of them was the shabbiness, the peeling and the pitted paintwork, the piles of rubble and the broken fences. Ukraine, to my searching eyes, looked second-hand; it looked like a junk yard.

To take my mind away from the wrecked scenery that surrounded us, I thought about Mother. I so wanted to go to the place where she was buried. So I could say a few words to her. At the age of 15, I'd been torn away from her, tossed onto the mercy of the wind. I'd been lucky and survived, when so many hadn't. I wished I could tell her I was okay, and that I'd found a wife and raised a family. The fact she'd lived until she was 90 made me feel a little better, but only briefly, when I considered she may have spent her days wondering what happened to her husband and her youngest son. I trembled when I thought about Father and his sudden death. I knew I had to tell her about that. That's why I was coming home.

My wife Maria chattered away to my niece and my nephews and I was grateful to her for that. I joined in the conversation now and again, but to be truthful, I had too much swirling around my head and my heart to be properly included.

For five hours we sat on that minibus, squirming and fidgeting. The seats were very hard and we were all getting a little bit sore and stiff. Halfway through our journey, we stopped at a petrol station to refuel and I went inside to see what I could buy with the Ukrainian currency I'd got.

'Welcome!' The shop owner was a small fellow, with thinning hair and a nodding smile you couldn't ignore. 'Please take a look around, I have much here that may be of interest to you.' I nodded back to him and then browsed through his wares. There wasn't much, just a typical selection of chocolates and candies and a rack of CDs. I flicked through them, but they were all of a modern style, so I wasn't interested. It was a shame to see such an enthusiastic fellow with so little to trade, so I bought a few chocolate bars from him. It was my first purchase with *hryvnia*, real Ukrainian money. I handed him the notes only too gladly as, in my mind, it cemented the fact that Ukraine was a free country, and its citizens and visitors had a currency to trade in. That's what I wanted to do. To see how people were faring in their day-to-day business, and give whatever money I could to them, even though it wasn't much. I wanted the Ukrainian economy to grow and prosper, and for Ukraine to get stronger.

After the refuelling was done, we all got back on the minibus, a little less sore thanks to that leg stretch and short walk.

Stefan, my nephew, who was driving the minibus, switched on the CD player and some traditional Ukrainian music arrived to accompany us on our journey. We sang along to '*Oy Chorna, ya si*

Chorna' a song about a young Ukrainian girl, and several others tunes followed that one. Maria and I led the singing and it filled me with great joy to hear so many of us sharing these great melodies in my beloved Ukraine.

The time passed quicker than I'd expected, and some familiar sights caught my eye. We passed by the lake where I used to go swimming with my friends. I looked across and there were groups of boys there, in their shorts, splashing around and fooling about just like I'd done with my friends all those years ago. A lump formed in my throat. We passed by the town hall, the place where the Nazis had based themselves during their occupation of the area, and where Father and I so narrowly escaped execution.

We'd arrived, and were heading into the heart of my old home town. Stefan drove the minibus around a few familiar bends and turns, and then, it wasn't long before I knew exactly where I was. Either side of us were groups of houses, some which I recognised, and others which appeared to be much newer. I scanned the dwellings on our left hand side, and my eyes fixed on one particular house. As the minibus slowed down, I couldn't take my eyes off it. The minibus stopped. Stefan turned the engine off and announced that we'd arrived. I put my hands together and whispered a prayer of thanks to the Lord. Then, I stepped down from the bus and stood looking at my old house. It wasn't much, but it was my home. It was where I was born and grew up. So many years had passed by, more than 50. For a few seconds, I gazed at the house. It hadn't changed all that much. The approach up to it had the same well-trodden track and there were neatly trimmed grass verges either side.

I walked up to the side of the house and I saw the door and the set of steps leading up to it. It was just as I remembered. As I stood there, I thought I could detect the aroma of fresh baking in the air, just like Mother might have done. The steps were freshly painted in the same shade of red that Father had always liked. It was so familiar.

I dropped to my knees in front of the house. Silently, I gave thanks to the Lord for leading me up to this moment. I placed the palms of my hands on the ground in front of the house and then I lowered my head and kissed the ground.

I was so happy to be back. A jigsaw which had been thrown in the bottom of a cupboard had finally found its missing pieces and put itself back together again. That was how it felt.

And I truly believe Ukraine will find its way, just like I found my way. There are many obstacles to overcome, but the human spirit and resolve can overcome them. I'd travelled many miles to reach that moment and in my heart the journey had been unending. At last, I got what I'd always wanted. Finally, I found freedom.

Ten years later ...

The waitress smiles at us as she wipes our table down, and Bronec and I grin back at her. All the staff in the café know us well, we're regulars here, and they often have a little joke with us. The café's just reopened after redecoration and the smell of paint is still in the air. The carpet beneath our feet is lush and thick. There are new light fittings and the walls have been painted cream, whereas beforehand, they were a deep red. It feels like we're in a completely different café.

'It's a funny feeling isn't it, sitting here?' says Bronec, 'it's just like being in a different world, don't you think?'

It's been a few years since I made that trip back to Ukraine, and I didn't even know Bronec then. I only got to know him in the last few years. Of course, we've talked about our lives and the journeys we've both made, but I've never really spoken to him in any detail about that visit. I haven't really spoken to anyone about it. It was important to rejoice and celebrate going back home, and, in many ways, it set me free, but it wasn't quite what I expected.

'Bronec . . . I know what you mean only too well.' There are two mugs of steaming hot coffee on the table in front of us. I stir a couple of spoonfuls of sugar into mine, and take a big mouthful. 'It reminds me of when I went back home to Ukraine. You know what? When I got off the minibus and saw my old house, I couldn't believe it. It looked the same, but I couldn't believe how small it was when I got inside!'

Bronec smiles, 'I know what you mean. Things are not always as we remember them.'

'You're right. You see, I went there with expectations. When I was a boy, my family had some really beautiful religious icons around the house. We had one of the Last Supper in the kitchen, the Holy Trinity and a portrait of Mary and Jesus in the living room, and one or two others. You know the kind of paintings I mean?' Bronec nodded, and I continued. 'Those paintings had the most beautiful frames, carved from oak, with very intricate patterns and a gold painted finish. They were very fine. But when I walked into the kitchen for the first time after all those years, the painting of the Last Supper wasn't there, and when I walked into all the other rooms I saw that none of those others remained either.'

I take another sip of my coffee and Bronec does the same with his.

'Well, I didn't want to make a fuss about it right there and then, because a big party had been laid on for us. There was food and drink on every inch of the kitchen table. We had a great time, and I was so happy to be back in the bosom of my family, back in my old home. We partied into the early hours. But it kept preying on my mind. So, the next day, when it was early and everyone was still either in bed, or just starting to stir, I asked Tanya, my niece, about it. Of course, she didn't know, or she couldn't remember anything about it. Maybe she was too young. So I turned to my brother's wife, Hala, and asked her the same question. She looked into my eyes, and I could see a great sadness deep inside her. She kept it well-hidden, as we all do, but it was there all right, I could feel it. She said she couldn't remember exactly, but she thought the paintings had been sold some years ago, many years ago in fact.'

Bronec nods as he listens, 'It sounds like those paintings were really something to you.'

'Of course they were! My Father held on to them through all the bad times, even the very bad times.'

'I know what you mean, but a very long period of time had passed before you went back home, so it was always likely those paintings would have ended up elsewhere.'

I take another mouthful of hot coffee and survey the new interior of the café. There is truth in Bronec's words, and what's happened to this café, one of our regular haunts, brings it home to me. The past clings onto us like strong glue, we can never pull ourselves away from it completely, and sometimes it's the little details that stick in our minds, we can't shake them away. The thought of one day seeing those paintings kept me going through times of turmoil, they gave me something to hang onto, but my life is settled now, so maybe the paintings aren't so important anymore.

More important is the visit I was able to make to Mother's grave. I'll never forget that. It wasn't the grandest of graves and a little overgrown. That didn't matter, because I could feel her there. I stood alone next to her for quite some time, and I told her everything that had happened to me and to Father. I put my hands together and gave thanks to the Lord for the union I was able to have with Mother. My heart opened like a flower and everything inside me was right there. I told her all of it. I walked away with the padlock smashed away from those words which had been locked inside me for so *many years.*

What really matters now is that Ukraine is free. I now realise my old home is that of my niece and nephews and I bless them and wish them luck, long life and prosperity as they journey through the new political and economic landscape. Of course, it's theirs to do with as they please, and it's good to see them caring for that old house, and constructing more buildings on that same piece of land. It's called progress, something Ukraine has missed out on under the misery of Soviet rule.

There are events and people from the past that should never be forgotten, some of them good, many of them bad. Now and again, I think about that crazy old man, Matviyko, who lived in that broken-down old shack near the lake, the one who laughed at us as we slid around on the snow stone, as he called it. Well, it feels like I've been sliding on the snow stone for many years, one way or another, trying to get up onto my feet. Only now can I really stand tall.

The present day and the future are what we must think about. Ukraine is building stronger links with the West and with its neighbours. Even though some of them may give us trouble on occasion, as each day passes we cement our place in world history and on the world map. Even though there are many Ukrainian diaspora such as I scattered across the world, we have a new identity and a new nation to be proud of, and it doesn't matter where we are in the world, we're all still part of it. Inside each and every one of us is a beating Kozak heart.

The End

Pronunciations

In order of appearance:

'Andriy' – two syllables, equal weighting. 'And' as in sand, 'riy' as in sea.

'Bronec' – two syllables, equal weighting. 'Bro' as in broth, 'nec' as in neck.

'Stefan' – two syllables, equal weighting. 'Ste' as in step, 'fan' as in fan.

'Bohdan' – two syllables, equal weighting. 'Boh' as in bob ending on a hard 'h' (the 'h' is sounded), 'dan' as in man.

'Holodomor' – four syllables, equal weighting. 'Ho' as in hot, 'lo' as in lot, 'do' as in dot, 'mor' as in morrow.

'Volodimir' – four syllables, equal weighting. 'Vo' as in bob, 'lo' as in lot, 'di' as in dip, 'mir' as in mirage.

'Kolhosp' – two syllables, equal weighting. 'Kol' as in colt, 'hosp' as in hospital.

'Miron' – two syllables, equal weighting. 'Mi' as in miller, 'ron' as in gone.

'Kozak' - two syllables, equal weighting. 'Ko' as in cot, 'zak' as in back.

'Novi Khutyry: *Novi'* – two syllables, equal weighting. 'No' as in not, 'vi' as in 'vee'. *'Khutyry'* – three syllables, equal weighting. 'Khu' as in hook (the 'k' isn't sounded), 'ty' as in took, 'ry' as in rink.

'Vinnitsya' – three syllables, equal weighting. 'VIN – NITS – YAH'.

'Mikola' – three syllables, weight on first syllable. 'Mik' as in 'mick',

'ola' as in collar.

'*Moscali*' – three syllables, equal weighting. 'Mo' as in moth, 'sca' as in scab, 'li' as in lea.

'*Katsap*' – two syllables, equal weighting. 'Kats' as in 'cats', 'ap' as in tap.

'*Hohli*' - two syllables, equal weighting. 'Hoh' as in hot ending on a hard 'h' (the 'h' is sounded), 'li' as in lit.

'*Taras Shevchenko : Taras*' – two syllables, equal weighting. 'Ta' as in tap, 'ras' as in rasp. *Shevchenko* – three syllables, equal weighting. 'Shev' as in dishevelled, 'chen' as in ten, 'ko' as in cot.

'*Ivan Franko: Ivan*' – two syllables, equal weighting. 'I' as in pizza, 'van' as in van. *Franko* – 'Fran' as in man, 'ko' as in cot.

'*Markovych*' - three syllables, equal weighting. 'Mar' as in marry, 'ko' as in cot, 'vych' as in 'rich'.

'*Kobzar*' – two syllables, equal weighting. 'Kob' as in cob, 'zar' as in arrow.

'*Paska*' – two syllables, equal weighting. 'Pas' as in pass, 'ka' as in cat.

'*Horilka*' – three syllables, equal weighting. 'Ho' as in hot, 'ril' as in kilo, 'ka' as in cat.

'*Varenyky*' – four syllables, equal weighting. 'Va' as in van, 'ren' as in rent, 'y' as in any, 'ky' as in hanky. VAR-EN-IH-KEY.

'*Pavlo*' – two syllables, equal weighting. 'Pav' as in have, 'lo' as in lock.

'*Khrusty*' – two syllables, equal weighting, silent 'k', this word begins with the 'h' sounded. 'hrust' as in crust, 'ty' as in dotty.

'*Popovic*' – three syllables, equal weighting. 'Po' as pot, 'po' as in pot, 'vic' as in 'rich'.

'Yaroslav' – three syllables, equal weighting. 'Ya' as in yak, 'ro' as in rock, 'slav' as in have.

'Oleg' – two syllables, equal weighting. 'O' as in on, 'leg' as in leg.

'Ukrayinska Povstanska Armiya': Ukrayinska – four syllables, equal weighting OOH-KRA-YEEN-SKA. Povstanska – three syllables, equal weighting. POV-STAN-SKA. Armiya – three syllables, equal weighting. ARR-MEE-YAH.

'Razoviy' – three syllables, equal weighting. 'Ra' as in ran, 'zo' as in got, 'viy' as in 'sea'.

'Slavka' – two syllables, equal weighting. 'Slav' as in slap, 'ka' as in cat.

'Uzhorod' – three syllables, equal weighting. 'Uzh' as in bush, 'ho' as in hot, 'rod' as in rod.

'Vysne Nemecke': Vysne – two syllables, equal weighting. 'Vys' as in vista, 'ne' as in neck. Nemecke – three syllables, equal weighting. 'Ne' as in neck, 'me' as in met, 'cke' as in 'scare'.

'Kazimir' – 'Ka' as in cat, 'zi' as in zig, 'mir' as in mirage.

'Samohonka' – four syllables, equal weighting. 'Sa' as in sat, 'mo' as in mop, 'honk' as in honk, 'a' as in hat.

'Borsch' - one syllable. BORRSHCH, with the 'o' as in bob.

'Kovbasa' - three syllables, equal weighting. 'Kov' as in cot, 'ba' as in bat, 'sa' as in sat.

'Nikolai' – three syllables, equal weighting. 'Ni' as is nit, 'ko' as in cot, 'lai' as in 'lie'.

'Sharivari' - four syllables, equal weighting. 'Sha' as in shall, 'ri' as in rip, 'va' as in van, 'ri' as in rip.

'Hohol' – two syllables, equal weighting. 'Ho' as in hot, 'hol' as in hollow.

'*Janowska*' – three syllables, equal weighting. 'Ja' as in jam, 'ow' as in low, 'ska' as in scan.

'*Oleksa*' – three syllables, equal weighting. 'Ol' as in bold, 'ek' as in echo, 'sa' as in sat.

'*Taras*' – two syllables, equal weighting. 'Ta' as in tap, 'ras' as in raspberry.

'*Kotlyarevsky*' – four syllables, equal weighting. 'Kot' as in cot, 'lya' as in yak ('l' sounded), 'rev' as in crevice, 'sky' as in 'ski'.

'*Haidamaki*' – four syllables, equal weighting. 'Hai' as in 'high', 'da' as in dad. 'ma' as in mat, 'ki' as in kilo.

'*Zaliznyak*' – three syllables, equal weighting. ZA- LEEZ- NYAK.

'*Miroslav*' – three syllables, equal weighting. 'Mi' as in mill, 'ro' as in rock, 'slav' as in slap.

'*Yarema*' – three syllables, equal weighting. 'Ya' as in yak, 're' as in red, 'ma' as in mat.

'*Fedor*' – two syllables, equal weighting. 'Fe' as in fence, 'dor' as in dorm.

'*Nazdorovya*' – four syllables, equal weighting. 'Naz' as in has, 'do' as in dot, 'rov' as in sovereign, 'ya' as in yak.

'*Korovai*' – three syllables, equal weighting. 'Ko' as in cot, ro as in rod, 'vai' as in 'vie'. KOH-ROH-V-EYE.

'*Ukrayinska Dumka*' - OOH-KRA-YEEN-SKA DUM-KAH.

'*Tryzub*' – two syllables, equal weighting. 'try' as in trick, 'zyb' as in hub.

'*Uskorz Wielki*' – USK-ORZ WEEL-KEY.

'Lemkovyna' – four syllables, equal weighting. 'Lem' as in lemon, 'ko' as in cot, 'vy' as in 'vih', 'na' as in nap. LEM-KOH-VIN-AHH.

'Myzichka' – three syllables, equal weighting. 'My' as in 'moo', 'zich' as in rich, 'ka' as in cat. MOO-ZICH-KAH

'Dryshba' – two syllables, equal weighting. 'Drysh' as in 'bush', 'ba' as in bat.

'Kolomyjka' – four syllables, equal weighting. 'Ko' as in cot, 'lo' as in lot, 'myj' as in 'me', 'ka' as in cat.

'Tarasivka' – four syllables, equal weighting. 'Ta' as in tap, 'ra' as in rap, 'siv' as in live, 'ka' as in cat.

'Zabava' – three syllables, equal weighting. 'Za' as in zag, 'ba' as in bat, 'va' as in vat.

'Pripyat' – two syllables, equal weighting. 'Pri' as in prim, 'pyat' as in pat ('p' and 'y' are both sounded).

'Mykhaylo' – three syllables, equal weighting. MIHH-EYE-LOH.

'Rivne' – two syllables, equal weighting. 'Riv' as in river, 'ne' as in net.

'Volodko' – three syllables, equal weighting. 'Vo' as in von, 'lod' as in plod, 'ko' as in cot.

'Mihasz' - (short form of Mykhaylo) two syllables, equal weighting. MIHH-ASCH.

'Hryvnia' - three syllables, equal weighting. HRIV-NI-YAH.

Notes

In order of appearance

'Holodomor' – Death by Hunger; 'holod' meaning hunger, 'mor' meaning death.

'Hetman' – Head of Ukrainian Cossack state. The meaning is thought to be head man.

'Kozak' – 'Cossack', Ukrainian style, both spoken and written.

'Kobzar' – Wandering Ukrainian minstrel.

'Paska' – Easter bread. Sweet egg bread, baked.

'Horilka' – Vodka; strong alcoholic spirit.

'Achtung' – A German word meaning 'attention'.

'Ostarbeiters' – A German term meaning 'Eastern Workers'. Forced slave labour gathered from Eastern Europe to work in Germany to support the war effort.

'Samohonka' – Home brewed spirit. Very powerful.

'Borsch' – Beetroot soup. Traditional in Ukraine and other parts of Eastern Europe.

'Kovbasa' – Sausage, delicatessen-style, usually home-made, smoked or with garlic.

'Sharivari' – Baggy trousers worn by Ukrainian Cossacks, usually tucked into boots.

'Hohol' – The haircut of the Ukrainian Cossack: the head shaved, with a lock of hair flowing from the crown.

'Tryzub' – The national trident emblem of Ukraine. An ancient symbol of freedom – the meaning is three-teeth; thought to represent the Ukrainian word for freedom: *volya*.

Translations

In order of appearance:

'choboti' – boots

'doshka' – wooden board

'paska' - Sweet egg bread, baked.

'Nazdorovya' – For your health. Cheers.

'Scotska horilka' – Scotch whisky.

'korovai' – Traditional, baked, plaited wedding cake – sweet, egg bread.

'britva' – cut throat razor.

'Ukrayinska Dumka' – A newspaper for the Ukrainian Community in Great Britain, the title of which translates as Ukrainian Thought.

'dryshba' – Best man (at a wedding).

'hopak' – Acrobatic Cossack style Ukrainian dance.

'kolomyjka' – Traditional Ukrainian folk dance.

'zabava' – A dance, an evening function where young folk would meet up to dance and get to know each other, accompanied by traditional music played by a live band.

Acknowledgements

Cover design by Isabel Szpuk and Simon Klymyszyn.

Many thanks to Paulo Brandão (www.paulobrandao.com) for his kind permission to use his wonderful photograph *frozen light in a snow weekend* as the basis for the book cover.

Thanks to Dr Michael M Naydan for his kind permission for the use of his translation of *The Days Pass, The Nights Pass* by Taras Shevchenko.

Thanks also to Lorna Clark for allowing the use of her father John Weir's translation of a section of *Haidamaki* by Taras Shevchenko.

Many thanks also to Ann Swinfen, author of *The Testament of Marian* (www.annswinfen.com), for her excellent guidance and keen interest.

Thanks also to Claire Whatley, short story writer and children's author (*Ingrid Wildsmith and the Curse of Zeus*) for editorial assistance, technical advice on writing and more encouragement than I could ever have expected or hoped for.

There are many others who encouraged me and gave me constructive criticism – thanks to all. Finally, I'd like to thank my wife, Isabel - for many inspirations and huge reservoirs of belief.

Printed in Great Britain
by Amazon